A Scattered People

A SCATTERED

An American Family

GERALD W.

Pantheon Books

PEOPLE

Moves West

McFARLAND

New York

The map on pages xiv-xv is by David Lindroth.
Library of Congress Cataloging in Publication Data
McFarland, Gerald W., 1938–
A scattered people.
Bibliography: p.
Includes index.
1. Ward family.
2. Pioneers—United States—Biography
3. Frontier and pioneer life—United States.
I. Title.
CT274.W37M34 1985 973 84-26623
ISBN 0-394-53841-2
Manufactured in the United States of America
First Edition

BOOK DESIGN: ELISSA ICHIYASU

For Jack Hillis, Britt Peter, and Bob Brown, wherever they may be

Contents

Chapter Two

TRANS-APPALACHIAN PIONEERS, 1805–1829   43

Chapter Three

UNFORESEEN DIRECTIONS, 1830–1850   87

Chapter Four

IN THE SHADOW OF CONFLICT, 1850–1865   131

Chapter Five

CHANGES OF MIND, 1865–1892   175

Chapter Six

JOE AND FLORA WARD: ON TO CALIFORNIA   223

Acknowledgments

E ven a quick reading of my footnotes will reveal that I visited many depositories of state and local records between 1975 and 1984. Inevitably, in the course of this research I accumulated a great debt to individuals. County and local officials as well as local historians and librarians were nearly always very helpful in answering my questions. A year (1978–1979) as a John Simon Guggenheim Fellow was instrumental in enabling me to complete much of the initial phase of research.

Three individuals deserve special mention here: Linda K. Kerber of the University of Iowa gave the next-to-last draft a particularly thoughtful reading; Wendy Wolf of Pantheon Books offered encouragement and good advice at all stages of the book's development; my wife, Dorothy Tuck McFarland, took time from her own projects to make helpful suggestions. As for the other individuals, many of them relatives, but many not, who graciously helped me in some way, large or small, I am going to content myself with a simple list of their names. I hope that these names, when linked with geographical locations, will provide some sense of the breadth of my travels, inquiries, and debts to others.

Morris Adair (Nashville, Tennessee); Gilbert S. Arnold (Southwick, Massachusetts); Mildred L. Bailey (Stamford, New York); Bernard Bailyn (Cambridge, Massachusetts); Robert Barnes (Perry Hall, Maryland); Mr. and Mrs. Delmar Bartels (Pawnee County, Nebraska); Reeves Ward Baughn (Garden Grove, California); Sam Ward Bishop and T. C. Bowen (both of Tazwell County, Virginia); Steve and Mary Buster (Emporia, Kansas); Edwin H. Carpenter (Huntington Library, San Marino, California); Esther W. Christoffersen (Richmond, California); Edwin N. Cotter (Lake Placid, New York); George Adair Fleming (Glendale, California); Carson Gibb (Annapolis, Maryland); Lloyd J. Graybar (Richmond, Kentucky); Jim Greenfield (Castleton, New York); Beth Hardy (Richmond, Virginia, research); Larry Jochims (Topeka, Kansas); Ruth Maricle (deceased; Auburn, New York); Marguerite McFarland (deceased; San Leandro, California); Richard A. McFarland (Placentia, California); Donna L. Root (Southwick, Massachusetts); Mabel and Guy Root (Mantua, Ohio); Charlotte Berger Schafer (deceased; Troy, New York); Cecil Steele (Indianapolis, Indiana); Bertha Ward Van Nortwick (deceased; Camarillo, California); D. E. Van Nortwick (Republic County, Kansas); Thomas L. Vince (Hudson, Ohio); Chester and Verna Ward (Osawatomie, Kansas); Mary and Lawry Weis (Rochester, New York); and Virginia Weis (Brockport, New York).

Many thanks to all of you, and my apologies to anyone I may have forgotten to mention.

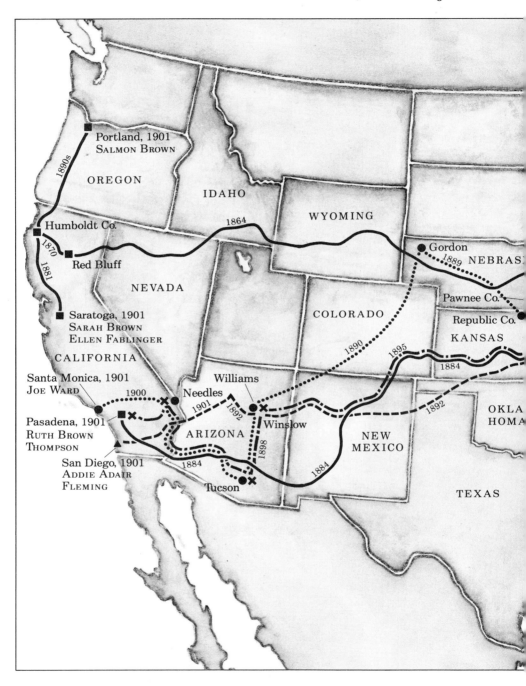

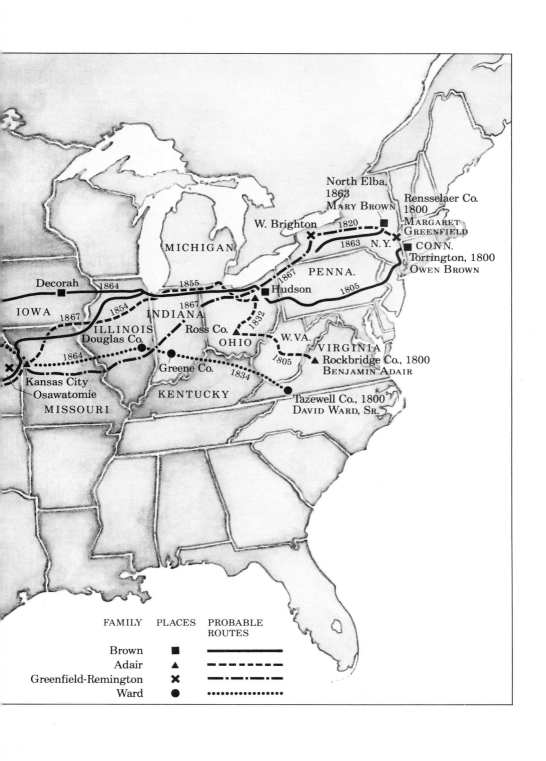

North Elba, 1863
MARY BROWN

Rensselaer Co. 1800
MARGARET GREENFIELD

W. Brighton — 1820 —

— 1863 — N. Y.

CONN.
Torrington, 1800
OWEN BROWN

MICHIGAN

Decorah — 1864 — 1855 — 1867 — PENNA.

1805

1867

IOWA — 1867 — 1854 —

INDIANA — 1867 — Hudson

ILLINOIS
Douglas Co.

Ross Co. — 1832 —

OHIO W. VA.

1805

VIRGINIA
Rockbridge Co., 1800
BENJAMIN ADAIR

— 1864 —

Greene Co. — 1834 —

Kansas City
Osawatomie

KENTUCKY

Tazewell Co., 1800
DAVID WARD, SR.

MISSOURI

FAMILY   PLACES   PROBABLE ROUTES

Brown   ■   ——————
Adair   ▲   — — — —
Greenfield-Remington ✕   — · — · —
Ward   ●   · · · · · · ·

FAMILIES

ON THE MOVE

E very May when spring at last comes to western Massachusetts, a small patch of phantom lilies blooms in my garden near the swamp. The annual reappearance of these modest flowers gently calls to mind the lives of certain nineteenth-century Americans who for more than a hundred years preserved bulbs of this particular stock. During the 1800s some of the lilies' caretakers left their birthplaces and moved west, and at least one migrant in every generation took phantom-lily bulbs along as mementos of the home left behind in the East. Doubtless it was comforting to know that even in a strange new land one would have near at hand sights and fragrances reminiscent of one's childhood. Among these families the habit of uprooting themselves to move farther and farther west persisted until, four generations after their forebears had left the East Coast, a few descendants reached California. The two scenes sketched below and the principal characters of each—Owen Brown, a migrant from Connecticut to Ohio in 1805, and his great-great-granddaughter Marguerite Ward, who was born on the Pacific Coast in 1900—represent the beginning and the end of that century-long journey across the continent.*

June 9, 1805. A farm west of Torrington, Connecticut. Two teams of oxen stand waiting, harnessed to heavily laden wagons. They belong to Owen Brown and Benjamin Whedon, two Connecticut Yankees about to start west for Hudson, a frontier village in the recently admitted state of Ohio.

The Brown segment of the party numbers seven: Owen Brown and his wife, Ruth, both in their early thirties, and five children—an eleven-year-old adopted son, Levi Blakeslee, and four of the Browns' own offspring (Anna, age seven, John, five, Salmon, three, and Oliver Owen, barely seven months old). The Browns are leaving many loved ones behind. Owen's ten brothers and sisters and his aged mother, as well as Ruth's parents, Gideon and Ruth Mills, and a multitude of other Mills relatives, all live in nearby Connecticut towns. But Owen's heart is set on moving west. He has sold his modest wood-frame house, his tanning business, and his farm. Although he has been ill much of the winter with fever and ague and is still not in good health, he is determined to delay no longer. Brown and Whedon urge their teams forward. The beasts lean into their heavy yokes, taking the first steps of a trip that will last seven full weeks.

August 17, 1900. A house on a dusty, small-town lane in Santa Monica, California.

In an upstairs room of the house an infant's piercing wail announces the birth of Flora and Joe Ward's second child, a daughter. The Wards arrived in Santa Monica from Needles, California, only six weeks earlier, on July 4. They decided that this quiet seaside village would be the perfect place for Flora to spend the last weeks of her pregnancy, and they rented rooms at Mrs. Hubbard's on Third Street. Joe continued to work for the Santa Fe Railroad as a fireman on a run between Needles and Los Angeles, while Flora stayed in Santa Monica and took care of her firstborn,

*There is a brief note on background references for each chapter and titled subdivision in the Sources section at the end of the book.

a toddler named Wallace Remington Ward. The new baby arrives on August 17 and is named Florilla Marguerite. Later she will be called simply Marguerite.

Between 1800, when all of Marguerite's forebears lived on the East Coast, and 1900, when she was born within easy walking distance of the Pacific, her ancestors had been migrating westward. Theirs was the story of a family on the move or, more accurately, of families on the move, since at the beginning of their journeys the various lines of Marguerite's ancestors were not yet linked by marriage or even connected by geographical proximity. Marguerite's Brown ancestors started west from Connecticut, the Roots from Massachusetts, the Greenfields from New York, the Adairs from Maryland, and the Wards from Virginia. Of necessity, therefore, before these separate branches could be joined in a single family tree, some or all of the families would need to move so that members from each of the lines could meet.

More than simple shifts of physical location were needed to bring these families together. As of 1800 the differences between them were so great that the likelihood of their becoming one another's in-laws seemed remote. Although all were members of the nation's white Protestant majority, the Browns and Roots were orthodox Congregationalists, bitter religious rivals of Baptist folk like the Greenfields. And these three Yankee families had little in common culturally with such Scotch-Irish Presbyterians as the Adairs of Maryland and the Wards of Virginia. In order for these families to intermarry, at least some individuals in each line would have to undergo significant changes in their attitudes toward either their own or another line's religious and ethnic background. Over a century's time many such changes did occur, and a description of how and why these personal transformations occurred will figure prominently in the narrative that follows.

Nearly all of Marguerite's ancestors who participated in the westward movement were common people, unknown to anyone outside their immediate circle of friends and relatives. When people of this sort are mentioned by historians, they are usually treated in the aggregate under such labels as "trans-Appalachian pioneers," "homesteaders," "rank-and-file soldiers," or "middle-class Americans." In my story of Marguerite's ancestors I have used individuals to try to convey a more intimate sense of the lives of ordinary Americans, but nothing in this emphasis on particular individuals is meant to imply that they were cut off from broader historical trends in this period. Quite the contrary was true. Marguerite's

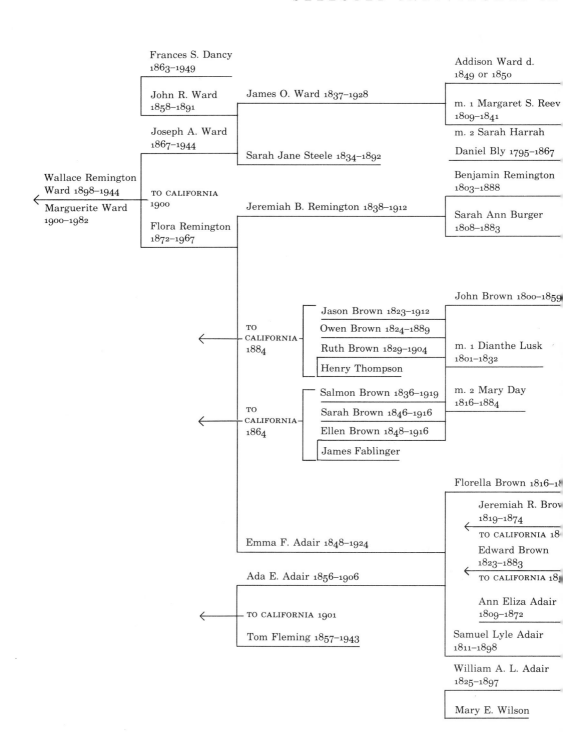

Frances S. Dancy
1863–1949

John R. Ward
1858–1891

James O. Ward 1837–1928

Joseph A. Ward
1867–1944

Sarah Jane Steele 1834–1892

Wallace Remington
Ward 1898–1944

Marguerite Ward
1900–1982

TO CALIFORNIA
1900

Flora Remington
1872–1967

Jeremiah B. Remington 1838–1912

Addison Ward d.
1849 or 1850

m. 1 Margaret S. Reev
1809–1841

m. 2 Sarah Harrah

Daniel Bly 1795–1867

Benjamin Remington
1803–1888

Sarah Ann Burger
1808–1883

TO
CALIFORNIA
1884

Jason Brown 1823–1912
Owen Brown 1824–1889
Ruth Brown 1829–1904
Henry Thompson

John Brown 1800–1859

m. 1 Dianthe Lusk
1801–1832

TO
CALIFORNIA
1864

Salmon Brown 1836–1919
Sarah Brown 1846–1916
Ellen Brown 1848–1916
James Fablinger

m. 2 Mary Day
1816–1884

Emma F. Adair 1848–1924

Ada E. Adair 1856–1906

TO CALIFORNIA 1901

Tom Fleming 1857–1943

Florella Brown 1816–1

Jeremiah R. Bro
1819–1874
TO CALIFORNIA 18

Edward Brown
1823–1883
TO CALIFORNIA 18

Ann Eliza Adair
1809–1872

Samuel Lyle Adair
1811–1898

William A. L. Adair
1825–1897

Mary E. Wilson

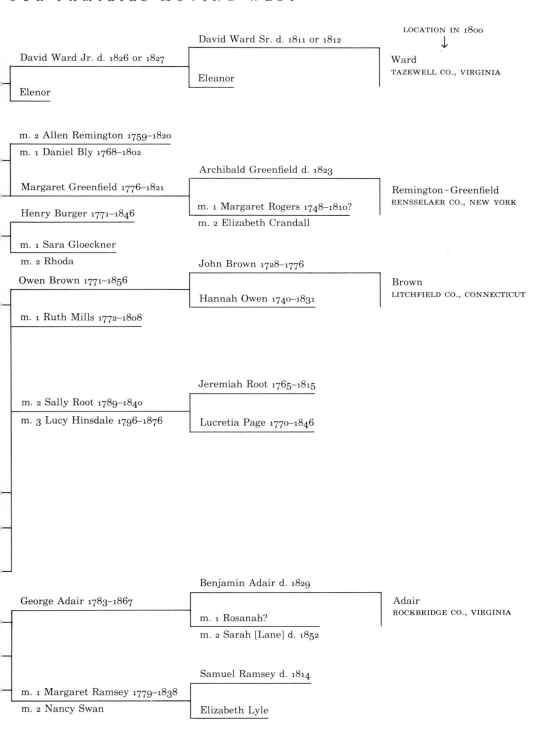

LOCATION IN 1800
↓

David Ward Sr. d. 1811 or 1812

Ward
TAZEWELL CO., VIRGINIA

David Ward Jr. d. 1826 or 1827

Eleanor

Elenor

m. 2 Allen Remington 1759–1820

m. 1 Daniel Bly 1768–1802

Archibald Greenfield d. 1823

Remington - Greenfield
RENSSELAER CO., NEW YORK

Margaret Greenfield 1776–1821

m. 1 Margaret Rogers 1748–1810?

Henry Burger 1771–1846

m. 2 Elizabeth Crandall

m. 1 Sara Gloeckner

m. 2 Rhoda

John Brown 1728–1776

Brown
LITCHFIELD CO., CONNECTICUT

Owen Brown 1771–1856

Hannah Owen 1740–1831

m. 1 Ruth Mills 1772–1808

m. 2 Sally Root 1789–1840

Jeremiah Root 1765–1815

m. 3 Lucy Hinsdale 1796–1876

Lucretia Page 1770–1846

Benjamin Adair d. 1829

Adair
ROCKBRIDGE CO., VIRGINIA

George Adair 1783–1867

m. 1 Rosanah?

m. 2 Sarah [Lane] d. 1852

Samuel Ramsey d. 1814

m. 1 Margaret Ramsey 1779–1838

m. 2 Nancy Swan

Elizabeth Lyle

ancestors changed their occupations and religious affiliations and succeeded or failed economically in ways that mirrored the experiences of
millions of ordinary Americans of their time. Moreover, her forebears
witnessed many of the nineteenth century's most notable events: the
completion of the Erie Canal, the panic of 1837, the beginnings of the
abolitionist crusade, the California gold rush, guerrilla warfare in Kansas
during the 1850s, John Brown's raid on Harpers Ferry, the Civil War, the
postwar homestead movement, the Chicago Fire, the 1876 world's fair in
Philadelphia, and the Ghost Dance War. I have mentioned the links
between these larger subjects and Marguerite's ancestors at every appro-
priate point, but in order to keep the focus on the common people themselves, I have, in all but a few places where the scarcity of facts requires
a more general approach, used an individual's life to introduce topics of
national import.

But why, one might ask, recount the lives of anonymous Americans
(a label applicable to all but one or two of Marguerite's ancestors), when
there were giants—Jefferson, Jackson, Lincoln, Emerson, Whitman,
Twain, Carnegie, and Rockefeller—in those days? One answer is that the
American dream, whether expressed as a concept ("a land of opportunity") or an ideal ("life, liberty, and the pursuit of happiness"), is a democratic vision in which common folk are supposedly the chief beneficiaries.
Moreover, few expressions of these democratic aspirations were more
characteristic of nineteenth-century Americans than the ordinary pioneer's act of pulling up stakes and heading west. And while the sweep of
westward migration can be described as a movement of people in the
aggregate, the process itself had an inner dimension that (insofar as it can
be reconstructed at all) must be understood through the lives of individual
pioneers. What motivated them to start west? When they reached their
new homes, did they find what they had hoped to find, or something else?
How did the realities of the migration experience affect their dreams?
Surely the best answers to these questions rest not in what the nation's
leaders, the century's giants, said the promise of American life was but
in what the common folk found it to be.

A Scattered People

BEGINNINGS: THE COLONIAL ERA

On March 20, 1630, the *Mary and John,* a three-masted ship under the command of a certain Captain Squib, weighed anchor from Plymouth, England. The ship carried 140 passengers whose destination was New England. Nearly all of them were farmers who hoped to obtain more and better land by moving to Massachusetts. Had Owen Brown, our Yankee migrant to Ohio in 1805, chanced to come across a copy of the *Mary and John*'s passenger list, he would have found on it the names of great-great-grandparents in five ancestral lines.

The voyage lasted ten weeks and a day, from March 20 to May 30, a fairly average length of time in transit for the period. We know nothing of the trip's particulars beyond the fact that the two ministers who were on board preached daily to their fellow passengers. However, to judge from logs of other ships en route to New England that same spring, it is fair to assume that the *Mary and John* encountered several bad storms and that heavy seas and gale-force winds compelled all the passengers to spend days at a time confined to the narrow, windowless space below the ship's deck. Nevertheless, if the recollections of a young bachelor passenger, Roger Clapp, are to be trusted, the emigrants did not suffer much. As Clapp put it in his Memoirs, "So we came by the good hand of the Lord through the deep comfortably, having preaching or expounding of the word of God every day for ten weeks together by our ministers."[1]

No sooner had the *Mary and John* come within sight of the Massachusetts coast than the colonists' luck took a turn for the worse. They had hoped to go directly to a site on the Charles River near present-day Boston, but when Captain Squib discovered that there were no pilots to

Early-seventeenth-century ship, from Joseph Furtenbach's
Architectura Navalis (1629).

guide the *Mary and John* into the harbor, he refused to risk the shoals
and unloaded his passengers and their goods on a barren peninsula outside the harbor (Nantasket Point). After some delays, the settlers
managed to move to Mattapan, which they renamed Dorchester (now part
of Boston). They were already running short of provisions, and many kept
themselves from starving only by digging for clams or by fishing from
several small boats that they hastily constructed. Fortunately for the
colonists, Indians came with corn to sell, and trading ships from Holland
and Ireland arrived with other goods.

Assistance from other humans was particularly valued in a land
where the white population was so scattered. When the *Mary and John*'s
passengers disembarked in May 1630, the only permanent European residents on the Atlantic seaboard south of Massachusetts were a few Span-
iards in Florida towns, a couple of thousand English in the colony of
Virginia, and a handful of Dutch in small outposts around the New York
area. Of the few white communities in Massachusetts, the largest was at
Plymouth, where the colony founded in 1620 by the *Mayflower* Pilgrims
numbered only a few hundred souls a decade later.

The arrival of the *Mary and John* marked the beginning of a new
phase of immigration to New England, the so-called Great Migration of
the 1630s. Following close in the wake of the *Mary and John* were eleven
ships of the Winthrop Fleet. This flotilla, organized under the leadership
of John Winthrop, governor of the recently chartered Massachusetts Bay
Colony, brought seven hundred settlers to Massachusetts in June and
early July 1630. Winthrop and many who accompanied him were Puritans, English Calvinists who wanted to purge the Church of England of
the Catholic influences that were growing stronger during the reign of the
Stuart king, Charles I. The church hierarchy's efforts to make its Puritan
critics conform led many of the latter to consider leaving England, but
economic aspirations determined their choice of New England as an eventual destination. To English people of Winthrop's era, land was wealth,
and not only did New England have vast expanses of land unoccupied by
other whites but, by European standards, the region's natural resources
were awesomely abundant: forests with trees of greater height and girth
than any in Europe, skies at times dark with passing flocks of birds, and
coastal waters with some of the world's richest fishing banks. And so the
English came, an estimated twenty thousand of them arriving in New
England between 1630 and 1640.

Regional differences made the English a varied lot. Among the colonists who arrived in 1630, for instance, the *Mary and John*'s passengers came from England's West Country, especially from the southwestern counties of Dorset, Devon, and Somerset. John Winthrop and most of the settlers who came in the Winthrop Fleet were from East Anglia, that is, from counties such as Suffolk, Norfolk, and Essex that were located northeast of London. At the time of the Great Migration most East Anglians customarily farmed enclosed fields that belonged to a single family or (at most) to two or three proprietors. West Country agriculture, on the other hand, was characterized by the open-field system, under which many families owned narrow strips of land in a common field and had to make cooperative decisions regarding which crops or animals to raise. Contrasting patterns of land use constituted but one of the many differences between the agriculture of the West Country and that of East Anglia, and the desire of English colonists to maintain their distinctive traditions led most of those who emigrated to the New World to sort themselves into towns with clear regional roots: West Country folk founded Dorchester and Newbury, and East Anglians established such towns as Hingham, Ipswich, and Watertown.

In religious matters the English colonists were split, broadly speaking, between Puritans from East Anglia and non-Puritans from the West and the North. Puritanism had only recently taken hold in England's West Country, and its few adherents there acted with such moderation that they did not become targets for persecution. By contrast, East Anglia had long been a hotbed of militant Puritan activity, and Winthrop and many other East Anglians had been harassed for their Puritan convictions. Once in New England the East Anglians, in working out precisely what they thought a pure church would be, soon settled on a new and more restrictive definition of church membership. Membership, they decided, should be limited to the "visible saints," those individuals who could publicly testify to a direct experience of being one of God's chosen. This doctrine not only limited church membership to the saints but had major political implications as well; Massachusetts stipulated that only church members could vote and hold office.

In the very years (1635–36) when the colony's Puritan leaders were consolidating their political and theological hegemony, Owen Brown's ancestors and a majority of the other West Country folk who had settled at Dorchester in 1630 decided to leave Massachusetts. Direct evidence about their motives is sparse. Apparently, they hoped that a move to the Connecticut River valley (a hundred miles west of Dorchester) would produce economic gains—better pasture land for their herds and a chance to tap into the rich western fur trade. But religion and politics also figured in the move. Dorchester's spiritual leader, the Reverend John Warham, was both a strong supporter of the relocation plan and a spokesman for the West Country tradition of religious moderation. Whereas Massachusetts's Puritan leaders wanted church membership reserved for the elect only, Warham had argued that "the visible church may consist of a mixed people, godly and ungodly."[2] This less restrictive standard for church membership had as its parallel in secular affairs a liberal view of political rights, which Warham and his followers adopted once they reached Windsor, their new Connecticut Valley home. In 1639, settlers from Windsor and two nearby towns (Hartford and Wethersfield) joined together to found Connecticut, a colony whose original charter rejected the Massachusetts precedent and made non–church members eligible to vote and hold office.

Connecticut's founders by no means went west into a trackless wilderness. The parties of settlers that left Dorchester for Windsor in 1635 and 1636 followed a well-established Indian trail across country to the Connecticut Valley. Once in Windsor, the immigrants turned their cattle and swine out into meadows that had been cleared by local Indians. These fields were not under cultivation in the mid-1630s, because smallpox, an Old World problem exported to the New, had caused an epidemic in 1633 that had decimated the Indian population of southern New England. The local Connecticut Valley tribes nevertheless welcomed the English newcomers as potential allies against more-powerful neighboring tribes. Consistent with English practice, Windsor's settlers purchased deeds to the land from local sachems, a process that was repeated over the years as the town expanded. In one such transaction in 1667, Owen Brown's great-great-great-grandfather James Enno bankrolled the purchase of one square mile of land from Massahogan and four other Indians. In the town's first few years there was a busy trade between the natives and the newcomers, Indians bringing pelts—beaver, fox, lynx, and others—to Windsor to exchange for the whites' cloth and metal goods.

European expansion in New England did not go unopposed. In July 1636, Indians killed a white fur trader near Block Island (off present-day Rhode Island). Massachusetts promptly sent an expedition under John

Endicott, who attempted to discipline the Pequots, the most powerful and militant tribe in the area, although the trader's murderers were most likely from another tribe. Endicott's efforts to humble the Pequots backfired, for the tribe became more rather than less belligerent. In October 1636 a Windsor man was tortured to death by Pequots, and the following spring a Pequot war party raided farms near Wethersfield, a settlement less than ten miles south of Windsor, killing nine whites and abducting two others.

Connecticut's settlers now went on the offensive. Captain John Mason of Windsor assumed command of a new force of ninety colonists; Windsor contributed thirty men in all, nearly half the adult male population. Two of Owen Brown's ancestors, James Eggleston and Nathan Gillett, joined the expedition. On May 10, the ninety whites and their sixty Mohegan Indian allies sailed down the Connecticut from Hartford to Long Island Sound. Just over two weeks later (May 26), Mason's forces made a dawn raid against a major Pequot stronghold, Mystic Fort (near present-day Stonington). The attackers surprised the Pequots, surrounded the fort, set it on fire, and killed all who tried to escape the flames. Four to six hundred Indian men, women, and children were slaughtered that morning, while only two whites lost their lives. Subsequently, other Pequots were hunted down and killed until the once-feared tribe was virtually exterminated. The significance of the Pequot War was not lost on other New England Indians, who, noting the colonists' ruthlessness in war, did not risk another general conflict with the white invaders for nearly forty years.

With the return of the victors to Windsor, the townspeople were again able to concentrate on building their new community. In 1639 they began to construct a meetinghouse near the center of town. In 1640 the town started recording deeds for land distributed in the 1630s. Ninety-two Windsor residents received 16,000 acres in the first round of land grants. The amount each settler got varied widely; the top 10 percent received 41 percent of the distribution, whereas the lowest 20 percent got only 3.5 percent. Yet even the smallest grant, William Hannum's, was for 10 1/4 acres. In a typical English village of the time, on the other hand, few, if any, residents in the bottom half of the village's status ladder owned any land at all. For English colonists accustomed to Old World standards of wealth, becoming a beneficiary of Windsor's liberal land policy was nothing less than a dream come true.

Attack on the Pequots at Mystic Fort,
May 26, 1637.

The method of land distribution and the practice of building a Congregational meetinghouse at the town's main crossroads were only two of the characteristic features of New England colonial society that were observable at Windsor as early as 1640. It is also clear that the destruction of the native Indian population through chance (disease) and intention (war) had begun. Moreover, colonists from the first used huge quantities of wood, a commodity relatively scarce in the Old World but plentiful in the New. By one estimate, a typical New England family burned thirty to forty cords (a pile four feet wide, four feet high, and three hundred feet long) annually in open-hearth fireplaces. It was said that a roaring fire was to the white settler what a blanket was to an Indian. All-wood houses, wooden fences that needed to be replaced every few years, and the practice of burning woodland acres to clear them for fields and pastures—all these depleted New England's forest resources until by the end of the colonial period Connecticut settlers were beginning to build stone fences because wood was increasingly in short supply. Most of the forest's larger animals—deer, moose, lynx, bear—also disappeared as southern New England lost its forest cover.

And what did the English bring to the New World from the Old? The same ships that brought colonists also carried things the emigrants probably wished they had left behind: black flies, rats, cockroaches, and sturdy weeds such as dandelion, nightshade, and stinging nettle—none of them native to North America. Other imports, however, were crucial to the newcomers' way of life: English law, Protestantism, sailing vessels, metal agricultural implements, honeybees, firearms, hardy clovers and grasses, and (most important of all for the Anglo-American farming economy) domestic animals of all types—cattle, goats, sheep, horses, and swine. The impact of these innovations, for good or ill, would not be fully felt for decades, even centuries. But by 1640, when the outbreak of civil war in England ended the first Great Migration, the white colonists' drive to populate North America and to reshape it to their liking was already well under way.

THE BROWNS OF
ANCIENT WINDSOR

I n 1892 an industrious historian-genealogist named Henry R. Stiles published a two-volume work entitled *The History of Ancient Windsor*. Stiles's use of the adjective *ancient* was not altogether extravagant, since the town's first white settlers had arrived in the 1630s. Such was Windsor's antiquity, indeed, that by the 1790s, a full century before Stiles's book appeared, some families had lived there and in nearby towns for five generations. By Stiles's day, however, few visible signs of seventeenth- and eighteenth-century Windsor still remained; when he began his research in the 1850s, he found only a very few old residents who could remember seeing the colonial era's more notable buildings.

Even more-drastic transformations have taken place in our time. Seventeenth-century Windsor and Simsbury (and their eighteenth-century offshoots, Bloomfield, Granby, and West Simsbury) are now suburbs or satellite towns of the bustling commercial city of Hartford. Interstate 91, the main northbound artery, passes through Ancient Windsor's countryside, but the traces of the town's preindustrial past that still exist are hidden from view. Both on and off the interstate, the dominant sights and sounds are modern ones: long lines of cars inching along in weekday traffic jams, suburban shopping centers, asphalt roads lined with ranch-style houses, and the roar of jets taking off from Bradley International.

The English colonial villages of Windsor and Simsbury had very different forms and rhythms. Windsor's founders built their first homes on tightly clustered lots along roads near the Connecticut River. The exterior features of many of these seventeenth-century houses had a rather medieval asymmetry: windows unevenly aligned with each other, an overhanging second floor, and a longer back roof (the so-called saltbox shape), the extended part of which covered an attached shed. These houses were relatively small on the inside, the most common type having only four rooms, two downstairs and two above. Utility was a governing principle throughout. To prevent heat loss in winter, windows were as few and as small as possible. Almost all space was used for multiple purposes; at various times each day the same room might serve as a bedroom, kitchen, workroom (for carpentry, spinning, and cheese making), school, place of worship, dining room, social hall, and then bedroom again. These

Seventeenth-century New England home: the Whitman House (c. 1660),
Farmington, Connecticut.

successive and sometimes simultaneous uses required simple and mobile
furnishings such as trunks and chests, which could serve equally well as
benches, tables, and storage spaces. Seventeenth-century estate inventories, with their lists of candlesticks, warming pans, and chamber pots,
testify to the lack of modern conveniences.

The clothing and household activities of Windsor residents also reflected a communal life-style relatively lacking in comfort, personal
possessions, and privacy. Each member of a typical household would have
had two changes of clothing, usually homespun cloth in an orange-brown
or russet shade, but occasionally dyed red, green, blue, or even purple.
Cooking and fire tending, women's chores, took great skill to manage in
open hearths large enough to stand in. Food preparation and consumption
still followed medieval styles; the colonists ate mostly stews and porridges
cooked in large pots and served in trenchers (wooden platters shared by
two or more trencher mates). Individual plates and drinking utensils were
rare. The common pot, communal mug, and shared trencher were the
rule.

By 1650 there were just over a hundred households of the type described above in Windsor, eight of them composed of people who would
become Owen Brown's ancestors. Of these eight houses, only one, the

Loomis homestead in Windsor center, survives today. Church buildings associated with Owen's forebears are equally rare, for although Congregational meetinghouses in the traditional New England style (with white clapboard exteriors and tall steeples) still dot the countryside throughout what was once Ancient Windsor and Old Simsbury, these are not the buildings in which Owen's ancestors worshiped. The older structures were torn down to make way for new meetinghouses at Windsor in 1794, Canton in 1815, Simsbury in 1830, and Bloomfield in 1890.

The elusive track of Owen's ancestors is followed more easily in old cemeteries at Windsor, East Granby, and Bloomfield, where many early settlers lie under rows of weathered reddish stones. One such headstone in Windsor's Old Burying Ground commemorates the progenitor of the Brown family, Peter Browne, who still spelled his name in the old way, with an *e* at the end (a practice his sons soon dropped). This Peter Browne first appears in Windsor records in 1658, when he bought a lot in town and married Mary Gillett, the American-born daughter of a West Country family that had come to Massachusetts in 1630 aboard the *Mary and John.* Mary and Peter Browne were Owen's great-great-grandparents.

Like the vast majority of Ancient Windsor's early residents, Mary Gillett and Peter Browne were English. Owen Brown's mother, Hannah Owen, however, was the great-granddaughter of John Owen, a Welsh immigrant, and the district of Windsor where he had lived was popularly known as Wales. Owen Brown's first wife, Ruth Mills, was a great-granddaughter of Pieter Wouter van der Meulen, a native of Holland who Anglicized his name to Mills after he settled in Windsor.

Windsor's founders, Owen's forebears included, were nearly all Congregationalists. Their denomination's monopoly hold on the town's religious life was rarely challenged prior to the mid-1700s. Even then, when Baptists rebelled against the Congregational establishment, the old orthodoxy managed to preserve its hegemony. Hegemony, however, by no means meant harmony, at least not in Windsor's Congregational parishes. In 1667 the efforts of Windsor's oldest church to choose a successor to John Warham, its first minister, triggered a bitter controversy that took fifteen years to resolve. Three of Owen Brown's ancestors—John Owen, John Hoskins, and Peter Mills—left the church as part of a splinter group whose leaders complained that they "perceived a deeprooted spirit of bitterness boiling in the breast of some of those of the old congregation here in Windsor against [them]selves."[3] A similar feud divided the "Second Society of Windsor" (the Poquonock parish) not long after it was founded in 1724 by a group of settlers from old Windsor, among them three of Peter Browne's four sons.

A force that did more to destabilize old New England communities than did religious controversies was the need for geographical expansion to accommodate internal population growth. This need was a fact of life that asserted itself very early in Windsor's history, mainly because the town's families were so large. For example, Owen Brown's eight pairs of great-great-grandparents had among themselves, respectively, twelve, thirteen, nine, nine, eleven, nine, seventeen, and eight children. Parents of such large broods often found that the family's landholdings, though generous by English standards, did not produce farms of satisfactory size (by American standards) when divided among so many heirs. Under such circumstances, land hunger exerted an insistent pressure on families to have some children move away from the older settlements. An option open to heirs was to trade or sell all or part of their inherited land in order to obtain a larger acreage of less-developed or even uncleared land on the outskirts of the old parishes. Peter and Mary Browne's sons made precisely this type of exchange in 1694, only two years after their father's death.

The large size of colonial families had a profound impact on the lives of many women, for whom the years from the age of twenty (give or take a few years) to menopause were devoted to childbearing. Peter Browne's wife, Mary, herself one of ten children, had twelve babies between 1659 and 1681. This pace of childbearing tied Mary to a reproductive cycle in which each round of pregnancy, birth, and lactation lasted only twenty to thirty months. Birthing was a social occasion over which the mother and her female friends exercised almost unchallenged control. Typically, a woman about to deliver gathered her closest female friends and relatives to assist her through her time of travail. In 1670, for example, when Mindwell Bissell was about to give birth to her fourth child, she asked her half sisters, Hannah Drake (Owen Brown's great-great-grandmother) and Elizabeth Loomis, and a midwife, Mrs. Walter Filer, to aid her. Mindwell lived on the east side of the Connecticut River, her three helpers lived on the west, and, because it was midwinter, the river was iced over. A passage was chopped through the ice, and the women were ferried across to attend Mindwell. On the return trip, however, the passage between the ice floes suddenly closed, and the canoe in which the women were riding was smashed. All three women went under the ice, but somehow they were rescued. Their miraculous escape came to the attention of Increase

Mather, an eminent Boston clergyman, who preserved the story for posterity by including it in his *Remarkable Providences.*

Not all the births in these prolific families were socially sanctioned. If, for example, a midwife testified before the town magistrates that the child of a couple married less than nine months had been carried to full term, it was taken as proof of premarital fornication. The couple were expected to confess their sin, accept punishment, and thereby be returned to good standing in the community. Although instances of premarital sexual intercourse were rare in Windsor's first fifty years, the frequency of sexual misconduct increased by the end of the seventeenth century. Just how far the breakdown of social control of sexual behavior had gone is evident in the case of Sarah Brown, Peter and Mary Browne's youngest daughter. In 1702 Sarah and her husband, Joseph Moore, were haled into court because she had borne a full-term child after only four months of marriage. Not only did Sarah and Joseph fail to express remorse but the jury backed them by refusing to follow the magistrate's instructions to convict the couple. Though this was a striking example of youthful defiance, it was not an isolated case. Throughout New England, the incidence of illegal and early births grew in the eighteenth century. The reasons for this trend are complex, but in land-poor districts it seems that some young couples forced their parents to let them marry (and to give them land) by presenting them with a pregnancy.

Given the fecundity of many colonial families, it was not uncommon for the need to arise to found new towns and parishes in every generation. The movement away from older towns by the original settlers' sons and daughters did not necessarily involve great distances. As the crow flies, it is barely fifteen miles (a day's travel in colonial times) from the Windsor lot Peter Browne purchased in 1658 to the Canton farm where his great-great-grandson Owen was born in 1771, more than a hundred years later. However, in the four generations of Brown men in direct line from Owen back to Peter, none of the sons was born in the same parish as his father: Peter and Mary Browne's son John (1668–1728) was born in Windsor; John and Elizabeth's son John Jr. (1700–1790) was born in Poquonock; Mary and John Jr.'s son John (1728–1776) was born in Wintonbury parish (now Bloomfield); and this third John and his wife, Hannah, moved to West Simsbury (now Canton), where their son Owen Brown was born on February 16, 1771.

Had the first Peter Browne of Windsor and his wife been able to visit West Simsbury on the occasion of their great-great-grandson's birth, they would doubtless have found that much had changed. In poking around her descendants' houses, Mary might have been struck by the much increased number of individual cups, plates, bowls, and mugs in use at mealtime. Forks were entirely new to her, an eighteenth-century innovation. Many of the ceramic items used in 1771 were thinner and harder, with a cream-colored glaze, in contrast with the pottery of Mary's day, most of it an undecorated buff or red clay with a yellowish-green finish. Meat was now frequently prepared in individualized portions, cut into even pieces with a saw rather than chopped with an ax into rough cuts for old-fashioned stews, the main meal of Mary's time. Outside the house, she might have noted that her descendants no longer broadcast table scraps and refuse out into the dooryard, as they had done, but buried trash in square pits away from the house.

But Mary and Peter would have found much that was familiar too. Most notably, perhaps, Peter would have been gratified to observe that his great-grandson John (Owen's father) was following a well-tested path, one Peter himself had trod a century earlier. John was an orthodox Congregationalist, a middling-prosperous farmer (ranking in the top third of local estates, though toward the bottom of that group), the head of a large and growing family, and a man connected through marriage to many of Windsor's founding families. Hints of the coming American Revolution, already in the air in 1771, might have given Peter a moment's pause. Only four years later, during the ruckus occasioned by the British attack on Lexington and Concord, John would spend three days marching toward eastern Massachusetts, turning back when his services were not immediately needed. In the fall of 1776, after the Revolution had broken out in earnest, Captain John Brown of Simsbury would march at the head of a militia unit to aid in the defense of New York City, only to die of camp fever two weeks into the campaign. But the actual move for independence and the battles that followed were still five or more years in the future at the time of Peter and Mary's hypothetical visit, so the political stirrings of 1771 might well have struck the old folks as not very different from the tumult and uncertainty that had accompanied the upheavals of their day —the Puritan Revolution and the Glorious Revolution of 1688.

The obvious continuities and relative stability to be found in Windsor, still an English colonial village in 1771, should not obscure the fact that forces were already present in American society that would disrupt these continuities—forces including, among other things, the ambitions of the colonists. The Browns and their neighbors had long been a restless people, as was evidenced by their original migration to North America and subsequently by their many small moves in Ancient Windsor and its environs. When Owen Brown struck out for Ohio in 1805, therefore, he was in many respects simply extending a family migration pattern into a new land in a new century.

THE ROOTS OF WESTFIELD AND SOUTHWICK

J eremiah Root was born on July 7, 1765, in the South Part (now Southwick) of Westfield, Massachusetts. Although he was less than six years older than Owen Brown, and although the two men lived in towns barely fifteen miles apart, he and Brown did not meet until each had made his separate way more than five hundred miles west to the Ohio frontier. There, in November 1809, a year after the death of his first wife, Owen married Jeremiah's oldest daughter, Sally. Whatever personal considerations went into forging this union, it had a compelling logic based on the two families' similar backgrounds.

The original Root immigrant to America was an Englishman named John Roote who came to Connecticut around 1640 and settled in Farmington, an early offshoot of Hartford. Like Peter Browne, his contemporary in nearby Windsor, John Roote of Farmington married a woman named Mary, had a large family (eight children), and was (as was his wife) a member in full communion of the local Congregational church. John and Mary Roote prospered. In a list of Farmington's taxpayers as of 1672, the Rootes ranked in the top 10 percent, seventh among eighty-four families in town. Despite their family's relative prosperity, the Rootes' older sons —John, Samuel, and Thomas—felt the need to leave Farmington and seek their fortunes elsewhere. In the late 1660s the three brothers, young men in their twenties, moved to one of the nearest areas where new land was readily available: the western frontier of Massachusetts, a part of the Connecticut River valley ten miles west of present-day Springfield.

Like Windsor, its neighbor to the south, Springfield was founded in the mid-1630s. However, whereas Windsor was a communal enterprise, established cooperatively by a group of colonists, Springfield owed much more to the leadership of a single man, William Pynchon. Pynchon chose Springfield's site upriver from Windsor with an eye to controlling the Connecticut Valley's rich fur trade. Putting his wealth to good use, he and his son John (who took charge of the family's New England ventures in 1652) were able to dominate Springfield's economic life. One-third of the local residents worked full- or part-time in the Pynchons' diverse businesses—grain mills, farms, construction projects, mines, and export trade. A large Pynchon warehouse at Agawam was the hub of valley commerce. Indian hunters and white farmers alike brought their goods to Warehouse Point to exchange for supplies. The local products—meats, grains, and furs—were then exported, the foodstuffs most often being sent to the West Indies aboard Pynchon-owned vessels.

As the fur trade began to decline in the 1650s, the Pynchons, ever the entrepreneurs, promoted the expansion of commercial agriculture in the valley by underwriting the establishment of such towns as Northampton in 1653, Hadley in 1659, and Westfield in 1667. Westfield fit well in the Pynchon master plan. The town's location on an old Indian trail meant that the new settlement was strategically placed to maintain control over whatever fur trade remained in the nearby Berkshire hills. But the town's long-term value to the Pynchon interests was as a producing center for grain and livestock.

Precisely how the three Root brothers were recruited as Westfield residents is unknown. Perhaps they were attracted to the area by reports from several Root relatives who had settled in nearby Northampton and who had worked for and traded with the Pynchons. In any case, the Root brothers were among the twenty or so men who shared in the initial division of Westfield land. This was a fact of no small importance, since under the colonial land system in Massachusetts a town's initial grant of land was made to a group of settlers. These so-called proprietors would then divide the land among themselves, granting various amounts to individuals on the basis of each grantee's wealth, social and political standing, and family size. Equally significant, the proprietors would leave some land undistributed, to be held in common until future divisions took place. Although latecomers to a town might be allowed to purchase proprietary rights (the right to share in future divisions of land), there was a tremendous advantage in being one of the original proprietors, whose families automatically participated in any further distribution of town land.

Building on their privileged position as founders of the town, the Root brothers became prominent figures in Westfield. John, the eldest, whose gravestone in the original town cemetery is said to be the oldest in Westfield, held various town offices and helped found the Westfield Congregational Church. Samuel, the next brother, was an early deacon of the church. His library contained a substantial number of Bibles, psalm books, and catechisms, as well as a variety of other books whose titles reflect the formidable otherworldliness of seventeenth-century New England Protestantism: *Thirsty Sinner, Preparation to Die, Barbarian Cruelty, Discourse on Witchcraft, Mourner's Cordial,* and *Groans of the Damned.*

Deacon Root's estate inventory indicates that he had military as well as religious interests. His armory contained a long gun, a musket, two carbines, a backsword and belt, and a handy assortment of gun rests, half-pikes, bullets, and powder. Such armaments were not kept merely for sport or show. It was a dangerous era, marked by frequent outbreaks of Indian and imperial wars. On several occasions military conflicts came uncomfortably close to Root's Westfield doorstep. In 1675–76 King Philip's War, a ferocious struggle between New England whites and Indians, brought widespread devastation to western Massachusetts. One in every

The footstone of Deacon Root's grave, Westfield, Massachusetts.

sixteen white men of military age was killed. Many colonial towns were damaged, and two frontier outposts (Deerfield and Northfield) had to be abandoned. Although Westfield was one of the few towns to escape direct attack, three Westfield men died in battle elsewhere. Moreover, this was not the last military threat to Westfield. In 1704, during Queen Anne's War (between the French and the English, with Indian allies on both sides), the house of the youngest Root brother, Thomas, was designated one of five Westfield residences to be fortified against possible enemy attack. Westfield again escaped damage, but at Deerfield, only thirty miles to the north, a combined force of Indians and French swept into town and killed or captured a majority of its residents.

Although the Roots prospered in Westfield during the late 1600s and early 1700s, the town proper eventually grew too crowded to contain their numbers and ambitions. Thomas Root had ten children by three wives. His son John had thirteen children, the second of which was John Jr. Early in the 1730s when a distribution of land was made in Westfield's South Part, five to seven miles from the old town center, John Root Jr. eagerly sought his share. He and his wife, Anna, then settled in a section of present-day Southwick (as the South Part was called later) that is even now known as the Root district.

In the 1750s, 1760s, and 1770s, the Roots of Westfield's South Part accepted the leadership positions in religious, political, and military affairs to which they were accustomed, given their family's status. John Root Jr. and his wife, Anna Loomis Root, were two of the eight original members of the Southwick Congregational Church. When the church's first officers were selected, John was named moderator, a clear indication of his high standing in the community. Moreover, the site chosen for the first meetinghouse was in the Root district, and while there were many reasons for this choice, one able historian of the church's early history has suggested that such "middle-aged prime-movers" as Anna and John Root brought their influence to bear on behalf of a location convenient to their homes.[4]

Anna and John Jr.'s oldest son, Gideon Root (1735–1804), was a soldier, a prosperous farmer, and an active promoter of Southwick's ecclesiastical and political independence from Westfield. During the French and Indian War, Gideon served as a private in several campaigns, among them the ill-fated Crown Point expedition of 1755. Three years later he married Huldah Nelson. Their ten children, including their second son, Jeremiah Root, were all born on the family farm in Southwick. In 1765

Gideon Root and fifty other residents of Westfield's South Part petitioned that Southwick be organized as a separate district. This was the first step of a process by which Southwick became an independent parish (1770) and an incorporated town (1775).

Gideon Root again went to war during the American Revolution. However, unlike some residents of the seacoast region of eastern Massachusetts (where anti-British feeling had been building since the Stamp Act crisis of 1765), Root and his neighbors in Southwick did not bestir themselves to drill and to stockpile arms until after Lexington and Concord in 1775. When war came, Root and many other farmers from New England's interior regions participated, but often they limited their active service to very short tours of duty. The record shows that in late August 1777 Root was a sergeant in one of the milita units assigned to try to stop British forces under General Burgoyne as they advanced from Canada down the Hudson River valley. After Burgoyne surrendered in early October, Root and several comrades apparently tired of hanging around camp and deserted, as a result of which they were denied pay for their earlier service. In 1779, however, Root again served for a month as a sergeant in the militia, this time in defense of New London. Two years later he was promoted to lieutenant, but by that time the major theater of military activity had shifted far to the south (to Virginia and the Carolinas), and Root did not again see combat. Three months under arms during the early years of the fight for independence was the sum of his Revolutionary War service.

Jeremiah Root's forebears were to Westfield, Massachusetts, what Owen Brown's were to Ancient Windsor. As late as the Revolution, more than a hundred years after each family had settled in its respective town, a fifth generation of Browns and Roots were being born on farms not far from where their ancestors had originally settled—Owen Brown just fifteen miles from old Windsor, Jeremiah Root only seven miles from Westfield. Both families remained orthodox Congregationalists, and both produced officers in the American militia during the Revolution. To be sure, the Roots, on the whole, were wealthier than the Browns, and Roots were among Westfield's founders, whereas Peter Browne had not arrived in Windsor until roughly two decades after the town's first settlers. But within the mosaic of religious and regional variations that made up American society in 1800, the Browns and the Roots—Yankees, farmers, Congregationalists, and townspeople—were found in the same part of the overall pattern.

MARGARET GREENFIELD'S BAPTIST HERITAGE

It is less than sixty miles from the Root family's Southwick farm to the Little Hoosick Valley in New York State, where Margaret Greenfield was born in 1776. During the 1770s, however, the cultural distance between these two locales was vast. The Roots of Southwick were residents of a settled community, a farm village complete with clapboard houses and a church and situated near a mature market town (Westfield). By contrast, Margaret Greenfield's parents lived in a raw frontier environment. Located just west of the New York–Massachusetts border, the Little Hoosick Valley (now part of Rensselaer County, New York) had been settled by a few Dutch homesteaders in the 1750s and 1760s. However, as late as 1770, when the Daniel Hull family, the first Yankee settlers, arrived, they found that the lack of a road through the southern part of the valley forced them to abandon their wagon and to continue the last few miles to their home site on foot, using an Indian trail that wound through "unbroken wilderness."[5] By the time Margaret Greenfield was born in 1776, more Yankees had arrived and occupied log homes scattered throughout the district, but they had been so preoccupied with clearing fields and building roads that they had not yet established churches, stores, or schools and would not do so until the early 1780s.

In two other important areas, land ownership patterns and religious preferences, the experience of Little Hoosick's settlers was distinct from that of Southwick's. New York had been New Netherland, a Dutch colony, until the mid-1660s, and the Dutch colonial inheritance remained influential even in Margaret Greenfield's day. Little Hoosick was part of the East Manor of Rensselaerswyck, property that belonged to the Van Rensselaer family under a semifeudal land system that had its origins in the Dutch government's practice of granting huge tracts to landlords known as patroons. Unlike the Roots of Southwick, therefore, Margaret Greenfield's parents did not own their farm but leased it from the lord of the manor, Stephen Van Rensselaer. However, an even more significant contrast between the Roots and the Greenfields was that Margaret's parents were Baptists, dissenters from the Congregational orthodoxy that ruled Southwick.

Baptists had long been a thorn in the side of New England's Congregational establishment. Throughout much of the seventeenth century, Congregationalists, dominant in every New England colony except Rhode Island, aggressively attempted to repress the Baptist faith. Baptists, though few in number, vigorously resisted and even won a few victories in their struggle for minority rights. These battles over religious freedom continued until the English imposed the Toleration Act of 1689 (granting Quakers, Baptists, and Anglicans freedom of worship), after which an uneasy truce set in. Outside of Rhode Island, however, Baptists remained a tiny minority in the population, their ranks kept thin by the social ostracism with which Congregational communities greeted Baptists. Coincidentally, the imposition of the Toleration Act occurred at the beginning of a period when colonial pietism was at ebb tide. During the four decades from 1690 to 1730, formalism and apathy prevailed in most New England congregations, orthodox and dissenting alike.

This complacency was shattered by the Great Awakening, a series of revivals whose major phase in New England dated from 1740, the year a leading English evangelist, George Whitefield, made his first North American tour. The New Lights, as those caught up in the revivals were called, were a diverse group, but they all shared a belief in the necessity of undergoing a personal conversion experience. Observing that many members of orthodox churches lacked this experience, the born-again Christians sought to revitalize their old congregations. Frequently they were rebuffed. Where reluctance among the orthodox hardened into intransigence, the New Lights usually felt compelled to "come out" of Congregational churches and organize themselves as "Separates." Most old-line Baptists also snubbed the New Lights in their congregations, and soon the born-again Baptists split off to form New Light Baptist churches.

In the 1750s and 1760s the New Light Baptists and some of the Separates drew together. By a complicated series of theological and political decisions, they joined under the Baptist label, though not without many losses from their ranks, especially among Separates who succumbed to social pressure and returned to the Congregational fold. These transformations were, of course, individual as well as group experiences, as can be illustrated by the lives of Margaret Greenfield's grandfathers—Joseph Rogers and James Greenfield.

Joseph Rogers's hometown of Exeter, Rhode Island, was a hotbed of New Light Baptist feeling in the late 1740s and early 1750s. Perhaps the intensity of the Holy Spirit's working there was prompted in part by Exeter's status as a recently organized town. Typically, settled ministers neglected such outlying districts, and the relatively less affluent people who inhabited them were often hungry for the emotional intensity characteristic of New Light preaching. Whatever the reason, a New Light Baptist church was organized in Exeter in 1750. Joseph Rogers, a strong-willed farmer in his late twenties, was an original deacon. The Reverend David Sprague, a dynamic preacher whose adherence to New Light views had already led to his dismissal from two old-line Baptist congregations, was chosen the church's first minister.

A hallmark of New Light belief was an insistence on personal piety, and church members kept a close eye not only on their own but also on each other's moral and religious fitness. Practiced rigorously, watchfulness sometimes had disruptive consequences, often producing dismissals, departures, and rancorous bickering among the New Lights. Elder Sprague broke off preaching at Exeter for a three-year period because a conference sponsored by the congregation had endorsed open communion between New Light Baptists and Separates (i.e., New Light Congregationalists), a decision he opposed. Not long thereafter Deacon Rogers also left the church, reportedly because he had "a grievous difficulty with another brother."[6] Rogers apparently soon relented and reunited with the church in May 1758. But peace did not prevail for long, for the very next year he was again at odds with one of the brethren. So, one supposes, relations among these crotchety individuals continued until 1766, when Deacon Rogers and his wife, Margaret, both now in their mid-forties, took their four daughters and left Rhode Island for Rensselaerswyck, New York.

Margaret Greenfield's other grandfather-to-be, James Greenfield, was a native of Connecticut. He was an original member and deacon of the Baptist Church of Montville (a town just north of New London, Connecticut). Greenfield and most of his Baptist coreligionists in Montville were Separates, that is, they had originally been Congregationalists but had begun to worship separately from Montville's orthodox Congregationalists as early as 1747. At the turn of the decade, in 1749–50, these come-outers had organized their own Separate-Baptist church in Montville and had chosen a forceful New Light evangelist, Elder Joshua Morse, as their minister. Such was the small world of Separates and New Light Baptists that Elder Sprague of Exeter, Rhode Island, was one of the clergymen who assisted at Elder Morse's ordination at Montville.

Deacon Greenfield's family background bore little resemblance to that of Owen Brown and Jeremiah Root. Their fathers were yeomen farmers. His father, Archibald Greenfield, was a mariner. The inventory of this Archibald's estate, taken in 1770, indicates that he was part owner of a "small schooner" (probably the *Swan*) and that he also owned or shared ownership of various small lots, houses, and wharfs along an estuary in Salem, Massachusetts.[7] But one must not conclude from this that Archibald Greenfield was wealthy. On the contrary, the record indicates that his debts nearly equaled the value of his modest assets. Even the large silver spoons he had willed to his grandsons were in pawn at the time of his death and very likely were sold to pay off his creditors.

By trade a roving man, Archibald the mariner covered quite a bit of territory in his lifetime. He first appeared in colonial records in 1717 in Newport, Rhode Island, recently married to Hannah Starr of Lyme, Connecticut. Subsequently, he owned land at both Newport and Lyme. After the birth of his two sons—James and Archibald Starr Greenfield—his marriage ended, either through divorce or Hannah's death. His sons were raised in Lyme while their father went on his way, next appearing in 1737 in deed records for Queen Anne's County, Maryland, where he was described as being from "Salem in Essex County in New England."[8] He married at least twice more. No farmer's daughters these, at least from what is known of them. Sarah Bacon of Salem, whom he married in 1749, was the daughter of a shipwright. Mary Gautier, a Marblehead widow he wed in 1757, was from a seafaring family. She had a son by her first marriage who, like his stepfather, was active as a sea captain–shipowner in the coastal trade between Salem and the Chesapeake region.

Archibald and Hannah (Starr) Greenfield's sons appear to have been raised by their mother or her family in Lyme, Connecticut. After coming to manhood, they took very different paths. Archibald Starr Greenfield's leanings were orthodox and entrepreneurial. He remained a resident of Lyme and followed his father's footsteps as a sea captain; his children also remained orthodox Congregationalists, entered business, and prospered. His brother James, meanwhile, married a New London woman and moved to that town's North Parish (now Montville), where he and his wife underwent conversion experiences in the late 1740s. They first joined the New Light Separates and then became members of the Montville Baptist

Church. James's sons were without exception farmers, all of them Baptists and none of them wealthy.

The Montville Baptists, like the New Lights everywhere, believed in acting as their brothers' keepers. When brethren were felt to be in conflict with each other or with the church covenant, Deacon Greenfield or another respected individual would be sent to mediate the difficulty. Even the deacon himself was not safe from scrutiny. The church minutes for January 13, 1768, report that "Deacon Greenfield and Brother Ebenezer Rogers manifested that they had settled their difficulty betwixt themselves." Amicable relations were not always restored, however, and the church minutes from the 1760s onward contain increasingly frequent references to members being dismissed from fellowship for "immoral acts" or "breaches of the covenant." A late example (November 20, 1773) includes the last recorded mention of Deacon James Greenfield. "Proceeded and took into consideration Deacon Greenfield and rejected him for the breach of Covenant and Immorality." Typically, no further details were given.[9]

About the time of the above entry, four of James Greenfield's sons—Raymond, Archibald, Enos, and Bethuel (and probably their father as well)—moved to the New York frontier, settling in the Little Hoosick district of Rensselaerswyck. Archibald, the second of James's sons, picked a hillside location just east of the Cherry Plain part of Little Hoosick. Although the precise date of his arrival is unknown, certain facts place it in the early 1770s. Cherry Plain's first settler arrived in 1770. Archibald's cousin Daniel Dennison came about a year later (June 1771). From old Rensselaerswyck rent receipts we learn that Archibald leased property between the homesteads of his cousins James and Daniel Dennison. Since all three men came from New London, Connecticut, and settled on adjacent farms of roughly equal quality, it seems reasonable to suppose that they moved about the same time. Archibald could not have arrived much later, since he was a bachelor when he left Connecticut, and his first child, Margaret, was born at Cherry Plain on February 24, 1776. The child's mother, whose name was also Margaret, was the daughter of Joseph Rogers, formerly Deacon Rogers of Exeter, Rhode Island, but now living in Stephentown, New York, a village just a few miles south of his son-in-law's farm.

Neither Margaret Greenfield's father nor her grandfather Rogers left a written record of their reasons for migrating to New York, but the prickly independence commonly found among the New Lights was undoubtedly a major influence. The minutes of the Exeter and Montville churches that Margaret's grandfathers had served as deacons abound with entries that reflect the contentiousness of the New Light breed. All New Lights were, in a term then popular, come-outers, people who had "come out" of (i.e., left) traditional Congregational and Baptist churches. But Joseph Rogers and James Greenfield had gone one step further down the come-outer's individualistic path and had broken with their New Light affiliations as well. Having placed this psychological and emotional distance between themselves and nearly all their neighbors, they perhaps found it a relatively easy choice—a relief, even—to move to the frontier, thus putting some physical distance between themselves and the communities whose conventions they had rejected.

Economic considerations also entered into the decision to move. Many of Rensselaerswyck's early settlers were marginal property owners who had sold small farms in settled areas in order to lease a much larger acreage on the frontier. Exeter, Rhode Island, a relatively poor community, was a likely source of this type of migrant, though Joseph Rogers, a church deacon whose father was a wealthy farmer, probably had a higher economic status than the average pioneer in Stephentown. Daniel Dennison of Montville (and later of Cherry Plain), however, owned only a modest farm in Connecticut, a relatively overpopulated farming area where prices for land were high. He exemplifies the logic behind the move to the Little Hoosick frontier. Selling out and going to New York was a reasonable gamble for a man trying to provide his large family with an adequate stake in life. Similarly, the move made sense for Dennison's cousin Archibald Greenfield, a young farmer with no dependents, but with no significant inheritance in sight either. Although few such pioneers would be permitted to buy farms under the prevailing land system in Rensselaerswyck, the terms of manorial leases offered less affluent migrants impressive inducements: no capital or down payment was required to obtain land, no rent was due for an initial period of five or ten years, and renters had the right to sell improvements they made on the property to the next leaseholders.

The lord of the manor, Stephen Van Rensselaer, had good reasons for offering such attractive terms. Obviously, if his manorial lands were occupied, his rental income would increase. But in the 1760s and 1770s the Van Rensselaers' promotional efforts took on a political dimension too. Anti-proprietor rent riots had occurred on neighboring manors, and the Van Rensselaers feared that similar disorders might break out in Rensselaerswyck. This danger was increased by the activities of expansionist-minded Massachusetts settlers who were not above encouraging rent troubles on patroon lands as a way of strengthening their colony's claims to disputed areas along the contested New York–Massachusetts border. The southeast corner of Rensselaerswyck was a ripe target for the Massachusetts expansionists. It was adjacent to the border and as late as 1765 was virtually uninhabited. In the mid-1760s, therefore, the Van Rensselaers moved to protect their vulnerable flank by promoting settlement of the East Manor, as they called the Stephentown–Little Hoosick area. From the Van Rensselaers' viewpoint, Baptists were ideal settlers because they would instinctively view any hint of Massachusetts expansionism as just another instance of aggression by that colony's power-hungry Congregational establishment.

Viewed in isolation, Margaret Greenfield's birth on the New York frontier in 1776 was an event of little significance to anyone but her immediate family. In a larger context, however, her birth was indirectly the product of broad currents in mid-eighteenth-century American life: the demography of overpopulation, the aggression of one colony against another, and a Baptist heritage rooted in revivalism and religious dissent.

DAVID WARD AND TAZEWELL COUNTY'S HEROIC AGE

Tazewell is located in the mountains of southwestern Virginia, nearly six hundred miles from Margaret Greenfield's New York State birthplace. Margaret's parents had migrated to Rensselaerswyck in the late 1760s and early 1770s. In the same period two Virginians, David Ward and Rees Bowen, moved their families to homesteads in the Clinch River valley, specifically to the part of the valley where the river's Maiden Spring branch runs below Short Mountain (approximately ten miles from present-day Tazewell). Aside from the similar timing of their moves to new homes, these Yankees and Virginians had little in common.

The Yankee homesteaders in the Little Hoosick area were mainly Baptists from English backgrounds, whereas the settlers on Virginia's Clinch Valley frontier were predominantly Scotch-Irish Presbyterians. Moreover, in the 1770s Little Hoosick's pioneers did not have to worry about Indian troubles, whereas the Virginians went through long periods when they thought of little else.

Among the many outbreaks of warfare between whites and Indians on Virginia's western frontier in the 1770s, none was more significant than Lord Dunmore's War in 1774. That August white Virginians launched a punitive expedition against the Shawnee tribe in the Ohio River valley, and nearly every able-bodied man in the Clinch Valley settlements marched off to join the campaign. Given the fact that Tazewell's pioneers, like most southerners of the time, lived on dispersed homesteads rather than in the tightly clustered town lots common in New England, the men's departure left the valley's women and children extremely vulnerable to attack. Rather than remain in their isolated cabins (the nearest neighbor was often at least half a mile away), the women went with their children to one of the valley's four fortified houses. David Ward's wife, Eleanor, probably stayed with her friend, neighbor, and future in-law Levisa Bowen, whose husband, Rees, had built a stockade around their cabin at Maiden Spring. Tazewell County lore honors Levisa for her resourcefulness during the Lord Dunmore's War emergency. It is said that, after observing Indian signs in the neighborhood, she dressed a black servant woman as a man and had her parade in front of the stockade with a musket to give the impression that the cabin's occupants were better defended than they actually were. The ruse was successful, and Levisa Bowen is credited with having prevented an Indian attack.

To speak of "Indian troubles" is, of course, to describe these events from the whites' perspective, according to which the Indians were always the aggressors. The facts regarding Virginia's war against the Shawnee in 1774 support a different view, however. Indeed, one leading authority on the subject asserts that "Dunmore's War was . . . brought on by the whites." The prize to be won was control of Kentucky's rich hunting grounds, a source of the Shawnees' livelihood coveted by the whites. From the 1760s onward, whites had entered the area—some, hunters like Daniel Boone, to collect furs, others to explore the possibility of permanent settlement. The Shawnee met these intrusions on their hunting grounds with great forbearance; nevertheless, in June 1774, after a series of nasty incidents in which Indians had more often been victims than aggressors,

Virginia authorities called out the backwoods militia, ostensibly to defend the colony's western border. But Clinch Valley frontiersmen like David Ward and Rees Bowen, who answered the call eagerly even though there was no imminent danger of Indian attack on their homesteads, were not inclined to commit themselves to the long periods of garrison duty required by a defensive war. The campaign therefore soon became an offensive one with goals the frontiersmen heartily endorsed: the defeat of the Indians, the opening of the Ohio Valley, and the opportunity for plunder; as one militia captain put it, "the plunder of the Country will be valluable, & it is said the Shawnee have a great Stock of Horses."[10]

In early September 1774 the Clinch Valley men rendezvoused with militia detachments from the Shenandoah Valley at Fort Union (now Lewisburg, West Virgina). Under Colonel Andrew Lewis's command, this combined force of approximately one thousand whites then made a wilderness march of twenty-five days northwest along the Kanawha River route to Point Pleasant, the junction of the Kanawha and Ohio rivers. A second column of Virginians, led by the colony's royal governor (John Murray, earl of Dunmore), was moving down the Ohio to join forces with Lewis's men, but the Shawnee took the initiative and attacked Lewis's camp at Point Pleasant on October 10. A bloody battle ensued, and the outnumbered Indians were forced to retreat. In order to avoid further losses the Shawnee leader, Chief Cornstalk, surrendered and accepted a treaty that stipulated that whites had the right to hunt in Kentucky and to travel unmolested on the Ohio.

Two Clinch Valley frontiersmen who gained reputations as Indian fighters in the Battle of Point Pleasant were Rees Bowen and David Ward. As we have seen, both had been among the earliest pioneers of Tazewell. Bowen had settled near a watercourse known as Maiden Spring. Ward lived several miles away in Ward's Cove, a spur of the broad valley in which Maiden Spring was located. At the time of their arrival in Tazewell the two men were not related, but over the years their children and grandchildren intermarried until the Wards and Bowens were cousins many times over.

Stories about Rees Bowen have a Bunyanesque quality. According to local tradition, Rees was "a giant in size and strength." It was "told as a fact that [his wife, Levisa] could step into [his] hand and that he could stand and extend his arm, holding her at [a] right angle to his body." Rees (sometimes spelled Reese or Reece) was renowned as a prizefighter and was said to have defeated all challengers. He is also immortalized in

Tazewell County lore as an explorer and a name giver, as the man who discovered and named the spring and river that, as an oft-repeated story states, "have ever since been known as Maiden Spring and Fork."[11]

The mantle of heroism local historians bestowed on Rees Bowen also covered his neighbor and kinsman David Ward. Ward's biographers emphasize the important role he played in the county's early political life. According to one such account, Ward was "a conspicuous figure among the frontiersmen because of his intelligence and excellent courage." The same author adds that David Ward was "known as one of the best Indian fighters on the Clinch," a high accolade, given the standards of Ward's time and place.[12]

A penchant for Indian fighting seemed to run in the family, for many of David Ward's relatives also participated in the Indian wars endemic to the Virginia frontier. An Augusta County cousin, Captain James Ward, had settled near Anthony Creek (now in Greenbrier County, West Virginia) in 1752, but Indian raids forced him to abandon his homestead. In 1758 Captain Ward's three-year-old son, John, was stolen by Indians. He remained with the Indians, married an Indian woman, and raised a family. At the Battle of Point Pleasant, John Ward fought for the Indians, while his father, Captain James Ward, died fighting for the whites. John Ward displayed the same tenacity as a warrior for his adopted people as his Ward relatives did for the white Virginians. Over the next twenty

Revolutionary-era American rifleman in canvas tunic, from a sketch by Baron Ludwig von Closen (1770s).

years he participated in a succession of frontier skirmishes, until he was killed in combat at Reeve's Crossing, Ohio (March 1793). Even in this last battle John Ward fought against members of his white family: a commander of one of the Virginia companies at Reeve's Crossing was John's younger brother, Captain James Ward.

David Ward and his relatives came to the Virginia frontier by a route and for reasons quite typical of Tazewell pioneers. David's grandfather was a Protestant from Ulster, Ireland, who had migrated to Pennsylvania along with three sons early in the 1730s. Like many Ulster Scots (or Scotch-Irish, as they were called in America), he soon moved on, taking his family down the Valley of Virginia to Augusta County, where his sons lived out their lives. Their sons, however, David Ward included, became homesteaders in newer areas of Virginia that major treaties with Indian tribes opened after 1763. Some of the things that drew David Ward to southwestern Virginia were obvious enough. Augusta County was becoming increasingly crowded, and the cost of farmland there was rising. By contrast, land on the headwaters of the Clinch River (then Fincastle County) could be had free by right of settlement.

The precise year when David Ward moved to Ward's Cove is uncertain—different sources variously report it as 1769, 1771, 1772, and even 1773. The important thing about these dates is not which is most accurate, but what they indicate about the settlement pattern that prevailed on the Clinch Valley frontier. Pioneers did not move there in a single, decisive trip. Instead, they first investigated the area in ways that left the door open to reversing their steps, if conditions on the headwaters of the Clinch did not prove sufficiently promising. For example, many potential homesteaders initially visited the valley as members of hunting parties, and David Ward probably joined one of the small companies of hunters that explored the area in 1769. Land records make it clear that 1771 was the year Ward laid claim to a tract of four hundred acres in the Cove. There is some evidence, however, that he did not actually bring his family to the Cove until 1772.

From 1771 onward David Ward was repeatedly chosen by his neighbors in the Clinch Valley to perform various civic duties: inspect roads, appraise estates, and serve on juries. By 1780 he had become a justice of the peace in Washington County (of which Tazewell was then a part). With this appointment David Ward, the son of a Scotch-Irish immigrant, acquired the privilege of being addressed as "David Ward, Gentleman," or "David Ward, Esquire." Although "Gentleman" status in a backwoods district by no means put Ward on an equal footing with George Washington or other members of Virginia's Tidewater aristocracy, Ward's career indicates what could be accomplished by an energetic man in the more recently settled parts of the state.

Ward's exploits during the American Revolution added to the esteem in which he was held. As early as 1777 his reputation as an Indian fighter won him the rank of lieutenant in the Washington County militia, but little was required of him as long as the chief theater of war was in the northern states. By the beginning of 1780, however, the British high command had shifted its attention to the southern states, and in May of that year British forces captured the key port of Charleston, South Carolina. For such northern farmers as Sergeant Gideon Root of Southwick (who last saw combat in 1779) and Corporal Archibald Greenfield of Rensselaerswyck (who had served for two days in 1776 and three in 1777) the fighting was for all intents and purposes over, but for David Ward and his neighbors the war had more than three years to go.

During the summer of 1780 the British won several important battles in South Carolina, thus opening the way for an invasion of North Carolina. Their advance began in September. The main British army under General Cornwallis marched on Charlotte, North Carolina, while a secondary force of approximately eleven hundred Tories led by Major Patrick Ferguson (the only British soldier in this contingent) was assigned to protect Cornwallis's left (i.e., western) flank. The fact that Ferguson had recruited many of his Loyalist followers from the western part of North Carolina alarmed revolutionaries from the same or adjacent mountain districts because they believed (correctly, as it turned out) that their homesteads were the targets of Ferguson's campaign. The Patriots therefore organized a counterforce of backwoods militia, about eight hundred men from the Carolinas and two hundred, David Ward and Rees Bowen among them, from southwestern Virginia.

At the Battle of King's Mountain (October 7, 1780), Ferguson's Tories, positioned on top of a heavily wooded ridge, used musket fire and bayonet charges to try to drive the Patriots down the steep slopes. The Patriot unit that suffered the worst casualties was the Virginia company in which Ward and Bowen served, and in the course of the battle Rees Bowen, who had recklessly refused to take cover, fell mortally wounded by a bullet in the chest. After an hour and five minutes of fighting, however, the Patriot riflemen won a complete victory, killing Ferguson and many of his followers and capturing the rest. This was the stuff of which legends are made, undisciplined companies of backwoods Patriots delivering a decisive blow, for the American victory at King's Mountain forced Cornwallis to delay his invasion of North Carolina until 1781, by which time the revolutionaries there were much better prepared to defend themselves.

After the Revolution, David Ward's stature as a leader in Clinch Valley politics continued to grow. During the 1790s he served as a justice of the peace in all of the counties whose organization preceded Tazewell's. He was also active in the campaign to establish Tazewell County, a goal that was reached in 1799. The following year he was named one of Tazewell County's first JPs, and in 1801 he was elected to the lower house of the Virginia legislature.

By the beginning of the new century, of course, Tazewell County's pioneer phase was over. The Indians had been driven out, lands surveyed and titles proved, the war for independence won, and the first comfortable homes built. Economic development brought with it a gradual increase of slave ownership, a key index of wealth in southern society, though as was typical of mountain counties, the number of slaves in Tazewell was not large. (In 1801, Tazewell's white adult males outnumbered adult male slaves by nearly four to one, and the county's largest slaveholder owned only seven male slaves. David Ward apparently never owned a slave, but his son John did own one for a time.) Despite the social and economic changes the years 1771–1801 had brought, the legacy of the early days lingered, perpetuated both through stories of pioneer times and in the attitudes of the first settlers' descendants. Long after most of the particulars of David Ward's life were forgotten, the inheritance of Tazewell County's heroic age lived on among the latter-day Wards in a love of tall tales, a penchant for risk-taking, and a readiness to head west when new frontiers beckoned.

BENJAMIN ADAIR: A NEW AMERICAN

The immigrant progenitors of these families came to North America over a period of more than a century. All of Owen Brown's forebears reached New England before the end of the 1630s. Jeremiah Root's great-great-great-grandfather Root came to Connecticut in 1640. Joseph Rogers's ancestors, and probably Margaret Greenfield's also, migrated to America in the seventeenth century. More recent immigrants such as David Ward's father and grandfather left Ireland for Pennsylvania in the 1730s. By contrast, the newest American of them all, Benjamin Adair, did not emigrate from England to Maryland until just before the American Revolution.

An illiterate newcomer with few financial resources, Adair left few permanent traces behind. He first appeared in colonial records in 1773, when he was listed in Baltimore County, Maryland, assessment rolls as a taxable man of sixteen years or more in the household of Joseph Hilton. If not married then, he wed soon thereafter, for his first child, a daughter named Margaret, was born in 1775. We next find Adair in 1780 and 1781, when he was named to act as joint executor of Frederick Caley's estate with the deceased's widow, Margaret. This Margaret Caley, who was probably either Adair's mother (remarried) or his mother-in-law, owned a small farm in Trueman's Acquaintance, Gunpowder Upper Hundred (Baltimore County), which Benjamin inherited after she died in 1785. The probate process took many years, and by the time the estate was closed, in 1798, Benjamin Adair had seven or eight children, including one son who had married earlier that year. Circumstantial evidence suggests that Adair's first wife (Rosannah?) died in the late 1790s and that he remarried, taking a young woman, Sarah (Lane?), as his second wife. He sold his Maryland property in November 1798 and moved to Rockbridge County, in the Shenandoah Valley section of Virginia, where he lived from 1799 to 1805. Sarah's two daughters were born during the family's six-year sojourn in Rockbridge County, bringing the total number of Adair children to ten. At no point during his six years in Virginia did Benjamin Adair own land.

Even in these bare facts about Benjamin Adair's life we can discern some traits that define him in relation to other Americans of the time.

Adair's port of entry, Baltimore, was the most popular destination for emigrants from the British Isles in the years immediately before the American Revolution. Many such emigrants soon went on to Pennsylvania, Virginia, or the Carolinas, but Adair remained in Maryland, where, fifteen years after his arrival, he had the good fortune to become a landowner. Maryland's early proprietors had favored a policy of distributing land in relatively large chunks to relatively few families. The result, comparatively speaking, was that landownership in Baltimore County, though nowhere nearly so concentrated in a few families' hands as it was in seventeenth-century New York, remained less widely distributed than in New England towns. When Adair inherited Margaret Caley's small farm in 1785, the very fact that he owned land therefore placed him above the more than 50 percent of Gunpowder Upper Hundred's white men—tenants, hired hands, and paupers—who did not. But Adair was still at the very lowest level of the landowning class, since, in an area where the principal market product was black beef cattle, his sixteen-acre parcel was one of the smallest properties.

Far above Adair on the social ladder were the gentry, represented in the 1783 tax lists by the 1 or 2 percent of the heads of households whose names were accompanied by a title—captain, major, or esquire. Typically, men like Acquila Hall, Esquire, and Captain James Bosley owned more than a thousand acres of land, twenty to thirty slaves, fifty to eighty head of black cattle, and two or three pounds of sterling silverware. That people of their class did not do manual labor was obvious from their clothing; gentlemen attired themselves in linen waistcoats and shirts with ruffled lace cuffs, and genteel women wore dresses of silk or fine linen. By contrast, the Adairs wore clothes made from coarse, practical fabrics—canvas and rough wool—and had small estates like that of Margaret Caley: sixteen acres of land, three head of beef cattle, and no silver plate. Her modest house, a gabled frame structure (twenty by eighteen feet) with a one-story stone addition (eighteen feet square), was later occupied by as many as eight or nine Adairs and was, in an appraiser's words, "much out repair" when they sold it in 1798.[13] Neither Margaret Caley nor the Adairs owned slaves. We do not know what Benjamin Adair's views on slavery were, but we do know that some of his descendants spoke out against the slave system in the 1830s and that one of their reasons for objecting to slavery was that they were disdainful of the social pretensions they associated with slaveholding. Owning slaves, like having fine clothes and silver plate, symbolized class distinctions that the Adairs, as newcomers and common people, resented.

Economic motives almost certainly figured in Benjamin Adair's decision to sell his Maryland farm and move to Virginia in 1799. He had eight children, one of which, his son Philip, was now married. Others would soon be coming of age. The family's destination in 1799, the Shenandoah Valley of Virginia, was a fertile farming region that had long attracted migrants who, like the Adairs, had limited means. The trouble was that by the time the Adairs reached Rockbridge County the frontier period, that is, the years when land was plentiful and cheap, had passed. Some earlier migrants to the valley, men like David Ward, whose father had brought him to Augusta County in 1758, had already moved on in search of less expensive land west of the valley. As we have seen, David Ward obtained four hundred acres of Tazewell land by right of settlement in the early 1770s, and this was at a time when economic conditions in the Augusta-Rockbridge area, where 60 percent or more of the local families owned land, were still relatively favorable. By 1800, however, a majority of Rockbridge residents were landless, and Benjamin and Philip Adair found themselves among this number. Even so, they made some small gains economically during their six-year stay in the county, increasing the number of horses they owned between them from four in 1799 to six in 1800, eight in 1804, and ten in 1805 (the year they left for Ohio). At about this same time David Ward and his oldest son, John, together owned eighteen horses and nearly seven hundred acres of land.

The obvious contrast between the Wards' well-established economic position and the Adairs' relatively marginal financial status must not be allowed to obscure what the families had in common—most notably, ties with a distinctive Scotch-Irish community in America. But even here there was a difference. While the Wards' Scotch-Irish heritage can be readily documented from their arrival in Pennsylvania onward, it was not possible earlier (i.e., in our narrative of the family's Maryland sojourn) to speak of the Adairs' cultural ties, because the record is so inconclusive. Neither of the two most tantalizing bits of evidence on the Adairs' pre-Virginia years—a grandson's statement that Benjamin Adair emigrated from England and the Baltimore County marriage license of Benjamin's son Philip, which shows that the wedding ceremony was performed by a Swedenborgian (a follower of the Swedish philosopher-mystic Emanuel Swedenborg)—documents Scotch-Irish ties. Since data on the Adairs' cultural affiliations during their early years in America are lacking, the relatively prolific information (mainly on Presbyterian church ties and on marriages to Scotch-Irish spouses) from the family's post-Maryland years becomes crucial to a delineating of the importance Scotch-Irish connections came to have for them.

After the family's move to Virginia, Benjamin Adair's daughter Martha married Daniel Lyle, and his son George married Margaret (Peggy) Ramsey. These marriages linked the Adairs with three Scotch-Irish families—the Ramseys, Lyles, and Keyses (Lyle in-laws)—who were among the earliest settlers in the Timber Ridge district, near present-day Lexington, Virginia. Although these three families had emigrated to America from Ireland, ethnically they were Scottish. Their ancestors had gone to Ulster, Ireland, in the early and middle 1600s as colonists in England's effort to subdue Ireland by populating it with Protestants. This "plantation of Ulster" (as the colonization of northern Ireland was called) was, of course, only one migration among many in which English and Scottish people participated in the 1600s. In the same years when these Lyles, Keyses, and Ramseys moved from Scotland to Ireland, other families described here —the Browns, Roots, and Greenfields—emigrated from England to New England.

In the early seventeenth century Ulster was no less a frontier than New England. Ulster Scots initially lived in shelters every bit as primitive as the American pioneers' log cabins. The Ulstermen also had to transplant Presbyterianism, the religion of the Scots, to a new land and wrest control of the Irish countryside from hostile natives. This latter task was no easy enterprise. The native Irish, driven from their lands into swamp and forest retreats, were just as much a menace to the Scots on the Ulster frontier as the Indians were to white pioneers in North America. As a result the Scotch-Irish migrants to the American colonies in the eighteenth century came as experienced homesteaders whose skills in anti-guerrilla warfare were readily adaptable to the American frontier.

Between 1717 and 1776 an estimated quarter of a million Ulster Scots joined the transatlantic migration. Deteriorating conditions in Ireland— rising rents, religious and political discrimination against Presbyterians, and economic disasters—provided the main impetus. Severe droughts and years of poor harvests accounted for a pattern of especially heavy migration during five peak periods: 1717–18, 1725–29, 1740–41, 1754–55, and 1771–75. The chief drawing power of England's North American colonies was the availability of cheap land, and as the location of the most readily available cheap land shifted, so did the ultimate destinations of the migrants. Before 1740 the most accessible inexpensive land was in Pennsylvania, a colony whose proprietor, William Penn, was tolerant of the Scots' Presbyterian convictions. These religious and economic factors combined to make Pennsylvania the most popular choice among such early Ulster migrants as the Ramseys and the Wards. By the 1740s, however, the magnet of newer lands opening up in the Valley of Virginia made that region the destination most frequently chosen by the settlers who came in the third great wave of Ulster Scot immigration.

Even today Augusta and Rockbridge counties—the Virginia counties where Benjamin Adair's Lyle, Keys, and Ramsey in-laws settled—claim to be the most Scotch-Irish counties in North America. In part, this was a product of geography. Staunton, the county seat of Augusta County, and Lexington, which is Rockbridge County's seat, were located squarely on the Great Wagon Road. This was the migration route that thousands upon thousands of Scotch-Irish took from southeastern Pennsylvania through the Shenandoah Valley towns of Hagerstown, Staunton, Lexington, Buchanan, and Roanoke. But more was at work in drawing such great numbers of Scotch-Irish to the Augusta-Rockbridge area than a convenient route. By the second quarter of the eighteenth century, the influence of land speculators and their promotional campaigns was a major factor in directing transatlantic migrants to specific destinations.

Benjamin Borden and William Beverley were the great speculator-developers of Augusta-Rockbridge land. The 92,100-acre grant that Borden obtained from Virginia covered a large part of present-day Rockbridge County. Beverley Manor, meanwhile, was a 118,491-acre tract that included most of the good farmland in what is now Augusta County. In order to promote land sales in these huge tracts, Borden and Beverley hired agents to recruit settlers abroad. Few of these were more enterprising than James Patton, himself a native Irishman and a shipowner-captain engaged in the transatlantic trade. Patton reportedly went to Ulster on twenty-five occasions, trading his goods and attempting to persuade Ulstermen to relocate in Borden's Grant or Beverley Manor.

Whether the Lyles who became Benjamin Adair's kin first heard about the Valley of Virginia through Patton or another agent is unknown, but the fact remains that they were among the earliest purchasers of Borden land. In 1742 Matthew Lyle, the first of several brothers to emigrate to Virginia, bought three hundred acres on the southwest side of Timber Ridge. Before then, there had been fewer than fifty homesteaders in that part of Borden's Grant. Matthew's brothers John and Daniel Lyle soon joined him in the Timber Ridge community, and by 1748 their future in-law Roger Keys was listed as having a homestead nearby.

At Timber Ridge and elsewhere throughout Borden's Grant, Scotch-Irish pioneers soon established Presbyterian churches. At the May 1748 county court, Matthew Lyle proposed the construction of Presbyterian meetinghouses at three locations—Timber Ridge, New Providence, and Tinkling Spring. A log structure had been in use at Timber Ridge since 1741, and the new stone building (still standing, though with major alterations) was completed in 1755. The congregation's formative years coincided with the revivals, known collectively as the Great Awakening, that swept through all of England's North American colonies. In the Great Awakening's New England phase, born-again Christians such as Margaret Greenfield's grandfather, Deacon Greenfield of Montville, Connecticut, called themselves New Lights and referred to those who rejected the revivalist's conversion-oriented credo as Old Lights. A parallel distinction arose in the middle and southern colonies among Presbyterians, who were divided by New Side evangelicalism and Old Side orthodoxy. Timber Ridge and the neighboring Presbyterian congregations went over to the New Side persuasion, modifying their inherited denominational forms to conform to eighteenth-century evangelical influences.

Signs of the pioneers' Scottish heritage remain in the Shenandoah Valley even today. Town names like Edinburgh and Glasgow are reminders of the settlers' national origins. The architecture of their early-day meetinghouses also drew on Old World forms. Except for the absence of the square bell tower that was commonly attached to Presbyterian churches in Ireland and Scotland, the mortared stone walls and narrow windows found in the eighteenth-century meetinghouses at Timber Ridge and Old Providence could be right out of the Ulster countryside—Dungannon, Ramelton, or Ancient Ballymoney.

Pause for a moment on a warm summer day and lean against the cool rock face of Old Providence Church. Let your eye follow the curve of the paved mourner's path as it crosses the green meadow to the church's original burying ground. There stand the old grave markers, some of stone and others of wood, nearly all of them badly weathered and settled into odd angles. Surrounded by these sights, you can easily imagine that you are in Scotland or Ireland rather than in Virginia. Still, appearances can deceive, for American society was not merely a transplantation of Old World forms to the new. Indeed, immigrants like Benjamin Adair left Europe in search of something different and better, and it was aspirations not unlike those that caused them to cross the Atlantic before 1800 that led many, Benjamin Adair included, to cross the Appalachian Mountains in the early nineteenth century.

TRANS-
APPALACHIAN
PIONEERS
1805-1829

S hortly after Ohio was admitted to the Union in 1803, representatives of three of our families on the move migrated to the new state.
Owen and Ruth Brown left Torrington, Connecticut, for Ohio on
June 9, 1805. Four months later, Benjamin and Sarah Adair joined a party
of migrants that started west from Rockbridge County, Virginia. Then, in
the summer of 1807, Jeremiah and Lucretia Root sold their farms in
western Massachusetts and moved to northeastern Ohio.

These decisions to go west were at once bold and conservative. It took
courage to leave the known for the unknown, to undertake the arduous

journey, and to start anew in a wilderness or a semiwilderness. But all three families were fundamentally conservative in their approach to westward migration. None of them went west until the threat of Indian attack had been greatly reduced by diplomacy (Jay's Treaty, 1794) and military victories (Fallen Timbers, Ohio, 1794), until land development companies like the Connecticut Land Company had been organized and had launched campaigns to promote homesteading in the area, and until liberalized government land policies (the Land Act of 1800) and the establishment of federal land offices in Ohio had facilitated settlement there.

These Adair, Brown, and Root migrants were by no means alone in their decision to head for Ohio. In the early decades of the 1800s, tens of thousands of easterners took note of the fact that the Indian threat was on the wane and that plenty of good land was now available in the Buckeye State. The rush to capitalize on these conditions contributed to a dramatic rise in Ohio's population, from 45,365 in 1800 to 230,760 in 1810 and 581,434 in 1820. Moreover, Ohio's swift growth was not unique. Indiana, the next state to the west, had only 24,520 residents in 1810; ten years later the number had swollen to 147,178 (an increase of 500 percent). The surge in population of western territories led to the admission of state after state in the early nineteenth century: Ohio (1803), Louisiana (1812), Indiana (1816), Mississippi (1817), Illinois (1818), Alabama (1819), and Missouri (1821). Of the present states east of the Mississippi, only Florida, Michigan, and Wisconsin still remained under territorial status in 1820. The trans-Appalachian frontier was well on the way to being settled.

A few heavily traveled roads bore the bulk of the Ohio-bound traffic. The future route of the Erie Canal from Albany to Buffalo, in New York State, was very popular with New Englanders. Other Yankees, however, among them the Browns and Roots who went west in 1805 and 1807, took another well-trodden path, the road through Pennsylvania from Harrisburg to Pittsburgh. Residents of the Upper South frequently used the so-called National Road, which ran from Cumberland, Maryland, to Columbus, Ohio, and points farther west. As we will see, however, Virginians like the Adairs who started west from the central Shenandoah Valley region often followed a road that wove its way through a series of west Virginia mountain passes before reaching Point Pleasant, where the migrants crossed the Ohio River into southern Ohio.

Scene on the National Road in Maryland, from a
painting by Thomas Ruckle (1889).

The routes taken by our Ohio-bound Browns, Adairs, and Roots, and the dates when they took them, are known, but other details about the journeys themselves are sparse. All we know about the Adairs, for example, is that they left Timber Ridge, Virginia, in early autumn and arrived in Highland County, Ohio, in December 1805. However, we can reconstruct some aspects of the Adairs' travels from the account of William Keys, another pioneer who left Rockbridge County for Ohio in 1805. Keys not only had been the Adairs' neighbor in the Timber Ridge area but was also their second cousin by marriage and would soon be connected to them through two more marriages between Adair and Keys relatives. The Keyses' migration party, which was about the same size as the Adairs', took an identical route to the same Ohio county that the Adairs would reach only a month later. Keys's migration narrative, quoted at length below, may therefore be taken as a fair approximation of what the Adairs probably encountered on the road to Ohio. But his narrative is also of more general interest, since it describes many features of westward travel that were typical of thousands of pioneer journeys in the early nineteenth century: the necessity of traveling in fairly sizable parties in order to handle the physical demands of wilderness roads, the family connections underlying the membership of many parties, and the relative ease with which the migrants acquired land once they reached their new Ohio homes.

We took our journey [Keys wrote] from the valley of the Old Dominion in September, A.D. 1805, with a strong team, large wagon and a heavy load. We proceeded on our way over the Allegheny mountains, Greenbrier hills, Sewell and Gauley mountains, Kanawha rivers and backwater creeks, often impassable by the rising of the river, and arrived at Point Pleasant, where we crossed the Ohio and left most of our troubles behind us. Our company consisted of two family connections, each of which were subdivided into one or two smaller families; and to give promise of a fair beginning, each of them had an infant specimen of young America to carry on the knee, and numbering twenty-three persons in all, eight of whom were full grown men.

We often had to exert all our united strength and skill to prevent our wagons from upsetting, and had often to double teams in order to ascend the steep mountain sides. None of our company met with any accident, but not so with all the emigrants who preceded us on the same route; we sometimes passed the fragments of broken wagon beds, broken furniture and remnants of broken boxes and other marks of damage by upsetting on the mountain side, where the wagon, team and all had rolled over and over down the steep declivity, for some rods, until stopped by the intervention of some trees too stout to be prostrated by the mass of broken fragments. By doubling teams, we could reach the mountain top, but to get safely down again called for other contrivances. One expedient frequently tried was to fasten a pretty stout pine tree to the axletree of the wagon with chains, so as to retard the downward course upon the horses. At the foot of such hills and mountains could be seen sundry such trees that had been dragged down for the purpose above named. We arrived at our Highland home in about eight weeks, constant travel, Sundays excepted. . . .

Our mode of travel over the whole length of the road, was like that of the children of Israel to the land of promise; we all took it on foot, except the aged mother, and women with young children—they rode on horseback where riding was possible. . . .

On or about the 20th of November, piloted by Judge Pope, we found a spring on our land, and, by first cutting a wagon road to it, landed all safe. We cleared away the brush, erected a tent, before which we kept a huge fire, and soon commenced building a cabin, which for all the world looked like log cabins in general, and being completed, we moved into it on Christmas day, A.D. 1805.[1]

During eight weeks en route to Ohio, the Keys party covered a little more than three hundred miles, averaging about seven miles a day. The Owen Browns' trip from Connecticut to Ohio in 1805 and the Roots' from Massachusetts in 1807—longer trips but over somewhat less rugged roads —took about the same length of time. What happened to these pioneers once they reached their destinations is the main subject of this chapter.

BENJAMIN ADAIR'S COUNTY FULL OF COUSINS

Benjamin Adair and his son Philip were not the sort of Americans whose lives are usually recorded in history books, but by a stroke of good luck we have an eyewitness account of their arrival on the Paint Valley frontier in south-central Ohio about forty-five miles north of the Ohio River. The scene, as remembered by one Thomas Rogers, took place in 1805. In August of that year Thomas and his brother Hamilton had settled on the west bank of a small but rugged river known as Paint Creek. One day in December, not long after the brothers had finished building their log cabins, they met "a company of Virginians encamped near the ford." Included in the party were John Tudor, Tudor's daughter Elizabeth and her husband (Philip Adair), and Philip's father (Benjamin Adair). The Rogers brothers, as the only settlers for miles in either direction along that stretch of the river, were glad to have company, and they invited the Virginians to stay with them until they could locate land and construct their own cabins. In a memoir set down many years later, Thomas Rogers recalled that Benjamin Adair, "the patriarch of the party," first went to look at some property about a day's ride away, but he soon returned to the Paint Creek area. Subsequently, he bought land in Ross County just across the river from Rogers's claim, and his son John made a down payment on a smaller parcel next to his. Philip Adair and John Tudor, meanwhile, settled on the west, or Highland County, side of the Paint near the Rogers brothers.[2]

Although each group of migrants to the Paint Valley frontier had its own story to tell, the many newcomers had much in common. Like the Adairs and their cousins William and Margaret Keys, the great majority of the pioneers were Virginians, and those who were not from Virginia came from neighboring states: Kentucky, the Carolinas, and Pennsylvania. Of course, New Englanders—the Owen Browns and Jeremiah Roots are examples—also moved to Ohio in the early 1800s, but they nearly always headed for the state's northern counties. Indeed, so distinct were these North–South migration bands that crossovers from one to the other were rarely found in the Paint Valley prior to 1830.

The adults who migrated to the Paint Valley frontier were mostly young people—either couples like William (age twenty-seven) and Margaret (thirty) Keys and Philip (twenty-eight) and Elizabeth (twenty-five) Adair, who were just getting started in life, or bachelors like the Rogers brothers, Thomas and Hamilton (both in their twenties in 1805). The married couples often had small children in tow, "an infant specimen of young America to carry on the knee," as the Keys migration narrative put it.[3] The older or grandparent-aged pioneers usually came west for reasons that had to do with their children. Benjamin Adair and William Rogers (the father of the Rogers brothers who shared their cabins with the Adairs in the early winter of 1805–6) came to help their older boys obtain land. Note also the motivation of William Keys's widowed mother, Esther Lyle Keys, who joined her son in moving because she did not want to be left behind in Virginia and to have the prospect of facing old age without her children near at hand.

The Adairs and Keyses were typical of Ohio's early settlers in that they traveled to the frontier in multifamily groups, rather than as individuals or as a single, nuclear family. At an even earlier date, particularly after the danger of Indian attack had diminished, it had not been uncommon for hunters, men with no intention of settling in Ohio, to travel alone or with only a few companions, each bringing a horse, a rifle, and little else. But Benjamin Adair and his family, like the great majority of Ohio-bound pioneers in 1805 and afterward, were farmers with plans to clear the land and build homes. To do this they brought teams, wagons, tools, and household items. The difficult task of moving these possessions over miles of wilderness roads prompted them to migrate in groups from which they could draw assistance—the Adairs in a party of nineteen, their Keys cousins in a group of twenty-three.

These groups also illustrate the important role that family ties played in westward migration. The Keys party comprised several subgroups, all of whom were Lyle and Keys kin. Similarly, there were three related households in the Adair party: those of Benjamin and Sarah Adair, of their son Philip, and of Philip's in-laws, the Tudors. The need for physical assistance on the trail west was obvious, but a more general impulse, which one might call a sense of collective family purpose, was also at work. For instance, nine of Benjamin Adair's ten children settled near him in the Paint Valley and all of them remained there, even after they had married and were raising families of their own, until his death in 1829. This broader sense of family also extended to blood relationships considerably less close than that of parent and child. The Benjamin Adair and William Keys parties, both of which arrived in the Paint Valley in 1805, very likely influenced each other's choice of the Ross-Highland area as a destination, even though they were rather distantly related, cousins-in-law only. Even if the two original groups had no common plan, their presence in the Paint Valley acted as a magnet that drew other relatives to that part of Ohio. Between 1805 and 1815 at least fifty of Benjamin Adair's Lyle, Keys, and Ramsey relatives arrived in Ross or Highland County, making those counties full of cousins. Unquestionably, some Americans moved west to escape from familial or parental authority, but among the Adairs and their Paint Valley cousins and in-laws, going west was, if anything, an escape with family, not from it.

The promise that drew most pioneers to Ohio was land. On this subject migrants divided into two types, settlers and speculators, though the two categories were by no means mutually exclusive. Benjamin Adair definitely belonged to the settler category. A man of limited means, he came to the Paint Valley in hope of obtaining a farm at the cost of a dollar or two an acre—about as high a price as he, even with help from his sons, could afford. The strategy of moving west to obtain more land worked fairly well for the Adairs. Although they encountered obstacles before reaching their goal, they finally managed to increase their holdings from 16 acres in Maryland and none in Virginia to more than 200 acres in Ohio. The second category of pioneer, the speculators and their agents, included such early residents of Highland and Ross counties as Nathaniel Pope and Henry and Nathaniel Massie. Such men usually had some land of their own to sell, but they also did a good deal of business as agents for large absentee landowners. As such they played a crucial role in breaking up large unoccupied tracts of 1,000 or more acres into small parcels of 50 to 150 acres, to be sold to settlers like Benjamin Adair.

Adair had dealings with at least two local land agents. He called on Nathaniel Pope not long after his arrival in Ohio but decided against buying land near Pope's settlement at Leesburg. Adair returned to Paint Creek and negotiated with Nathaniel Massie. In December 1805 he signed an agreement to purchase 150 acres from Massie. The terms seemed attractive, $1.66 2/3 an acre, with half the $250 purchase price payable immediately and the other half due a year later. Massie, incidentally, was acting as agent for John Graham, a Revolutionary War veteran from Richmond, Virginia, who had received 1,000 acres of Ross County land as a military bounty. Like many veterans, Graham had no intention of becoming a resident of Ohio but was simply trying to make some money by selling his bounty lands through Massie.

As attractive deals sometimes have a way of doing, especially for men of limited means, Benjamin Adair's agreement with Massie did not turn out to be such a bargain. Adair had trouble meeting the second and final payment. After all, how could he raise cash while he was still clearing the land? Massie gave Adair an extension on the final payment in 1806 and again in 1807. Then, in 1807, Graham discharged Massie as his agent, and in return for the immediate payment of an amount equal to the outstanding debts against his Ohio land holdings, Graham sold Massie the right to collect what he could from settlers like Adair who still owed money. Massie continued to give Adair extensions until Adair finally completed payment in 1813, a full seven years after the debt had been due. If Massie appears flexible and generous, it should be noted that Adair paid interest at such a steep rate that he had to pay Massie a total dollar figure more than twice the original purchase price. Even then, after he had made the final payment, Adair's troubles were not over, since Massie died later in the year without providing him with a deed. Adair never succeeded in gaining clear title to the land in his lifetime.

A land of promise for many, the Ohio frontier was for all a place of hazards and hardships. By the time the Adairs and their relatives began homesteading along the Paint, the danger of Indian warfare was greatly diminished, though it revived, briefly, during the War of 1812. Paint Valley militiamen were mobilized in 1812 in response to fears that Britain's Indian allies, ably led by the great Shawnee chief Tecumseh, might go on a rampage. Few local men actually saw combat, however, and most, like their fathers during the Revolution, served only briefly. Benjamin Adair's son George was mustered in for one month and William Keys for two. Other problems of frontier life, such as the so-called squirrel invasion of 1807, during which hordes of hungry squirrels stripped the settlers' cornfields bare, posed no serious threat to the pioneers' survival, although many families spent the next winter on sparse diets of cabbage and turnips.

Paint Valley pioneers regarded the natural world around them with a mixture of fear and wonderment. Game was generally plentiful in the heavily wooded hills around the valley, but the abundance of animal life was a mixed blessing. Deer and wild turkeys supplied the pioneers with meat, but bears and other predators were notorious for carrying off the settlers' sheep and hogs. In the spring, rattlesnakes came out of hiberna-

These two drawings from *Davy Crockett's Almanack* (bear, 1836; snake, 1838) depict some of the hazards of frontier life with a tale-spinner's unbridled enthusiasm.

tion and often appeared in great numbers. Old-timers recalled seeing the newly emerged snakes "rolled up in large bundles or faggots, half the size of a barrel, each one having his head sticking outward, and all forming a most frightful circle of heads, glaring eyes and forked, hissing tongues." According to another story, William Pope was on a ride in 1802 when he stopped, tethered his horse, and walked "two or three rods" down a path to a spring. He

was just in the act of stooping down to take a drink when his eye detected the presence of a huge rattlesnake, very close to him. He happened to have the wiping stick of his gun in his hand with which he soon killed the snake. By the time, however, he had accomplished this, he saw others and he took his tomahawk and cut a pole and kept on killing till they became so numerous that he grew alarmed and started for his horse—literally killing his path through them to where he had left his company. . . . Pope wore buck skin breeches and heavy blue cloth leggins. During the fight with the snakes several struck him on the legs and fastened their fangs in his leggins, [and] hung there till he cut them off with his butcher knife.

Later, Pope's companions counted the dead snakes and came up with a total of eighty-four.[4]

A Narrow Escape from a Snake.

Pope's behavior was typical of the white men whose watchword in dealing with predators and the natural world was, according to a contemporary observer, "extermination." This attitude is evident in one old-timer's boast that he had killed "one hundred and sixty bears, ninety-six panthers, one hundred and six wolves, one thousand elk and deer, eleven buffalo, and other game in proportion; also ninety-six Indians." Tales of bear-killing exploits were repeated endlessly (and no doubt expansively). Like the wild animals native to the region, forests were also, according to an opinion widespread among early settlers, "enemies to the advancement of man and his plans." William Keys noted further that pioneers rarely expressed any regret over the almost complete devastation of the groves of oak, ash, maple, hickory, and other hardwoods that had once covered the Paint Valley countryside.[5]

Stories about fighting Indians, killing the biggest bear (or the most rattlesnakes), and clearing the land were told with great gusto by male pioneers. But the violent exploits the frontiersmen recalled with such relish reflected conditions about which early women settlers often had very different feelings. Although this contrast between men's and women's attitudes toward frontier life is rarely evident in records left by the Adairs and their neighbors, it is suggested in a few Paint Valley pioneer narratives. For instance, when her husband was away, Mrs. David Ross, a resident of Union Township in Highland County, reportedly "would leave the house and stay in the woods until he came back, for fear of the Indians." The narrator goes on to contrast her feelings with those of her husband, of whom it was said that he "had a brave pioneer heart . . . and enjoyed his isolated condition quite well." Mrs. Ross's apprehensions were not unique. John Proud, "a great hunter," was once away on a trip, leaving his wife and children "in their solitary cabin, which his wife had to defend all night, standing with the ax in her hands to keep the wolves out, as it had no door except what was very commonly substituted in those days, a blanket or quilt." Such cabins, women's principal place of work, left much to be desired. As one old-timer acknowledged, these "little uncomfortable log cabins and shanties . . . would not be used at this day [the late 1850s] for sheep pens." Cooking over an open fire, keeping house in one room with a dirt floor, giving birth with few, if any, women friends to help, and minding children as wild animals prowled nearby, many pioneer women must have found their new lives arduous, to say the least, in comparison with the lives they had known in Virginia. Little wonder, then, as we will see in subsequent chapters, that when a younger generation of men, sons of the Ohio pioneers, were champing at the bit to head west for newer frontiers, their mothers and wives were not always eager to go.[6]

Violence, as one of the prevailing white male responses to a frontier environment, did not go unchallenged in the early decades of Paint Valley life. To be sure, all pioneers participated to some degree in the work of driving out Indians, exterminating predators, and cutting down forests. However, when the frontiersmen's aggressive attitudes carried over into white society and took the form of disorderly conduct—brawling, drunkenness, rape, and even murder—many pioneers found this unacceptable. They therefore worked to create a countervailing force through such institutions of social respectability and social control as churches, schools, and courts.

It was with this second, civilizing orientation in frontier society, and especially with churches as instruments of social control, that Benjamin and Sarah Adair's children, cousins, and in-laws were associated. Like most of their relatives, the Adairs were Presbyterians. The church they attended, the Rocky Spring Presbyterian Church, was located on a hillside near the junction of the Paint and Rattlesnake creeks, only a short distance from the Adair homestead. Services were held at this site as early as 1806, but the congregation did not have a regular minister until the Reverend Nicholas Pittinger took over in April 1810. In that same year Benjamin Adair's son George was elected one of the church's first five elders. All the officers of the church were men, although in actual numbers women constituted a slight majority of the congregation's members.

The church's records, dating from 1810 and known as the "Rocky Spring Session Book," have been preserved. A large part of the volume consists of simple notations of members' names, baptisms, and the like; almost nothing was recorded regarding the congregation's religious practices, even though we know from other sources that protracted revival meetings had an important place in its early history. Scattered passages, however, provide revealing glimpses into the church's inner workings and into the private lives of its members. These passages show how the Rocky Spring Presbyterians dealt with cases of slander, gambling, intoxication, Sabbath-breaking, and fornication in their ranks.

That church members sometimes behaved in the brawling, disorderly ways so characteristic of the surrounding frontier community is clear enough from these cases, but it is also obvious that church-going settlers generally disapproved of such behavior. They had no special role to play where state and local laws were at issue and civil courts had jurisdiction. It was in the sphere of private morality, outside the civil legal code's purview, therefore, that these Christian settlers felt responsible for applying sanctions. However, the neighborhood surveillance needed to spot transgressors was somewhat inhibited by the settlement pattern that prevailed in the area, for nearly all Paint Valley pioneers lived on dispersed farms, much as they had done in southern states where the proportion of town dwellers was very low. Despite this limitation on their ability to keep neighbors under close scrutiny, Rocky Spring Presbyterians tried hard to be their brothers' and sisters' keepers. In the first twenty years after the church was organized, several dozen disciplinary cases were brought before sessions of its board of elders. The incidents considered by the board involved male and female members in about equal numbers, but the types of transgressions attributed to men and women differed. Only men were accused of intoxication, gambling, and breaking the Sabbath. With one exception in five cases, only women were tried and convicted of fornication. In two other cases touching on sexual offenses, women were accused of slander for having told neighbors that a male member of the congregation had tried to seduce them.

The two slander cases involved a great deal of neighborhood gossip, and for that reason they exposed the mind of these Presbyterian respectables in a particularly intimate way. At the session that heard Mrs. Susannah Lamb's case, for example, nearly all of her neighbors testified, including Philip Adair's wife, Elizabeth, and Rachel Lunbeck (another Adair in-law). Several witnesses repeated what Mrs. Lamb had told them —that one day between dawn and sunrise the man in question had come to her house and called to her to come outside and see her cabbage plants and that when she had gone out to the cabbage patch, "he caught hold of her and did not behave decently." Unfortunately for Mrs. Lamb, there were no independent witnesses to the alleged incident, and several neighbors, indeed, came forward to charge that she was wont to tell tales; so the elders accepted the man's denials and rebuked Mrs. Lamb, suspending her from communion with the church until she gave "evidence of repentance."[7]

The other slander case came before the August 1820 session. In it Samuel B. Strain appealed for redress against Jane Watts. According to Strain and other witnesses, Mrs. Watts had told neighbors that he had attempted "unlawful entercourse with her" and had also made "an attackt of a simmeler kind" on her daughter Sally. The incident with Mrs. Watts involved an indecent proposal Strain allegedly called out to her as she was passing his house. In the Watts girl's case, Sally had been out one evening hunting for a lost calf when supposedly "Sam'l B. Strain did pursue her running and spitting on his thumbs and caught hold of her." According to the Watts family's version of the incident, Sally rejected his overtures, whereupon "he let go telling her that if she ever told it nobody would think anything of her."[8]

Strain's defenders claimed that on a previous occasion Jane Watts had falsely charged a man with having attempted to seduce her. In support of this charge, one of Strain's relatives stated that nine years earlier Jane Watts and her husband had been tenants on James McMurtry's plantation in Barren County, Kentucky. Supposedly, an altercation about working a cornfield had prompted Mrs. Watts to spread stories about McMurtry's having made "an attempt on her chastity." A similar quarrel between Mrs. Watts and Strain's wife was said to explain why she would spread malicious stories about Mr. Strain. A Watts relative then rose to say that Jane's accusations against McMurtry had not been believed, because "the people generally thought she talked too much." Two witnesses challenged the testimony against Jane Watts, however, saying they had been acquainted with her in both South Carolina and Ohio (but not in Kentucky) and had. never considered her "dishonest or given to talebearing."[9]

Whatever the truth was, the session brought to light important information about the part of Paint Valley society with which the Adairs were most closely associated. Mrs. Watts provided yet another example, albeit an unhappy one, of how westward migration did not necessarily break an individual's former associations. She had certainly not escaped her past, for although she had moved several times (from South Carolina to Kentucky and then to Ohio), stories of her having been approached with sexual propositions had followed her from place to place. Strain's defenders used this to their advantage. As one witness said, "it seemed strange that she should be so often attacked in a similar way." The board of elders agreed and voted to suspend Mrs. Watts from communion with the church.[10]

This result was quite consistent with another feature of the social world inhabited by the Paint Valley Adairs. The Rocky Spring Presbyterians' disciplinary process worked to the advantage of male elders like Samuel B. Strain and against the interests of women like Susannah Lamb or Jane Watts and her daughter. In every case where the choice was between believing a woman's word or a man's, the elders of the church

Benjamin Adair's mark on his Last Will and Testament (1819).

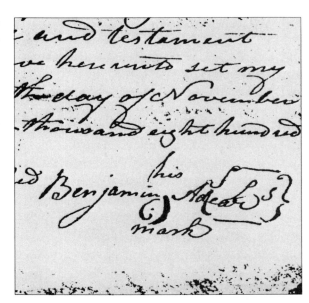

took the man's side. Mrs. Watts was at a further disadvantage because her economic status was lower than her accuser's. Strain had long been a landowner, while Jane Watts, according to four witnesses, had at various times lived with families as a servant or a tenant.

Although the social control that Rocky Spring Presbyterians exercised among themselves discriminated against some people, notably against poor and widowed women, the practical consequences of church ties for members who remained in good standing were, on the whole, positive. For the Adairs, the Rocky Spring Presbyterian Church was the principal source of friends, future spouses, and educational and religious inspiration over a period of twenty or more years. Even more broadly, however, the church was a primary means by which pioneers like Benjamin Adair, who had several times left former homes to move west, established roots in a new settlement.

The other ties that were crucial to Adair's sense of belonging were, as was mentioned earlier, those with his family. Despite his moves from Maryland to Virginia in 1799 and from Virginia to Ohio in 1805, he was not cut off from valued family connections of long standing. John Tudor, his son's father-in-law, originally a neighbor in Baltimore County, Maryland, and then a companion on the road to Ohio, later lived just across Paint Creek from Adair's farm. Direct links with Maryland were also retained. As late as the mid-1830s, one of Benjamin Adair's Ohio-born descendants went east to Baltimore, presumably to visit relatives there. An even greater continuity existed in contacts between the Paint Valley Adairs and their cousins and in-laws in Virginia. One of Benjamin Adair's older daughters married a Lyle and stayed in Virginia, but her brothers and sisters kept in touch with her. Moreover, Adair's Ohio homeland quickly became a county full of Lyle, Ramsey, and Keys cousins, many of whom exchanged news with him about Virginia relatives. And with his wife, his nine children who came to Ohio, and their spouses, cousins, in-laws, and neighbors who formed the Rocky Spring community, Benjamin Adair had a wealth of relationships on which to draw in his new home. As one neighbor recalled, "old man Adair . . . had the pleasure of seeing all his children settle in life around him and united with the church."[11] It was an epitaph he would have liked.

JEREMIAH ROOT'S OHIO GAMBLE

As she hurried up the steps of the First Congregational Church of Aurora, Ohio, Lucretia Root noticed nothing unusual about the day. It was cold, but that was normal for January in northeastern Ohio, and she was hurrying, but that was only because she was a little late for Sunday service. As she slipped inside the church, however, every eye turned to look at her, and the expressions on her neighbors' faces were so solemn that Lucretia felt something must be seriously amiss. She wondered anxiously if it might concern her husband, Jerry, who was visiting his brother in Massachusetts. At the end of the service the minister, the Reverend John Seward, asked her to stop by the parsonage, and her apprehension increased when she arrived at Seward's cabin and found the room full of her friends, all sitting in complete silence. After Lucretia had taken a seat, Seward cleared his throat and began to read from a letter.

"My dear Madame," he read, "God is great and his works are wonderful. His ways are in the great deep and past finding out, and though clouds and darkness are round about his throne, yet in his sacred word he has assured us that justice and righteousness are the seat of his habitation forever. Man that is born of a woman is but a few days and full of trouble. *Imperfection* and *mortality* are stamped upon his nature. Written in letters of blood, this life is emphatically called a *veil of tears*. Disappointment and trouble, sickness, pain and death are the common lot of all. Prosperity charms us. Adversity tries us, and the one is placed over against the other to the intent that man should find nothing after him. Our friends and acquaintances fail us. The nearest and dearest ties of nature are dissolved. The widow's moan and the orphan's tear attends us, while death like some able day's man lays all in the dust. We are lost in the forgetfulness of the grave, and mankind live only in the memory of their actions. This being the case, it becomes us to bow with submission to the will of that God whose name is Jehovah, to improve Time in preparation for Eternity, and thereby answer the end and design of our creation, to bear the ills of life with an equal and constant mind. Enjoy the *good* and forget the *evil*, and always maintain a consciousness of doing right. This will beam happiness upon our minds, make the journey of life agreeable, avert the ready shafts of calumny and reproach, and be a firm support in death. Having thus prefaced my address, and as I fondly hope prepared your mind for the reception of *Melancholy Tidings* it is my painful task to announce them. *Your kind and affectionate partner, the husband of your youth, Jeremiah Root, Esquire, is no more!!"*[12]

Lucretia was stunned. Her dear husband of more than twenty-seven years was dead. She was scarcely able to concentrate as Seward continued to read, adding the further details that Jerry had died on December 26, 1815, at his brother's house in Southwick, that he had been ill for ten days, the last two of them in great "pain and distress," and that Jeremiah's Southwick relatives were making arrangements to return his horse and personal effects to Ohio.

Only later did Lucretia learn that this letter had been addressed to her but that because the phrase "Mournful Intelligence" was scrawled on the envelope, the postmaster gave the letter to Seward to deliver to her. Seward not only decided to open the letter but also reported its contents to the congregation before Lucretia arrived at church. He took it upon himself, furthermore, to invite her friends to be at the parsonage when he read the letter to her. It seems doubtful that Seward's manner of delivering the news lessened the shock for Lucretia.

Although there is no record of Lucretia's thoughts later in the day that fateful Sunday, they almost certainly turned to memories of her life with Jeremiah—their early married years in Southwick, the births of their seven children, and the hopes and dreams they shared in deciding to move to Ohio in 1807. Doubtless, too, her husband's death at the age of fifty forced Lucretia to see the move to Ohio in a new light. A venture that had once seemed a reasonable financial gamble, given Jeremiah's good health and Ohio's promise, was now, with Jeremiah dead, in grave danger of failing.

Jeremiah Root and Lucretia Page were married on February 5, 1788, in Southwick, Massachusetts, Jeremiah's birthplace. Jeremiah was twenty-two, Lucretia not quite eighteen. It was a promising match: both were self-reliant, ambitious, and Congregationalist. Both of their fathers were Revolutionary War veterans. Since the Westfield-Southwick area had been home to the Roots for many generations, it was natural enough that Jeremiah and Lucretia made their first home in Southwick. Also, Jeremiah was still young and needed help from his father, Lieutenant Gideon Root, to get started in farming.

Jeremiah and Lucretia Root's oldest children were born in South-wick: Sarah (Sally) in 1789, Abigail in 1792, and most likely Polly (in 1794) as well. Cozy though it was to be under the Root family's protective wing and to benefit from its established reputation, Jeremiah was too full of his own plans to rest content with the situation. As long as he remained in Southwick, he would not quite be his own man. Economically, he would always be second in line behind Gideon Jr., his older brother. Socially, he would be, in the eyes of many, lower in status than his father and brother, always a second son, albeit from an important local family.

By 1795, the year his son Jeremiah Jr. was born, Jeremiah Root had moved his family to Washington, Massachusetts, a village in the Berk-shires about forty miles by road from Southwick. It was not a major move as distance goes, but it signaled Jeremiah's determination to set out on his own. Over the next decade he worked diligently to become financially independent, first by acquiring clear title to 150 acres of land in Washing-ton and then by making a down payment on a second farm, this one in nearby Chester. By 1800 Jeremiah had moved his family to the Chester place, a choice 48-acre farm adjacent to the Congregational meetinghouse and complete with a house and two barns.

Reading between the lines of official county records makes it clear that Jeremiah's pursuit of economic independence led him to stretch his resources to the limit. Rental income from his farm in Washington appar-ently helped him meet the heavy mortgage payments he owed on the Chester place. In 1803, however, an installment came due when he was low on cash, and he had to obtain a second mortgage from a Boston bank. By 1806 his risk had paid off. Through hard work, timely loans, and good luck, Jeremiah Root acquired clear title to two farms, a total of nearly two hundred acres that was worth perhaps $4,000 on the open market.

At about this time talk among Jeremiah's neighbors in Washington, Chester, and Middlefield turned frequently to the topic of Ohio, and more specifically to discussions of Ohio's Western Reserve district. This huge tract of nearly four million acres in northeastern Ohio had been opened to settlement late in the 1790s by the Connecticut Land Company, which had purchased most of the land from the state of Connecticut and then surveyed it. Whole townships were subsequently sold to either a single investor or groups of investors, and now these investor-speculators were seeking to entice settlers from older districts such as the Berkshires to move west. In 1806 several acquaintances of Jeremiah Root decided to exchange their Berkshire farms for Ohio land owned by David King and Ebenezer King Jr., who had purchased a major share in town 5, range 9, and as yet unnamed town later called Aurora. Jeremiah was intrigued by what he heard about Ohio, and there is strong evidence that he made an exploratory trip to Aurora in 1806 to look things over.

The investment potential of Ohio property struck Root as excellent, and by January 1807 he was ready to put all his resources into buying western land. His was a modest speculation, speculative in the sense that the future value of any given farm in the still largely unsettled Western Reserve was uncertain. It was modest because Root's capital was by no means unlimited. He could raise approximately $4,000 by selling his Berkshire farms. That sum placed him considerably ahead of Benjamin Adair, who had trouble raising $250 to purchase his farm on the Paint. Yet Root's resources did not begin to compare with those of David King and Ebenezer King Jr. of Suffield, Connecticut, the major figures in the Big Beaver Land Company, from which Root obtained his Ohio land, and men typical of the large-scale investors who purchased whole townships at $10,000 a crack. But even the Kings were small fry compared with a giant of the western land trade like Oliver Phelps, also of Suffield, whose outlay for Western Reserve lands alone was $248,185 and who, in partnership with Nathaniel Gorham, controlled even larger acreages in western New York.

A reciprocal relationship existed between the large and small investors in western lands. Large speculators like the Kings were in a position akin to that of the owners of an automobile franchise with a large inventory. The Kings' inventory consisted of real estate. The Jeremiah Roots were not unlike people who had an old car (in this case a farm) they wanted to trade in. Although the analogy is not precise—mainly because most western lands were uncleared and therefore not immediately usable, as a new car would be—the comparison holds fairly well. Each party to the transaction received something of value. The wealthy landholders reduced their inventories of Ohio land. The smaller farmers received a reasonably good price for their old farms and the chance to acquire a larger acreage by moving west.

Jeremiah Root's experience provides a good illustration of just such an exchange. David King and Ebenezer King Jr. gave him a good price for his two farms—$2,300 for his land in Washington, and $2,100 for his home place in Chester. In paying Root top dollar for his Berkshire farms, the Kings actually lost money on that part of the transaction, since they resold the Chester place for only $1,800 shortly after receiving title from

Root. In so doing, however, they had induced Root to invest heavily in their Western Reserve holdings. In 1807 he purchased 660 acres of undeveloped land from the Kings, three times his Berkshire acreage. Then, in 1810 and 1811, he bought more parcels from the Kings, bringing his total property in Ohio to nearly 1,000 acres. True, he had to go into debt again, borrowing more than $1,500 to complete the deal. But what did it matter? Jeremiah Root was in his early forties, his prime, and was confident he had the energy to clear his land and pay off the loans. Besides, his experience with borrowing in order to buy his Berkshire farms had been encouraging. Why shouldn't it work again?

For the trip west the Roots joined forces with a group of their friends and neighbors. An acquaintance of Jeremiah's, Joseph Eggleston, had gone to Ohio in 1806. Joseph returned to Massachusetts in the summer of 1807 to claim Parley Leonard as his bride. After the ceremony, the newlyweds started for Ohio with a party of thirty-two migrants, five families in all, including Jeremiah Root's, all of them friends of the bride and groom. Little is known of the trip itself, except that the colonists took a Pennsylvania wagon road that followed roughly the same route as the present-day Pennsylvania Turnpike.

From the first, Jeremiah Root's Ohio gamble went well. He played an energetic part in establishing all of the new community's major institutions and quickly found his way to the top of the local elite. When Aurora's first church was founded in December 1807, he was chosen an elder. In the very next year Portage County was organized, and Jeremiah, named one of the new county's first justices of the peace, was suddenly Jeremiah Root, Esquire. In 1809 his daughter Sally married a prominent Portage County man, Owen Brown, a widower from nearby Hudson and one of Jeremiah's colleagues on the county court. Then came the War of 1812, during which Jeremiah was commissioned a lieutenant, the same rank his father had held in the Revolution. Thus, honors and titles whose achievement might have been long delayed had he remained in Southwick were soon his in Ohio.

Jeremiah's ties with his Southwick relatives had always been close, and they remained so, although some strains surfaced in the years after his move to Ohio. Jeremiah's father had died in 1804, but Lieutenant Gideon's widow, Huldah Root, lived until 1813. She was never fully reconciled to Jeremiah's decision to go west; according to one of his daughters who met the old lady, she mourned his loss to her dying day. Evidence of the emotional pressure on Jeremiah, which at times must have been as heavy as his mother's heart, may be glimpsed in a letter the widow Root sent her son in 1810. "What feelings does it give me," she wrote, "to think that my dear children are scattered to the remotest parts of the earth never, perhaps nevermore to set eyes on them. When I think of it my heart swells with grief."[13]

Jeremiah made at least one trip from Ohio to Massachusetts while his mother was still living, for we know that he visited her in 1811, when she was seventy-three years old. According to his daughter Abby (who was present), on the day that he was to begin his return trip to Ohio, his mother threw "her arms around his neck and kissed him, and looking through her tears she said, 'Goodbye my son, God bless you.' And putting a pair of blue and white striped mittens on his hands, she said, 'I have knitted these for you, and it may be the last thing I can ever do for you.' "[14] Her words proved prophetic, for she died in 1813 without having seen Jeremiah again.

Other evidence of the Root family's opposition to Jeremiah's move west is found in a letter, quoted below, sent to him by his brother Gideon not long after Jeremiah had become a Portage County justice of the peace in 1808. In the opening passage, Gideon alluded to the family's displeasure with Jeremiah's decision to leave Massachusetts. Later Gideon referred to Ohio as a "rude wilderness . . . where beasts of prey roam the forests," reflecting the negative image the frontier had in the minds of many easterners. Finally, mixing praise with a dash of reproach, Gideon gave his version of Jeremiah's motives for migrating, acknowledging that the needs of a large family (by 1805 Jeremiah and Lucretia had seven children) had made the move logical, but implying that what Jeremiah had really been after was the "vanity" of higher social status.

"The tender ties of near and dear relatives are broken," brother Gid wrote. "The most tender sensibility is alienated. The serene charm of friendship ceases to please, and clouds and darkness veil the temple of true felicity. It must be so, or why have I seen a man, a friend and brother, in the prime of life and usefulness, quit his native home, the lap of ease and plenty, a circle of friends and relatives, social intercourse and agreeable society, in exchange for a rude wilderness where poverty growls and beggary starves, and where beasts of prey roam the forests and where fiercer beasts of men infest the recent ground. But to this my friend will object and say the design is a laudable one. I exchange my condition to better it. A numerous family demands my care. The rough ways must be made smooth . . . and what farther—a little *honorary distinction* is pleas-

WESTERN EMIGRATION.

JOURNAL

OF

DOCTOR JEREMIAH SMIPLETON's

TOUR TO OHIO.

CONTAINING

An account of the numerous difficulties, Hair-breadth
Escapes, Mortifications and Privations, which the
Doctor and his family experienced on their
Journey from Maine, to the 'Land of Pro-
mise,' and during a residence of three years
in that highly extolled country.

BY H. TRUMBULL.

Nulli Fides Frontis.

BOSTON--PRINTED BY S. SEWALL.

Antimigration propaganda typically showed the pioneer (here, Ohio immigrant
Jeremiah Simpleton) returning much the worse for the experience.

LANDS

in New-Connecticut,

THAT part of the Connecticut Reserve, or New-Connecticut, to which the Indian title has been extinguished, lying West of Pennsylvania, and South of Lake Erie, having been surveyed and divided.

THE subscriber offers for sale a large quantity of Land, in the following Towns, viz.

In No. 2, and No. 12, in the first Range,

ADJOINING the Pennsylvania Line, the former of which has settlements adjoining, both in Pennsylvania, and the town immediately West. The latter is about 24 miles from Presque-Isle, and has settlements at a few miles distance in Pennsylvania, is about six miles from the Lake, and lies on the Ashtebula Creek.

In the Third Town in the Second Range,

Adjoining the Town in which is the Salt Spring, and adjoining the Town called Young's Town, in which is a settlement of fifteen families. This Town is about 60 miles from Pittsburg, and through it runs the Big Beaver River.

In No. 1, and No. 8, in the 4th Range,—In No. 7 in the 6th Range, No. 8 in the 7th Range, and No. 10 in the 8th Range.

Through the last three Towns a road is laid out from the Salt Springs to the Lake, and through No. 10, in the Eighth Range, a road is likewise laid out from the Pennsylvania line, to the Town of Cleaveland, both of which are to be cut and compleated early the ensuing Season.

In No. 9 in the 8th Range, No. 7 in the 9th Range, and No. 13 in the 3d Range.

Also, 29 lots lying in the four best Towns as selected by the Surveyors.

The Tract of Country in which the above Lands are situated, having been explored and divided the last season, is well known to be a most excellent tract of Land, well watered, and its waters good ; its situation peculiarly favorable, lying on Lake Erie, its rivers, and the boatable waters of the Ohio. The part of the Tract now offered for sale, being large and much diversified in its situation, and most of the Tracts either lying on the Rivers, the great Roads about to be opened, or near Settlements ;—the subscriber presumes there is no part of the Lands in the whole Tract, which are more inviting to the settlers. He expects to be on the Lands in the month of June, after which time constant attention will be given, and all applications attended to with care and dispatch. A small part of the purchase money will be expected to be paid down, for the remainder a convenient Credit will be given.

SIMON PERKINS.

Agent to the Erie Company.

PRINTED AT J. TRUMBULL'S PRESS, NORWICH.

1798 poster advertising Ohio lands. Note that the last line promises "convenient Credit."

ing, some vanity to be excited. You have it, and here permit me to express a pleasure on hearing that you have received public testimonials of respect from the people with whom you reside. . . . Well it is *Jeremiah Root, Esq.* now. He has got what he went after."[15]

If the phrase "he has got what he went after" came to Jeremiah Root's mind on the occasion of his fiftieth birthday, July 7, 1815, he doubtless would have agreed that his brother's statement was accurate. Unlike another Jeremiah—the fictional hero of a satirical antimigration tract, Dr. Jeremiah Simpleton, who abandoned Ohio and went back to New England after three years filled with "Numerous Difficulties, Hairbreadth Escapes, Mortifications and Privations"—Jeremiah Root had stayed and had done well.[16] During his eight years in the Western Reserve, he had become a church elder, a lieutenant in the militia, and a public official with the title of esquire. Although he still owed $1,500 on his land, he was making good progress toward clearing and paying for his thousand-acre parcel. By 1815 he was one of the richest men in Aurora, ranking fourth among fifty-four taxpayers in the township and paying an annual tax of $16.92, more than three times the average his neighbors paid. Moreover, this represents only part of Root's estate, since his favorite farm was just across the line in Bainbridge, Geauga County.

His one continuing regret was that in seeking his destiny in Ohio he had upset his Southwick relatives. Jeremiah did his best to reassure his family in the East. When he visited Southwick in 1811, he took his daughter Abigail along and placed her in a Massachusetts boarding school. It was his way of showing that in casting his lot with the West he had not forgotten either his loved ones in Southwick or the superiority of eastern education. The wisdom of his course was confirmed three years later, in 1814, when Abby, now back in Ohio, met and married one of Portage County's best-educated men, a Hudson physician, Dr. Jonathan Metcalf. As Jeremiah started east in November 1815 for yet another visit with his family and friends in Southwick, he was unquestionably in a good position to speak with pride about what he and his family had achieved since their move to the Western Reserve.

When news of Jeremiah's death reached Lucretia later that winter, it must have struck her as ironic that her husband had, in death, literally gone home to the very relatives who once had accused him of deserting them. She was in no position, however, to allow such thoughts to distract her for long from pressing practical concerns, for Jeremiah's Ohio venture, which was hers as well, was now in jeopardy. Over the past five years, he had taken out several substantial mortgages to finance additional land purchases. At the time he had been in his mid-forties and in good health, and like many other upwardly mobile pioneers who borrowed to get ahead, he had felt that the potential for accelerating his family's rise in social status greatly outweighed the risk of failure. His death, however, threatened his family's well-being and forced Lucretia and their oldest son, Jeremiah Jr., to try to keep the family solvent.

Although Jeremiah Jr. was barely twenty at the time of his father's death, he was old enough, and capable enough, to step into his father's place and make the Roots' Ohio gamble work. For six years, from 1816 to 1822, Jeremiah Jr. devoted himself to helping his mother clear the debts against his father's estate, and only after this obligation was fulfilled did he marry a neighbor, Huldah Harmon, and start a family with her. Although Jeremiah Jr. did not follow his father's example and pursue a career in politics, he, like his father, made the most of economic opportunities. Indeed, it is a final proof of Jeremiah Sr.'s business acumen in betting on Ohio's future, that Jeremiah Jr., a major beneficiary of his father's investments, became so wealthy that he was able to retire from active farming when only forty-two.

Lucretia Root outlived her husband by more than three decades, spending most of her later years in the homes of her children. Even in old age Lucretia was an impressive woman, and her grandchildren remembered being slightly awestruck when they came under the steady gaze of her dark eyes. She died on May 29, 1846, at the age of seventy-six, while visiting her daughter Abigail Root Metcalf in Hudson, Ohio.

SQUIRE BROWN OF HUDSON, OHIO

On October 16, 1804, Owen Brown returned to his home in Torrington, Connecticut, after a brief trip to the frontier town of Hudson, Ohio. He had gone to Hudson to explore the prospects for moving there and, liking what he had learned, had bought a small plot of land and begun to clear it. Although he had been taken ill in Ohio and still suffered from recurrent attacks of fever and chills, his determination to move west was undiminished. His eagerness to migrate stemmed partly from his belief that the move would be financially rewarding, but, of equal importance, he had met his future neighbors and had been favorably impressed. The people of Hudson, he wrote, were "very harmonious and middling prosperous, and mostly united in religious sentiments."[17] Moreover, the town's founders were committed to establishing a community whose hallmarks were Christian piety, educational advancement, and a moral, law-abiding citizenry, all goals that Brown shared.

Hudson's founders were not the only Americans in the early national period with plans for the development of the American West. Federal legislators passed laws requiring that much of the nation's vast wilderness be divided into rectangular tracts, a practice that gave western settlements the right-angled layouts many retain today. Similarly, private entrepreneurs' policies tended to channel the flow of migrants into given areas, and this produced lasting results. The Connecticut Land Company, for instance, sought to sell whole townships to groups of investors from a single eastern community in hopes that "the solidarity of a common background" among the township's purchasers would facilitate rapid settlement, while also encouraging the preservation of the New England heritage in Ohio. On the local level some Western Reserve communities became "covenanted towns," that is, communities whose founders began their enterprise by making "a special compact with God and with each other." At Tallmadge, a town only ten miles south of Hudson, an experimental religious colony of this sort flourished briefly between 1807 and 1812 under the Reverend David Bacon's leadership.[18]

Hudson also had one individual who was the settlement's leading spirit during its formative years—David Hudson, lately of Goshen, Connecticut, for whom the township was named. It was he who, together with five partners, in 1798 purchased the as yet unnamed Ohio township that was located approximately two dozen miles southeast of present-day Cleveland. In 1799 Hudson traveled to the townsite and surveyed its twenty-five square miles of land, nearly one-third of which he owned. Then in 1800, accompanied by his family and a handful of other settlers, he made a second trip from Goshen to Ohio to become a permanent resident of the Western Reserve. Hudson's dream was to transplant the best of New England to Ohio, and in pursuit of that goal he personally recruited settlers for the community, concentrating on attracting migrants whose special skills were needed by the fledgling town. His success as a recruiter was illustrated by two new colonists who arrived from

Connecticut together in 1805—Benjamin Whedon, a schoolteacher, and a tanner named Owen Brown.

The road had not been particularly smooth for Owen Brown. In 1776, when he was five years old, his father, Captain John Brown, died of dysentery a month after leaving home at the head of a Revolutionary militia unit. With eleven children to support, and none of the boys old enough to run the farm, Owen's widowed mother was in a bad spot. "For want of help," Owen remembered, "we lost our crops and then our cattle, and so became poor."[19] In an effort to make ends meet, the widow Brown sent several of her children to live with relatives. Owen spent 1777 at his grandfather's in Bloomfield.

Owen was at home only sporadically during the fifteen years between his father's death and his twentieth birthday. In his preteen years he was boarded out with various neighbors and relatives, with the result that his education followed an erratic course. As a teenager he became even more itinerant, spending winters on the road as an apprentice shoemaker and summers at home working his mother's farm. The Brown family's fortunes began to improve in the late 1780s as Owen and his brothers came of age, but the legacy of the lean early years lingered. Owen's limited education in academic subjects was markedly evident whenever he grappled with the complexities of spelling and grammar. And, though it was true that Owen's experience of poverty taught him some useful lessons in the value of thrift, self-reliance, and hard work, his intense determination to do well in life had its origin in a persistent fear that he might fail.

Early in 1793, less than a week before his twenty-second birthday, Owen Brown married a neighbor, Ruth Mills. Her father was a minister, and as well-educated and devout Christians her family belonged to what Owen called "the better class of people."[20] Owen and Ruth were also very much in love. Unfortunately, their hopes for a family were initially crushed when their first two children died in infancy. After the second died, they adopted a boy named Levi Blakeslee. Eventually, however, they produced their own children as well, four of whom were living when the Browns left for Ohio in 1805.

During these first twelve years of married life, Owen worked hard to make his businesses—shoemaking, tanning, and farming—succeed. Quick to grasp opportunities for doing even better, he moved his family three times in this brief period: from West Simsbury to Norfolk, from there to Torrington, and finally from Connecticut to Ohio. It may be that it was relatively easy for a man who had moved so often from childhood onward to uproot himself again and again, but one must not assume from this that he liked the life of a rolling stone. Nor would it be accurate to say that his motives for going to Ohio were solely economic. Brown certainly hoped to do well financially in Ohio, but he was after something else too. As a man whom circumstances had frequently uprooted, he felt a deep need to belong somewhere, and the fact that David Hudson had handpicked him for membership in a new community must have struck him as a good omen: Ohio might be the place where he could, at last, put down permanent roots.

The Browns, accompanied on the trip west by Benjamin and Deborah Whedon, followed a route that took them through Pennsylvania. Owen's son John, who was five years old at the time of the move, later recalled how proud he had been of sharing the responsibility of driving the family's cattle. There were occasional bursts of excitement, as when members of the party found and killed large rattlesnakes, but for the most part the journey was uneventful. After seven weeks on the road, the Brown-Whedon party arrived in Hudson, Ohio, on July 27, 1805.

Owen Brown was unquestionably a valuable addition to David Hudson's growing community. To be sure, Brown was not so prosperous a middle-class emigrant to the Western Reserve as Jeremiah Root. Brown's Torrington property sold for $1,200, whereas Root's Berkshire farms

Owen Brown
(1771–1856).

brought a combined price of $4,400. Nor was Brown, who had had no opportunity to go to school regularly during his impoverished youth, as well educated as most of Hudson's pioneer leaders. But he came equipped with many skills the settlement needed—skills acquired from his wide experience as a tanner, shoemaker, builder, and stockman. He also fit in well in other ways. Like David Hudson, he was a Congregationalist in religion and a Federalist in politics. Moreover, his devotion to his family and his seriousness in matters of the soul won his neighbors' admiration. It was observed in this respect that although Owen Brown stuttered badly in ordinary conversation, he "was very able in prayer, and in his approach to the throne of Heavenly Grace the impediment in his speech almost entirely disappeared."[21]

According to Christian Cackler, a pioneer resident of Hudson, the town as of 1805 was part of a nearly "unbroken wilderness, filled up with wild men and wild animals. Probably forty Indians to one white man." By frontier standards Owen Brown's views on the Indian question were a bit odd. He wrote that the local Indians "were very friendly and . . . were a benefit rather than [an] injery." Most of the Indians were forced from the area around the time of the War of 1812. This was, Owen said, "rather against my wishes." He believed that Indians should be protected under the law just as whites were, and with his customary independence of spirit he backed his words with warrants for the arrest of two white men who murdered an Indian in 1806. David Hudson and a few others supported Brown, but the more general reaction among settlers locally was to be annoyed with Brown. The accused men were soon freed.[22]

Settlers' attitudes toward local wildlife paralleled their view of the Indians. The popular opinion, it seemed, was that the only good varmint was a dead varmint. Bears and wolves did pose a threat to smaller domestic animals, and Christian Cackler, for one, recalled that his family would not risk raising a sheep or hog unless their "eyes were on it most of the time."[23] Individual settlers fought back by killing four-legged predators (and rattlesnakes too) in great numbers, sometimes organizing their war on the wildlife into what was called a circle hunt. As many as two hundred men and boys would surround a swampy area and then drive through it, killing all the animals—literally hundreds of deer, bear, wolves, and smaller animals—caught in the roundup. Although it was said that Owen Brown did not like to hunt, his tannery did a heavy business in skins that hunters brought him.

It took several decades for Hudson's pioneers to transform the raw wilderness of New Connecticut (as the Western Reserve was sometimes called) into a mature community comparable to what they had known in old Connecticut. Initially, all settlers, whether rich or poor, lived in small log cabins, most of them either twelve by fourteen feet or fourteen by sixteen feet. It was to just such a structure, half-completed during his brief visit in 1804, that Owen Brown brought his family in 1805. One could sympathize with Ruth Brown if, on seeing this rude home (which the Browns occupied for more than ten years), she felt some nostalgia for the house, modest though it had been, that she had just left in Torrington. To be sure, only a year after the Browns' arrival David Hudson had a frame house (one of the first in the Western Reserve) built for himself, and a few other local pioneers were able to follow suit over the next five years. Such achievements, together with the early presence in Hudson of a significant number of college-educated migrants, gave the town a reputation throughout the Western Reserve and even in the East of being unusually advanced for a frontier community. But improvements long remained the exception rather than the rule. Primitive physical conditions were so much a part of life in early Hudson that when Dr. Jonathan Metcalf, an eastern-educated physician and Owen Brown's future brother-in-law, sent to Pittsburgh in 1813 for glass panes to install in his log cabin's windows, it struck his neighbors as "a great piece of extravagance."[24] Most occupants of log cabins made do with oilcloth windows. Similarly, though a few Hudson residents had frame houses, most lived in log cabins well into the 1810s, and during that decade Hudson was, at times, virtually cut off from the rest of the world because wilderness roads were impassable during the spring mud season.

Owen Brown never shrank from hard labor or community obligations, but there must have been times when his heavy workload tested his energies to the fullest. During his first ten years in Ohio he had land to clear and stock raising to supervise, while also setting up and operating a tannery on the banks of Brandywine Creek near the center of Hudson. With surplus income from these business activities, he purchased parcels of undeveloped land from which he later sold small lots, making at least four such sales one year when the real-estate market was strong. Meanwhile, he was much in demand in the public sphere. He was respected as an arbitrator of disputes over land titles and often rode sixty or seventy miles to referee cases. He held a succession of committee posts in Hud-

son's First Congregational Church. From the very first he was also active
in county government, serving on a number of grand juries before being
elected to the first of several three-year terms as a county commissioner
in 1813. These services earned him the title of esquire, and his neighbors
thereafter called him Squire Brown.

Although Owen's children were young when they arrived in Ohio,
they soon learned the significance of their father's statement that Ohio
was not "a land of idleness." From an early age Owen's oldest son, John,
was expected to accept adult tasks. At age six John learned the rudiments
of merchandising by selling rawhide whips to local settlers. At age eight
and nine he worked as an apprentice, learning his father's trade at the
family tannery. When, during the War of 1812, Owen Brown contracted
to supply beef to American troops stationed in Michigan, the twelve-year-
old youngster not only accompanied his father on trips to Detroit but was
also responsible for driving "wild steers and cattle through woods" over
distances of more than a hundred miles. Referring to himself in the third
person, John made it clear that he would have considered it an insult had
someone suggested that he was too young to handle the cattle drives
alone: "He would have thought his character much injured had he been
obliged to be helped in any such job."[25]

During these busy years tragedy struck the Brown family. John was
eight at the time, December 1808. On the ninth of that month Owen's wife,
Ruth, gave birth to a daughter, who lived only a few hours. Later in the
day Ruth also died. "All my early prospects appeared to be blasted," Owen
wrote later, remembering how shattered he had felt as he buried the love
of his youth in Hudson Cemetery. For Ruth's headstone, Owen chose the
following inscription:

> She was a dutiful child,
> A Sprightly youth, a Loving wife,
> A tender parent, a Kind neighbor
> and an Examplary christian.

"These were days of affliction," Owen recalled. "I was left with five (or six,
including Levi Blakeslee, my adopted son) small Children the oldes[t] but
a little one 10 years old."[26]

Eleven months after Ruth's death Owen married again, taking Jeremiah and Lucretia Root's daughter Sally, a woman eighteen years his
junior, as his second wife. Although Owen from the first respected Sally

and soon came to appreciate her common sense and good judgment, he never experienced the spontaneous affection for her that he had felt for Ruth. For her part, Sally found the first years of married life quite trying, not because Owen regarded her as his helpmate rather than as his sweetheart (an attitude she accepted), but because she had walked into a difficult situation with Owen's older boys. The problem was not the size of Owen's family; she had six brothers and sisters of her own. What was new, and hard to endure, was that at the age of twenty the new bride found herself facing three boys—Levi Blakeslee, who was in his mid-teens, and John and Salmon Brown, aged nine and seven respectively—whose minds were set on rejecting their stepmother. John later admitted that Sally was "a sensible, intelligent, and on many accounts a very estimable woman; *yet he never adopted her in feeling;* but continued to pine after his own Mother for years." Salmon joined John in playing practical jokes on their stepmother, one of which (rigging a ladder to the barn loft so that the steps would give way when she climbed up) injured more than her pride. Levi Blakeslee, only five years younger than Sally, was no less obstreperous in resisting her authority. Owen Brown reflected on these familial conflicts and blamed himself for being so frequently absent from Hudson on business, ruefully concluding that "it was an injery to my family to be away so much."[27]

In April 1811 Sally bore a daughter, Sally Marian, the first of her eight children. A son, Watson, was born in 1813 and another daughter, Florella, early in 1816. By this time Owen's worldly prospects had improved a great deal. He was about to move his tannery to an enlarged site north of town and to build a frame house near the new tannery. Eager to see his sons educated, he sent John and Salmon, aged sixteen and fourteen, east to study at Plainfield Academy in Massachusetts, the first step toward a hoped-for career in the ministry for John. The experiment was not a success. John felt like an awkward frontier giant among younger boys, and Salmon, who tended to be flippant, did not fit in well either. After less than a year at school, divided between Plainfield and Morris academies (the latter in Connecticut), the two Brown boys headed home, their discomfort and failure in the East underlining the need for good schools in the Western Reserve, where pioneer children could learn and at the same time fit in socially.

David Hudson's solution to the problem of educating western youngsters was the building of an academy and college at Hudson. Such a project, of course, would buttress Hudson's vision of his town as one noted for morality, Christian piety, obedience to the law, and educational excellence. In spite of his persistent lobbying, however, it was 1822 before the idea of a college in the Western Reserve was endorsed by the Portage Presbytery, the ecclesiastical body to which the Hudson Congregationalists belonged. Even then there was much debate over the prospective college's site. Eventually, Hudson was chosen, and in 1826 Western Reserve College received its charter from the state.

The townspeople of Hudson quickly organized to build the college. Owen Brown served on the construction committee. On April 26, 1826, the day the cornerstone of the first college building was laid, "a procession [formed] at Mr. Hudson's house which moved to the meeting house for prayer and singing, and then to the college campus."[28] After a dedication address was given in Latin, a committee of local Masons laid the cornerstone. With these solemn ceremonies, the local populace launched an educational enterprise that was intended to make Hudson into a western version of the New England college town.

No account of the people and institutions that sustained the New England tradition in early-day Hudson would be complete without mention of the First Congregational Church. Organized in 1802, it remained something of a missionary outpost without a permanent minister until the Reverend William Hanford arrived in 1815. Early in the 1820s a substantial new meetinghouse was completed. Owen Brown, who had served as the principal contractor for the building of the meetinghouse, was also a member of the visitation committee that in 1820 and 1821 made a house-to-house canvass of Hudson's residents "to awaken their attention to the concerns of their souls." The personal approach paid off in goodwill, at least according to Squire Brown's neighbor Lora Case, who remembered the occasion when Brown stopped by and expressed regret at not having seen him in church of late. Thinking that Brown was simply looking for financial support, Case replied, "We are in the woods, clearing our farm and it is not paid for yet," to which Brown responded, "That is not what I mean. It is your presence which is better than money."[29]

The church also tried to enforce high moral standards among its members. During the 1820s the church minutes record problems with "immodest language" and unspecified "difficulties" between husbands and wives.[30] No case, however, excited more comment than Deacon Benjamin Whedon's. Whedon was excommunicated for not exercising proper control over his household and, worse yet, for not expressing regret for his laxity in allowing his wife and adopted son to hold a puppet show and dance at his house.

The 1820s were fruitful years for Owen Brown, but they were not without their difficulties. Early in the decade the aftershocks of the panic of 1819 caused him considerable financial distress. As he put it, "Money became scarce, property fell, and that which I thought well bought would not bring its cost. I had made three or four large purchases in which I was a heavy loser." Squire Brown's older boys were sometimes a care, too, especially Salmon. Owen did what he could to support his son's law studies in Pittsburgh, but he worried constantly because Salmon showed no "evidence of being a Christian." Like Salmon, John was restless, apparently needing to get out from under his father's watchful eye, even though there was a close and lasting bond between father and son. John first established his own tannery. Then, with his father's encouragement, he married. Finally, in 1826, he sold out and moved to northwestern Pennsylvania. Indeed, by 1826 all of Owen's children from his first marriage had come of age and he could take satisfaction in the fact that he had ten living heirs, five by his first wife and five by his second. Squire Brown's businesses also flourished in the late 1820s, with the result that he would soon make his largest land purchase ever, a fine farm and house east of town on the Aurora Road. The man who had for so long wandered from place to place seemed at last to have found the community where he truly belonged.[31]

As for the town, David Hudson's village struck most observers as a quiet success in the late 1820s. Orramel Hinckley Fitch, a traveler to the Western Reserve in 1827, found most Ohio communities "new and dreary," but he described Hudson as "a pleasant village," albeit one without "much business." The arrival in October 1827 of the first class of Western Reserve College students created stirrings in Hudson, but they represented progress of the type that meshed perfectly with David Hudson's aspirations for the town. In the First Congregational Church, too, peace seemed to prevail. A visiting committee in 1829 concluded that "with few exceptions there was the appearance of harmony among the members of the church." To Owen Brown, David Hudson, and other local pioneers, therefore, it must have seemed in 1829 that their vision of the town's future was well on the way to being realized.[32]

MARGARET GREENFIELD AND HER SON BENJAMIN

The story of Margaret Greenfield's son Benjamin differs significantly from those of our other trans-Appalachian pioneers. It comes last in sequence because Margaret's son was a full generation younger than Benjamin Adair, Owen Brown, and Jeremiah Root, and was still a boy when these men and their families left for Ohio in 1805 and 1807. He did not migrate west until 1820, and when he moved, he went as an unmarried seventeen-year-old who in all likelihood was traveling alone. A more significant contrast between Margaret's son and our other migrants arose from the conditions under which he began his trip. The Adairs, Browns, and Roots had all achieved a degree of economic security in their former East Coast homes and were risking that relatively secure position in following the rainbow to improved fortunes in the West. Margaret's Benjamin, on the other hand, left Hancock, Massachusetts, in 1820 because he had virtually nothing to lose.

To understand why Benjamin's future in Hancock seemed so bleak in 1820 it is necessary to discuss his mother's life, for she was in large part the cause of the insecure status that sent him west. Not that his mother wished him ill—on the contrary, Margaret had done her best to help him —but her efforts had been undermined by factors largely out of her control: the deaths of two husbands and the era's prevailing prejudices regarding women in general and widows in particular.

Benjamin's mother, Margaret, was born in February 1776, the daughter of Archibald and Margaret (Rogers) Greenfield. The Greenfields were tenants on Van Rensselaer manor lands, and the section of the Little Hoosick Valley where they lived was in an early stage of frontier development, lacking churches, schools, and stores. Distant events, however, soon stirred the community. While Margaret was still an infant, her father volunteered for militia duty in the American Revolution and received the rank of corporal in the Sixth Albany Regiment. His very brief service consisted mainly of responding to alarms caused by Tory activity in the area. Of Corporal Greenfield's daughter Margaret little is known except that she learned to read and write. Judging from the scratchy, somewhat unsteady appearance of her signature, however, she did not often have occasion to use a pen in later years.

The Little Hoosick Baptist Church was one of the first community institutions to be established in the Greenfields' neighborhood, and it was to have a crucial place in young Margaret's life. Like Margaret's parents, most local settlers were from Connecticut and Rhode Island, and many were Baptists. When some of these Baptists gathered on December 30, 1783, at the recently completed frame house of Daniel Hull, Esquire, and began to organize a church, they drew on their past experience for models and adopted a constitution patterned after the covenant of the Baptist Church of Exeter, Rhode Island. This was the congregation that Margaret's grandfather Joseph Rogers had served as deacon many years earlier. His daughter, now Mrs. Archibald Greenfield, had formerly attended the Exeter church, as had eight of seventeen of the Little Hoosick congregation's founders.

Jonathan and Eunice Bly were two of the founders who had also been members of the Exeter church. Although the Blys were slightly older than Archibald and Margaret Greenfield, the two families drew together quite naturally. The Blys well remembered Mrs. Greenfield as one of the Rogers girls from the Exeter church. Moreover, there was the matter of proximity in a relatively small community. The Blys and Greenfields lived a mile and a half apart on opposite sides of the main north–south road through town, and the stores, school, and church that were built along the main road by 1790 were logical meeting places for the parents and their children.

The families were joined by the marriage of the Greenfields' daughter Margaret to Daniel Bly, one of Jonathan and Eunice's sons. Although the precise date of the wedding is unknown, most likely it took place in the summer or fall of 1792, shortly after Margaret's grandfather Rogers gave her a family Bible and Jonathan Bly gave his son a twenty-seven-acre lot on the southeast corner of the family property. Here, on the banks of Rocky Brook, the newlyweds built their home. Daniel was in his early twenties and Margaret only sixteen. In 1796 Jonathan Bly deeded another plot of almost fifty acres to the young couple. Since he had eleven children for whom to provide, Jonathan Bly was being quite generous, and Daniel and Margaret had much to be thankful for. In the decade between 1792 and 1802, Margaret and Daniel had three children, a son and two daughters. Although the increase in their family obligations made the income from their farm seem less substantial, their financial status was nevertheless secure. Daniel and Margaret had their youth and a farm that, if not large, was at least, according to a contemporary evaluation of the soil, "considerably good."[33]

In the first years of the new century, however, fate dealt Margaret Bly a series of hard blows. Her grandfather Joseph Rogers died in 1800. He had always been very kind to her, and his death removed a strong and fairly affluent force in the community that might have aided Margaret through difficult times. Then, in August 1801, Margaret's father-in-law, Jonathan Bly, died, followed less than a year later (July 3, 1802) by her husband.

Margaret's situation after Daniel's death was not an enviable one. At twenty-six she was a widow with three young children: Daniel (seven), Margaret (five), and Lydia (two). Her husband's death deprived her of the man who had done the farm work on which her family's income depended. As was often true in that period, her husband's will left the farm property to his children rather than to his wife. Margaret, therefore, could not raise capital by selling the land. She could only manage it as best she could until Daniel Jr. came of age and took possession of it. Tenants and renters were difficult to find in a labor-scarce society, and in any case rental income would not make her economically independent. Margaret's only recourse, one commonly followed by widows in agricultural areas during the era, was to turn to relatives for support. Clark Bly, her deceased husband's oldest brother and her nearest neighbor, gave her what help he could with labor and finances. Of her Greenfield relatives, her brother Joseph Rogers Greenfield was the most forthcoming with assistance. Remarriage would have been another way for Margaret to resolve her dilemma, but practically speaking her chances of finding a second husband were not good. She had little personal wealth, only her household goods and a few farm animals. Moreover, she would bring to any marriage the financial burden of three young children.

Margaret's son Benjamin, her fourth child, was born on October 2, 1803. The record is mute regarding his father's name, and the community's reaction to the birth of Margaret's illegitimate child cannot be gauged directly. She belonged to the Stephentown Baptist Church, but the minutes of its meetings did not mention the congregation's disciplinary actions, if any. The church records do contain notations of dismissals next to the names of some members, and the absence of any such notation next to Margaret's name indicates that she was not excommunicated. Unquestionably, however, Benjamin's birth increased Margaret's economic burdens and did nothing to enhance her chances for remarrying.

At this critical juncture in Margaret's life, the figure of Allen Remington, a farmer from nearby Hancock, Massachusetts, entered. Although Hancock was separated from Berlin (as Margaret's town was now called) and Stephentown by a steep mountain ridge, the towns, especially their southern sections, had considerable contact, thanks to Baptist denominational connections and the local farm-marketing process. Allen Remington had come to Hancock from Rhode Island after the Revolution. He and his father had previously lived briefly at Exeter, Rhode Island, and they had relatives in Stephentown, so it was likely that Allen met the widow Bly through either the Rogers family or her Bly in-laws. In 1809 Allen asked Margaret to marry him.

Remington was a widower with nine children, at least four of whom (and possibly as many as six) were still very young. In remarrying, Allen was careful to protect the economic interests of his heirs. Before he and Margaret were wed, they signed a marriage agreement establishing the legal rights of both parties. Should Allen die first, those of Margaret's children born prior to 1809 would receive a settlement equal only to the value of her personal property at the time of the marriage, and she would receive a yearly stipend of twenty dollars. This effectively placed responsibility for her care, in the event of Allen's early decease, on her family and not on his. Despite this stipulation and the sixteen-year difference in their ages (he was forty-nine, she thirty-three), Margaret's decision to marry Allen Remington made good sense. It was, indeed, her best hope at the time.

The wedding was in mid-1809, after which Margaret and her children moved to Hancock. The combined households of Allen and Margaret Remington numbered sixteen, including his widowed mother. This crowded household in Hancock was the home Margaret's son Benjamin knew from early childhood onward, and his stepfather, Allen Remington, was the only father he ever knew. He took his stepfather's family name for his own and in later life always gave Hancock as his place of birth and Allen Remington as his father's name.

In 1816 Daniel Bly Jr., Margaret Remington's oldest son, came of age and wanted to settle his father's estate. Besides Daniel Jr.'s legal claims to his inheritance, another factor gave some urgency to the process: Daniel had fallen in love with a Hancock woman, Phoebe Gardner, and wanted the estate probated so that he and Phoebe could afford to migrate to western New York. The estate was liquidated with the help of Daniel Jr.'s uncle Clark Bly and stepfather, Allen Remington. Remington lent Clark Bly money with which to purchase the Bly farm from Daniel Jr., and young Daniel then used the proceeds to finance his move west.

Daniel and Phoebe's destination was Henrietta, a town in the Genesee Valley of western New York. How the town of Henrietta came into being illustrates once again the role wealthy speculators played on the trans-Appalachian frontier. When Massachusetts ceded its claims to western lands after the Revolution, the state was given a large area in western New York, which it was to sell to its citizens but which was to be under New York's political jurisdiction. A syndicate headed by Oliver Phelps and Nathaniel Gorham, two of the era's most ubiquitous land speculators, emerged as top bidders for six million acres of land. Soon, however, Phelps and Gorham had trouble raising cash and sold a substantial part of the Genesee section of their purchase to Robert Morris, former secretary of the treasury and a member of their original syndicate. Morris, in turn, drew in British investors, including Sir William Pulteney, for whose daughter the town of Henrietta was named. Finally, in 1799, the British investors, working through a peripatetic American agent named James Wadsworth, sold ten thousand acres in Henrietta Township to two Dutch brothers, Willem and Cornelius C. Six. By this complex process of international land speculation, the segment of the Phelps-Gorham tract in which Daniel Bly Jr. settled came to be known as the Holland Purchase.

Daniel Bly Jr. and Phoebe Gardner were married on May 28, 1817. Not long thereafter Daniel traveled west to Genesee country to locate a farm. Perhaps he had already made contact with the Holland Land Company's office in Albany. Almost certainly he was familiar with advertisements promising that the company's available properties were "not surpassed by any interiour lands in the United States, for healthfulness, good and abundant waters, and choice of markets for their rich products."[34] In any case, Daniel soon negotiated a purchase agreement with a Holland Land Company agent, making a down payment on 157 acres of rich land along the Genesee River in the northwest corner of Henrietta. Having made these arrangements, Daniel returned to Rensselaer County for his bride.

In the fall of 1817 or early spring of 1818, the Blys loaded wheat seed and other goods on an oxcart and started west. For part of the trip they rode a Mohawk River flatboat, completing the journey via the wagon road through Auburn and Canandaigua. The newlyweds immediately set about clearing their land. The down payment for their property and the expenses of the trip west left them no free cash whatsoever, but they were by all accounts happy. And, having led the way west to Henrietta, they formed the nucleus of what became a settlement of relatives that eventually included Daniel's half brother Benjamin Remington.

In 1820, when Benjamin Remington joined the Daniel Blys in Genesee country, he was barely seventeen. The timing of his departure from Hancock is explained by more of those sudden turns of events that seemed to haunt his mother's life. The first major change came in the summer of 1820. Margaret's father, Archibald Greenfield, decided to leave Berlin and move to Sempronious Township in Cayuga County, then a semiwilderness district in west central New York. Economically, Archibald's decision seems inexplicable. He owed no debts on his Berlin farm, and the town tax list for 1810 shows that he was well off compared with his neighbors, his assessed worth of $1,800 placing him 26th among 355 taxpayers. It is unlikely that, at the age of seventy or thereabouts, he sold his comfortable home of fifty years and moved to a log cabin on a half-cleared hilltop in Cayuga County in the expectation of striking it rich. Oral family tradition had it that he went to Cayuga to claim the land bounty to which he was entitled as a veteran of the Revolution, but extant records do not support this story, even though his farm was located in the military tract. More promising clues to the timing and motives of Archibald's move in 1820 are found in personal relationships. His brothers Raymond and William had moved to Sempronious ten years earlier and had probably been urging him to join them there. His first wife, Margaret's mother, had close ties in the Berlin-Stephentown area, however, and had probably opposed a move west, especially since it meant giving up a comfortable old age. But she had died in the late 1810s, and Archibald's second wife, perhaps, did not have the same leverage or similar reservations. The issue then became preserving what one valued most. In the 1770s Archibald and his brothers had moved from Connecticut to New York, partly in order to preserve their Baptist heritage; moving again in 1820 would enable Archibald to return to close physical proximity to his brothers, thus preserving his most cherished family ties.

A second and more crucial event in Margaret Remington's life, and therefore in Benjamin's as well, was Allen Remington's death later in 1820. The consequences were felt almost immediately. Under Margaret's prenuptial agreement with Allen, she was to receive only a small sum equal to her personal property at the time they married plus a stipend of twenty dollars a year. Perhaps she and her two young sons by Allen Remington would be welcome to stay on the family farm in Hancock under the care of its new proprietor, Allen's oldest son, Jonathan, but the position of her son Benjamin was more precarious. The estate was not large, and the Remington heirs were numerous. Moreover, although Benjamin had taken his stepfather's family name, he was not included among Allen Remington's heirs. There was little future for him in Hancock, except possibly as a hired hand, and it is not clear that Jonathan Remington would have welcomed him in that capacity. Benjamin's most viable option after his stepfather's death was to head west, stopping to see his grandfather in Cayuga County, but making his half brother Daniel's homestead his final destination. He knew he could count on a warm reception in Henrietta, both as a brother and as an additional hand to help clear Daniel's homestead.

In 1821, less than a year after Benjamin went west, his twice-widowed mother, Margaret, died at the age of forty-five. As a footnote to the story of her life and the difficulties she had faced but not entirely conquered, it is worth mentioning that her children and heirs brought a suit against Allen Remington's estate, claiming one-third of the estate's proceeds, the amount that Massachusetts law would have assigned them as Margaret's heirs. Allen Remington's eleven children countered by introducing the marriage agreement Margaret had signed with their father in 1809. The court ruled that the document was valid and that Margaret's heirs— Daniel, Margaret, Lydia, and Benjamin—were entitled only to the value of the household goods and the two cows and eleven sheep their mother had brought with her to Hancock. Each of her four heirs, therefore, received $37.12 1/2. The division among Allen Remington's eleven children, on the other hand, brought them $229.26 apiece. Even the larger sum was not a fortune, of course, but the difference between the amounts received by the two sets of heirs provides a small object lesson in the vicissitudes of widowhood during the early national period.

So with a legacy of $37.12 1/2 and not much else, Benjamin Remington began to make his way. Fortunately for him, his early adult years coincided with good times nationwide in the 1820s, and he almost at once began to make strides financially. In this respect his story parallels those of Benjamin Adair, Owen Brown, and Jeremiah Root, each of whom had gone west in hope of improving his lot, and all of whom had made at least modest gains. But what had been gained could also be lost if circumstances changed, and there were many signs as the 1820s drew to a close that major changes were in the air. The opening of the Erie Canal in 1825 not only lowered freight rates between New York City and Buffalo to a tenth or less of former prices but also contributed to a canal-building fad and an economic boom that swept much of the nation. By 1829, the year when Andrew Jackson, the first westerner to be elected president, was inaugurated, the children of Ohio pioneers now talked of moving on to newer states—Indiana, Illinois, and even Missouri. Benjamin Adair, Owen Brown, Jeremiah Root's heirs, and Benjamin Remington had done well enough in the 1820s, but what would happen to them and their families in the changed and often treacherous times ahead was another matter.

Chapter Three

UNFORESEEN
DIRECTIONS
1830-1850

T here are periods in history when all old standards of behavior and belief come under attack and a once-familiar world seems turned upside down. The 1960s were one such era, the 1830s another. Although many of the causes and events that captured the American public's attention in the 1830s are no longer household words, even a partial listing suggests the sweep and intensity of change 150 years ago. There were new isms to contend with: abolitionism, Mormonism, Transcendentalism, Christian perfectionism, and vegetarianism. Masons and Catholics became targets of hostile crusades. Established ways of thinking were challenged by such varied new ideas as those in Ralph Waldo Emerson's "American Scholar" address, the writings of phrenologists, and proposals for extending higher education to women. Politically, Americans were confronted by one crisis or innovation after another: Nat Turner's slave rebellion, the nullification controversy, President Andrew Jackson's veto of the charter of the United States Bank, the establishment of the Texas republic, and the emergence of a mass-participatory, two-party system that pitted Whigs against Jacksonian Democrats in election campaigns that for the first time featured national nominating conventions and party platforms. Economically, a frenzied speculative boom in banking, canal building, and land sales was followed by the panic of 1837 and a depression that lasted beyond the decade's end. Few American lives were left untouched by the events of the era, and some—like that of Owen Brown's son John—were transformed.

Prior to 1830, when the new era's causes first began to reshape his thinking, there was virtually nothing in John's life to suggest that he would later become the passionate activist known to us as John Brown the abolitionist. After an apprenticeship with his father, he set up in 1817, at the age of seventeen, his own tannery in Hudson, Ohio. Three years later, encouraged by his father, John married a neighbor, Dianthe Lusk. Although his business went well enough, he was impatient to escape Hudson, where he lived in the shadow of his dynamic and successful father. In the mid-1820s, therefore, he took Dianthe and their three children to northwestern Pennsylvania, settling in Randolph Township, an undeveloped district that had been bypassed by earlier migrants intent on reaching richer lands farther west. In a burst of activity he cleared his land, built a log cabin and a barn, opened a tannery (the first business enterprise in the area), and helped organize a church and establish a school. Lean, intense, and often dogmatic, John Brown was known to his neighbors as a devout, ambitious, and utterly conventional man.

Antimasonry, one of the new causes that flourished in the 1830s, was the external prod that first jarred John out of his conventional path. The movement's origins were recent, dating from 1826, when Masons in western New York had abducted and apparently murdered William Morgan, a renegade member of the lodge who was preparing to publish an exposé of its inner workings. Over the next several years, official investigations in New York brought to light the impressive political power of Masonry and the fact that Masons in public office not only obstructed attacks on the order but also shielded fellow members against punishment for criminal acts. Triggered by these revelations, a truly popular, grass-roots Antimason movement sprang up and spread quickly, gaining adherents in particularly large numbers in upstate New York, northern Ohio, Massachusetts, and Pennsylvania. Where Antimasonry was strong, it generally resulted in a drastic reduction of membership in local Masonic lodges. The movement also led to the formation of an Antimason party that named its presidential candidate in 1832 at the first national party convention ever held in the United States.

John Brown had become a member of Hudson's Masonic lodge in 1824, but he resigned a few years later as evidence emerged that Masons sometimes allowed loyalty to the order's oaths to outweigh patriotic devotion to the Republic's laws. Then, as Antimasonry gained momentum in 1830, John briefly became active in the movement. Behind his growing opposition to Masonry were patriotic, religious, and partisan motives of the sort quite typical among the order's opponents. As a devout Calvinist, John shared a widely held prejudice against Masonry as a substitute, secular religion that violated God's First Commandment: Thou shalt have no other gods before Me. Politically, like many Antimasons, he was neo-Federalist and anti-Jacksonian, and President Jackson's membership in the order helped make Antimasonry into a convenient vehicle for opposing Jackson and his political allies. In 1830 John began to speak out against alleged Masonic atrocities, denouncing them so vehemently that for a time he became apprehensive about possible counterattacks on his person. "I have aroused such feeling in Meadville," he wrote his father, ". . . as leads me for the present to avoid going about the streets at evening and alone."[1]

John was soon preoccupied with other worries. By 1831 it was clear that his business was not going well. He had made the common mistake of opening a business in a newly developed area that was not yet mature enough to support it. There simply were not enough hides or customers in the region to make his tannery pay. Then Dianthe died on August 10, 1832, three days after giving birth to a son (who lived only a few hours), her seventh baby in twelve years. John was sick and depressed for several months after Dianthe's death, but in less than a year he married again. His new wife was Mary Day, a local blacksmith's seventeen-year-old daughter. Their first child was born ten months later.

Even as John's attention focused on his personal woes, abolition, the cause in whose service he would eventually become famous, burst on the scene. During the 1820s the most widely endorsed solution to the problem of slavery had been colonization (the deportation of freed blacks to Africa), a program promulgated by the American Colonization Society under such eminent leaders as James Madison, John Marshall, and James Monroe. The viability of this thoroughly racist, conservative approach was challenged in 1831 by two events. In January a fiery antislavery editor, William Lloyd Garrison, began publishing a newspaper called the *Liberator* in which he called for the immediate abolition of slavery. In August a black minister, Nat Turner, led a slave insurrection in Southampton, Virginia, that left fifty-seven whites and more than a hundred blacks dead. Angry southerners reacted by demanding that "incendiary" literature like the *Liberator* be banned from the federal mails and by passing laws that subjected free blacks and slaves to still more restrictive legal codes. In New England and New York, meanwhile, Garrison and wealthy white philanthropists such as Arthur and Lewis Tappan began organizing abolitionist societies. Their adherents, though always a tiny majority, succeeded in establishing more than two hundred local antislavery societies by the mid-1830s.

Colonizationists and proslavery advocates forcefully tried to suppress the growth of abolitionist sentiment. When a woman named Prudence Crandall opened a school for black girls in Canterbury, Connecticut, she was jailed and her students were threatened with prosecution under an outdated vagrancy law. Had they been convicted, the youngsters could have received up to ten lashes on the bare back. At Western Reserve College in Hudson, Ohio, three faculty members were forced from their positions in 1833 because of the stand they had taken favoring abolition over colonization. In 1834 the conservative trustees of Lane Theological Seminary in Cincinnati, Ohio, ordered student activists to disband their antislavery society and to close the night school, library, and Sunday school they had established for free blacks. Later in the year anti-abolitionist rioters in New York City went on a three-day rampage during which they sacked Lewis Tappan's house and several churches that were believed to have abolitionist pastors. In 1835 Garrison was attacked and almost killed by an anti-abolitionist mob in Boston.

Stirred by these and subsequent events during the 1830s, John Brown came to think of himself as an abolitionist. Although he first read the *Liberator* at his father's place in Hudson in 1833 or 1834, and although his biographers have cited evidence that connects him with antislavery views prior to that date, the earliest contemporary source documenting his desire to aid blacks is a November 1834 letter from John to his brother

Frederick. "Since you left me," he wrote, "I have been trying to devise some means whereby I might do something in a practical way for my poor fellow-men who are in bondage." His plan, he reported, was to "get one negro boy or youth," a free black or one freed by or purchased from a slaveholder, and to raise him "as we do our own." John was also mulling over the idea of starting a school for free blacks, but nothing came of either plan because he was soon overwhelmed by financial problems. Nevertheless, he was thinking in new ways, and later in the 1830s he would take his first steps toward doing something for blacks and the abolitionist cause.[2]

In the summer of 1835 John abandoned his tanning operation in Pennsylvania and returned to Ohio. It was ironic that he had to leave New Richmond for want of business there just as an inflationary boom was gaining strength in most of the country, Ohio included. Initially, the good times had solid foundations, but as the boom accelerated a get-rich-quick spirit was fed by three sources: canal schemes, easy money, and land speculation. The success of the Erie Canal had led many states to try to emulate New York's achievement. Pennsylvania put forth an incredible plan to build a canal that would cross the Alleghenies and link Philadelphia and Pittsburgh. In Ohio a north–south canal that ran from Cleveland, on Lake Erie, through Akron to Portsmouth, on the Ohio River, was completed in 1833. Land prices along the canal soared, attracting many speculators who hoped to get rich quickly. Contributing to the ease with which they were able to invest in land was a dramatic surge in bank credit. In the early 1830s largely unregulated state banks sprang up in town after town, their numbers doubling in seven years. Most of them printed unsecured bank notes and put this paper currency into circulation by lending it to all comers. The result was a fourfold increase in bank loans based on promissory notes from 1830 to 1837. With canal schemes, good times, and general optimism feeding inflation and raising land prices, the logical thing to do was to buy land, especially since credit for such purchases was readily available. Land sales surged. The federal government alone sold 3.8 million acres in 1833 and more than 20 million acres in 1836, a staggering fivefold increase.

In 1836 John Brown lived in Franklin Mills (now Kent), less than ten miles southeast of his former home in Hudson. At the height of the boom it seemed that investment opportunities surrounded him on every side. When the north–south Ohio canal had reached nearby Akron, the prices of some town lots had risen to twenty times their former level. In 1836 the

Pennsylvania and Ohio Canal Company was building an east–west canal to link Akron with Pittsburgh, and its route would pass right by Franklin Mills. Local land prices were already rising in anticipation, and the sooner one invested, the greater the profits that would surely follow. So, early in 1836 John plunged in with both feet, borrowing thousands of dollars from relatives, friends, and banks to set himself up as an investor-developer. In a manner typical of all such promotions, he gave his property a promising name (Brown and Thompson's Addition) and began to set out home, hotel, and industrial lots along wide streets with such names as Franklin, Prospect, Haymaker, Pennsylvania, and Cuyahoga. In 1836 all this was still pastures and farm fields, but one had to be pretty sleepy not to notice that the industrial revolution had come to the United States, and by the logic that propelled such farsighted projects there was no reason why Brown and Thompson's Addition could not become a leading industrial center once the canal was completed.

The above-mentioned investments made John Brown a participant in a classic American land boom. Unfortunately for him, the boom soon turned into an equally classic bust. In July 1836 the Jackson administration issued the so-called Specie Circular, which stipulated that from mid-August onward the federal government would require purchasers of federal land to pay in specie (gold or silver currency). Paper money, those notorious unsecured state bank notes, would no longer be accepted. The new policy was extremely deflationary, and land prices slumped immediately. Moreover, confidence in the banking system was undermined. The result was a financial panic in March 1837, and with its arrival the speculative bubble burst beyond repair. Banks failed; businesses closed their doors; the canal company suspended construction work; and thousands of land speculators like John Brown who had borrowed money to buy land at prices far in excess of what it would now bring were ruined.

The 1830s were far from over in March 1837, of course, but the changes the decade had already brought in John Brown's life were immense. Much of his energy in subsequent years would go into a battle to get back on his financial feet, but he had also started down the path toward a career as an abolitionist. Canals, crashes, and causes—watchwords of the 1830s—had all touched him and pushed him, along with many of his contemporaries, in unforeseen directions.

BENJAMIN REMINGTON AND ADDISON WARD: THE WEST'S UNCERTAIN PROMISE

In a book published in the late 1840s, Orsamus Turner offered a capsule description of a pioneer's progress from frontiersman to prosperous farmer. In the first of four pictures that accompany the text, the pioneer is shown after six months in the new country living in a rudely built, chimneyless log hut surrounded by dense virgin forest. A second illustration represents the pioneer family's circumstances a year later, by which time some improvements are visible, including a chimney added to the cabin and mortar to its walls, an expanded forest clearing, and a dooryard enclosed by a zigzag fence of split rails. Ten years later, according to a third picture, the clearing has become a field, and the settler has built a small barn, planted an orchard, replaced the rail fence with a picket fence, and constructed a large cabin next to the original hut. The accompanying text suggests that after less than a dozen years in his new home the farmer is likely to have become a captain in the militia and that his children will doubtless have begun to attend a newly organized school nearby. In a fourth and final panel, which depicts a scene forty years after the pioneer's arrival, he lives in a handsome stone house surrounded by large, well-tended fields, his material success readily apparent for all to see.

Turner's portrait of a pioneer's progress was idealized in that it described the experience of those who succeeded and not of those who failed. To be sure, there were many success stories to tell. Among the members of our families on the move, for instance, were two half brothers, Daniel Bly and Benjamin Remington, who settled in the very area Turner was describing (the Genesee Valley in western New York) and who, after a decade or more of deprivations, achieved the civilized comforts they had lacked initially: good housing, educational opportunities, increased social status, and economic well-being. If Daniel and Benjamin read Turner's books (and they very likely did, since Daniel is mentioned in one), they must have found that the life of Turner's hypothetical pioneer closely

These scenes and those on the next two pages show a pioneer family's progress, as logged by Orsamus Turner in *Pioneer History of the Holland Land Purchase of Western New York* (1850).

paralleled their own. But one must not assume from this that moving west guaranteed success. On the contrary, westward migration was a chancy business, and for the many pioneers whose stories had unhappy endings —men like Addison Ward, who tried his luck as a homesteader in Indiana and Illinois only to go broke and die at a relatively young age—the so-called promise of the West was little more than a cruel hoax.

Daniel Bly occupied his homestead on the banks of the Genesee in Henrietta in 1818, a little more than a decade after the first farmers had moved to the area. The years before his arrival had been hard ones for local settlers. In part their difficulties were traceable to conditions that were typical of early days on nearly all frontiers: the struggle to clear the land combined with the lack of sizable towns and adequate transportation facilities through which to market produce once pioneers finally had something to sell. But Genesee Valley farmers also suffered some blows particular to their area. Harvests were very poor from 1812 to 1815, and 1816 proved to be the worst year of all. To make matters worse, in 1817 the Holland Land Company, which controlled most of the land in Henrietta, more than doubled the price of land per acre for settlers who had

not yet paid for their homesteads in full, with the result that many pioneers were forced out altogether.

Daniel Bly's timing proved to be just about perfect, since things took a turn for the better in the Genesee Valley in 1817, the year before his arrival. That autumn local harvests were at last satisfactory, and from 1818 to 1824 they were positively bountiful. More important, Genesee Valley farmers benefited from national trends in transportation and commercial agriculture that, in turn, stimulated the rise of new market cities in America's interior regions. Before the War of 1812, the major cities of the United States—Boston, New York City, Philadelphia, Baltimore, and New Orleans—were all seaports. But in the nineteenth century a transportation revolution—initially in water transport (canals and steamboats) and later in land transport (railroads)—led to the growth of inland cities: Pittsburgh, Chicago, Cincinnati, St. Louis, and the like. In the 1820s, however, when these new trends first became evident, no American city grew faster than the Genesee Valley's market town, Rochester, which went from a tiny hamlet in 1820 to a bustling city of 10,000 by 1830. Although some of Rochester's growth would have occurred regardless, the key to its explosive expansion in the 1820s was the Erie Canal. Authorized by the New York legislature in 1817, this massive public-works project set

Turner's pioneer family's progress, continued.

a standard of success that many other states soon tried to match. Even before construction crews arrived in Rochester, in 1821, the pace of the town's economy was accelerating in anticipation. When the final link between Rochester and New York City was completed, in 1823, the effects were dramatic. With shipping charges lowered to one-tenth of their previous price per ton, flour shipments from Rochester rose from 26,000 barrels in 1818 to 200,000 a year by the late 1820s. It was a golden opportunity for farmers like Daniel Bly and Benjamin Remington in nearby Genesee Valley towns.

Bright prospects, of course, did not assure success or eliminate all hardship for pioneers. Even if one found an excellent homestead, as Daniel Bly did, paying for the land could be a demanding task. Arriving after the Holland Land Company imposed its new price of $10 an acre (the old price had been $4), Daniel needed fourteen years (1818–31) to complete the purchase of his contract, paying $2,198, interest included, for a 150-acre farm. Scarcity of cash often forced severe economies on early settlers. According to one reminiscence, Daniel Bly went barefoot two summers because he did not want to wear out his one pair of boots. At $7 a pair, boots were too valuable to be worn when the weather was warm. Transportation in the Genesee Valley was still rudimentary. Before 1820 the

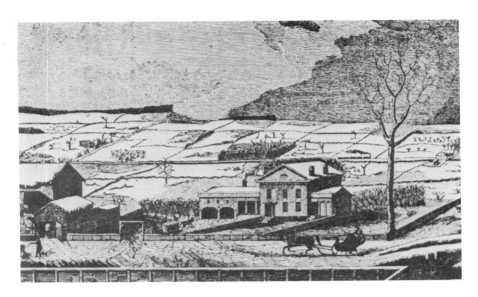

road along the river from Henrietta to Rochester was little more than a stump-ridden cart path. One crossed the river on a raft of logs lashed together, poled across by either Daniel or Phoebe Bly. Predatory animals were no longer a major menace in 1818. The last attack by wolves on a Henrietta settler took place in 1815, though Bly memoirs record that the family often heard wolves howling in the neighborhood. Abundant game —including deer, waterfowl, and hundreds of passenger pigeons—were found near the Blys' log cabin.

Benjamin Remington arrived in the Genesee Valley in 1820. Initially, he lived with his half brother, Daniel Bly, helping clear Daniel's farmland and very likely joining the Blys in worship at the Henrietta Baptist Church. Soon, however, Benjamin began to make his own way and found employment as a teacher in Rush, the next town south of Henrietta, not long after a log schoolhouse was built there in 1822. Benjamin also participated actively in the New York State militia, and like the archetypal pioneer in Orsamus Turner's sketch, he became captain of his local unit in 1833, only thirteen years after his arrival in the valley. Two years later he completed the purchase of a small farm on the banks of the Genesee in the southwest corner of Brighton, just across the road (which was also the town-line road) from Daniel Bly's Henrietta homestead. Before another year passed, on March 26, 1836, Benjamin married Sarah Ann Burger, whose family had settled in Henrietta in 1830. He was thirty-two, she twenty-seven.

It would be interesting to know how Benjamin and Sarah Ann responded to the protracted religious revival led by Charles G. Finney, one of the most influential evangelists of the day, in nearby Rochester in 1830–31. For six months people from Rochester and the surrounding countryside flocked to hear Finney, who preached almost daily and three times a day on Sundays. Every local Protestant church gained members, and for a time, one Finneyite remembered, "You could not go upon the streets and hear any conversation, except on religion."[3]

The revival mixed some old things with many new ones. Throughout the late 1820s parts of western New York had caught fire with revival spirit so often that the area became known as the Burned-Over District. News of Finney's successes in Rochester, however, helped spread revivalism through much of the northern United States, leading to a second Great Awakening reminiscent of the religious fervor that swept the American colonies in the mid-1700s. Finney was an innovator in revival method, theology, and Christian moral reform. He was adept at using so-called extraordinary methods: door-to-door evangelizing, prayer meetings that lasted until dawn, an anxious seat in front of the congregation reserved for sinners in particular need of prayer. He also encouraged women to participate prominently in public prayer. In theology, he rejected Calvin's dark view that men and women were innately depraved and argued that God had given human beings free will, which they could exercise to choose good rather than evil. Moreover, if Christian self-control could change individuals, the combined efforts of many Christians could bring moral improvement in the world. Consistent with this belief, from 1831 onward Finney and his followers increasingly emphasized the Christian's duty to make God's kingdom a reality on earth by eliminating such social vices as prostitution, intemperance, and slavery. Overall, Finney's exhortations suited the optimistic mood of the early 1830s, when many Americans' personal experience seemed to confirm that hard work and good habits could make a difference.

Scene along the Erie Canal,
from a watercolor by John Hill (c. 1830).

Precisely where Benjamin Remington and Sarah Ann Burger fit into all this is impossible to say, although it seems unlikely that they were able to ignore a six-month-long revival happening less than five miles up the road. What we do know is that sometime in the 1830s or 1840s Benjamin abandoned his Baptist roots and Sarah Ann her Lutheran ties to become Methodists. Finney was a Presbyterian, but his influence spread well beyond that denomination. Moreover, the popular Methodist hymn "Rock of Ages," which speaks of a "double cure" for sin (justification, the act of faith that makes the believer worthy of salvation, and sanctification, the development of pure conduct here on earth), could be understood as being quite congruent with Finney's point that conversion should also produce a reformed life. Thus, although we know little for certain about Benjamin's religious life, we would expect that his personal successes in this period seemed to him to validate the positive view of human nature and life on earth that Finney and other evangelists were advancing.

Benjamin continued to prosper after the 1830s. Indeed, in many respects he could have served as a model for Orsamus Turner's idealized description of a pioneer's progress. In 1847 Benjamin expanded his farm by buying another small parcel from Daniel Bly, and in the 1850s and 1860s he further extended his holdings. He and Daniel Bly both built

Benjamin Remington
(1803–1888). *Opposite:*
Benjamin and Sarah Ann
Remington's children.
Left to right: Jeremiah,
Edwin, Margaret.

comfortable houses for their families in this period; Bly, in fact, claimed that his was the first brick house in Henrietta. Finally, consistent with Turner's sketch in which the successful pioneer confirms his solid standing with his neighbors by winning election to office, Benjamin Remington was elected Brighton town supervisor in 1851.

Sarah Ann's contribution to her husband's success also deserves attention. Without her efforts in the private sphere as a homemaker and mother, Benjamin obviously would not have had as much time and energy to devote to militia meetings and town politics. A nineteenth-century version of the "feminine mystique" gave mothers special responsibility for overseeing their children's moral and educational development, a task Sarah Ann was evidently well prepared to undertake, for, according to her descendants, she had a good education for her time. We know that one of her brothers had graduated from Union College in Schenectady, New York, in 1824. Very likely it was his influence, combined with Sarah Ann's, that led her older son, Jeremiah, to attend Union College in the 1850s. Similarly, her hand is evident in both of her sons' choice of a Methodist preparatory school in eastern New York where some of her Burger relatives lived, as well as in the tasteful, well-groomed appearance her three children presented when they stepped into the daguerrotypist's

Benjamin and Sarah Ann Remington (1808–1883) with their daughter Margaret in front of their West Brighton, New York, home in the 1870s.

studio in the mid-1850s. By that time Benjamin Remington, a man who some thirty years earlier had been an orphan with almost no estate, had become a prosperous farmer, a militia captain, and a town official. For him the West's promise had been fulfilled.

Addison Ward, a pioneer whose migration story ended far less happily than Benjamin Remington's, was born in Tazewell County, Virginia, on the family homestead in Ward's Cove. This fine piece of land had been settled in the early 1770s by his grandfather David Ward Sr., the Indian fighter, Revolutionary War veteran, pioneer political leader, and the subject of our earlier sketch. Addison's father, David Ward Jr., was apparently one of David Sr.'s younger sons. When the old man died in 1811 or 1812, the mantle of family leadership fell on David Jr.'s brother John, who inherited their father's settlement tract in the Cove. David Jr. did not receive any land from his father's estate; however, in 1817 he was able to purchase a large parcel (532 acres) in the Cove from a Ward relative. Four years later, in 1821, David Ward Jr. wrote his will, describing himself as being in "perfect health, but of an advanced age." From this document we learn that Ward's wife was named Eleanor, that he had eight children (four sons and four daughters), and that the youngest two sons, Addison and Hiram, were "under age and have not been educated."[4] David Ward Jr. lived another six years and was very likely able to see that his boys received their basic education before his death in late 1826 or early 1827. With his passing, his son Rees was left as the oldest male in this branch of Wards.

Rees had always been headstrong and impetuous. At a very young age he had married his neighbor Elizabeth Bowen, thus forging a double bond between himself and Rees Bowen, revered Tazewell County Indian fighter and soldier. Young Rees Ward had been named after the old hero, and now they were linked in a second way by Ward's marriage to Rees Bowen's niece Elizabeth. In 1830 or thereabouts Rees Ward, in debt and no longer tied to Tazewell County by his father's presence, apparently took the lead in urging his younger brothers Hiram and Addison to join him in selling their inherited lands and moving west. The sales were completed in February 1831, the last date when their names occur in Tazewell County records. By the mid-1830s, if not sooner, the three Ward brothers—Rees, Hiram, and Addison—had accomplished the rest of their plan by relocating in Greene County, Indiana.

Today the absence of any interstate highway nearby makes Greene County seem out of the way to a cross-country traveler. To reach it from Indianapolis, one gets on Kentucky Avenue (also State Highway 67) and heads southwest toward Vincennes. About halfway through the forty-seven miles it takes to reach the junction with U.S. 231, the road narrows from four to two lanes. From the junction it is another thirty-one miles to Switz City, where one turns west on a still-narrower road that covers the last six miles to Linton. For perhaps half an hour now you have been in Greene County, but the approach to Linton brings you into Grant and Stockton townships, the part of the county where the Ward brothers settled in the 1830s. Until the last few miles before Linton much of the land is good, flat farmland, but from there on the terrain becomes rough and hilly, much less promising. A historical marker less than a mile from Addison Ward's former farm in Stockton Township indicates that this was the theoretical center of United States population from 1930 to 1940, a distinction since passed on to points farther west.

Greene County itself was organized in 1821 and had attracted many settlers before the Ward brothers arrived in the 1830s. Among the earliest pioneers were several of the neighbors with whom the Wards later became friendly, notably the families of Robert and John Harrow. When the Harrows came in the early 1820s the district was sparsely settled, and Robert Harrow's son liked to reminisce about the cold winter's morning on which a settler had had to walk three miles to his nearest neighbor's cabin to obtain a coal to start his hearth fire. By the 1830s the territory was growing more populous, but social conditions remained relatively primitive. As late as 1834 the county commissioners were debating how to deal with the hogs that disrupted the judicial process by grunting and fighting under the courthouse floor.

The rush to obtain western land that contributed to boom times nationally in the mid-1830s had a strong impact on Greene County too. An old-timer recalled that "every thing was prosperous" locally in those years and that "various townships were being rapidly filled up" by new-comers eager to purchase whatever federal land was still available in the county.[5] The Ward brothers came to Greene County at about this time, and although we cannot date their arrival precisely, we know it was between 1831 and 1834, for not long after reaching Indiana, Addison Ward married Margaret Susan Reeves, and their first child, Susannah, was

E. W. Clay captured the social disruption caused by the panic and depression of 1837 in this cartoon, "The Times" (July 4, 1837).

born in Greene County in July 1835. Their second child, a son named James Osborn Ward (but always called Jim by his family and friends), was born in February 1837. Later that year Addison acquired title to eighty acres of United States government land just north of Linton in Stockton Township. His brothers Rees and Hiram lived nearby.

Although the Wards shared the boom-time mentality of the mid-1830s, as relative latecomers to Greene County they started the race to get ahead at a disadvantage. There was some very desirable open prairie in Stockton Township, but most of this prime land had been snatched up by neighbors like the Harrows who had arrived ten or more years earlier. By contrast, the eighty acres that Addison Ward bought from the government were mostly broken and rocky terrain that needed to be cleared of its thick forest cover. Moreover, the Wards had stretched their resources to the limit in coming to Indiana and getting started there. Rees, always a bit of a plunger, had gone into debt to buy land on the assumption that flush times would continue and that the value of everything, including his property and crops, would keep on rising.

But flush times did not last. The panic of 1837 was followed by a depression, the effects of which were first felt in the urban and manufacturing regions of the East and in every section of the country where commercial agriculture had become the rule. *Niles' Register* estimated that 90 percent of the factories in the East had closed by early autumn 1837, throwing an equal percentage of the industrial labor force out of work, and in Philadelphia that same summer a majority of the white-collar workers previously employed in the city's famous commercial district were on the streets looking for jobs. Private and public construction projects slowed or ground to a halt, leaving many workers unemployed. In New York City alone perhaps six thousand building tradesmen lost their jobs in 1837. During the winter of 1837–38, the number of people trying to crowd into the poorhouses of major cities was so great that many shelters turned away hundreds every night. Because so many unemployed people were ready to take any sort of job, wages in some industries were driven down by as much as 50 percent.

The depression's immediate impact was slight in rural parts of Indiana like Greene County where agriculture was not yet highly commercialized. It also helped that Indiana's banking system had been managed in a way that, for the times, was almost uniquely conservative. Moreover, crops were good in 1837 and prices still not greatly depressed, with the result that Greene County farm income remained adequate. State bankruptcy statistics show no great change in 1837 from the averages for the immediately preceding years. But Indiana had not been totally immune to the speculative fevers of the mid-1830s and had, in fact, passed an ambitious public-works act in 1836 that committed the state to build 840 miles of canals, more than 300 miles of turnpikes, and 90 miles of railroad track. Though the slowdown in these construction projects late in the 1830s hurt the state's economy, it was the ripple effects of the national turndown that finally brought a full-fledged depression to Indiana. By 1839 there was a surplus of agricultural production over demand, and consequently the prices of farm goods dropped sharply. In Greene County latecomers like Rees and Addison Ward who were still clearing their land were particularly vulnerable to any reduction in their income. Despite his debts, however, Rees held on until 1843 before he sold out, but his younger brother Addison found the odds too great by 1840, and that June he sold his eighty-acre farm in hopes of obtaining sufficient funds to keep going as a tenant farmer. Less than a year after he lost his farm, he lost his wife. Margaret's death on March 2, 1841, left him with three children (Susannah, Jim, and David), the oldest of whom was barely six.

The fragmentary record of Addison Ward's life from his first wife's death until his own death less than ten years later can be summarized quickly. In November 1841 he remarried, taking as his second wife Sarah (Sally) Harrah, the sixteen-year-old daughter of his neighbor John Harrah (as the Harrows had come to spell their name). Sometime later in the 1840s Addison and Sally Ward, with the three children from Addison's first marriage, moved west to Illinois. Their first son, John, was born in 1847 and twin boys, Joseph and William, in 1849. Not much later, either in late 1849 or early 1850, but on an unknown date, at an unknown place, and of unknown causes, Addison Ward died.

There was no practical way for Sally Ward to survive on her own in Illinois. She was a twenty-five-year-old widow with six young children, no land, and no immediate prospects of remarrying. She did the only thing she could do, therefore, and returned to her family in Greene County, Indiana. The 1850 census shows her and the three younger Ward children living with her parents, John and Margaret Harrah. Her stepchildren (Susannah, Jim, and David), meanwhile, were boarding nearby in another Harrah household.

In later years Addison Ward's children could not give an accurate account of their father's origins and youth, a lapse traceable to the break caused by his death. His oldest son, Jim, for example, knew nothing about his aunts and uncles, except for the two, Rees and Hiram, who had accompanied Addison to Indiana. Jim even believed that his father had been born in Greenbrier County, West Virginia, and that he had lived in Kentucky for perhaps twenty years before coming to Indiana, neither of which notions was true. Both, however, were true of members of the Harrah family, Jim's stepmother's people. The younger Ward children who grew up in their Harrah grandparents' home and the older ones who boarded nearby with David O. Harrah (whose wife was a Ward, but from the Greenbrier branch that had come to Indiana by way of Kentucky) both heard the same version of the family's past. Without being aware of what they had done, therefore, Addison Ward's children had adopted the Harrah family history as their own. It was a poignant illustration of how badly the West's promise sometimes worked out. Addison Ward had lost all around. He had lost his farm and his first wife in Indiana and his own life in Illinois, and his children, as a consequence, had lost track of their family's true history.

Addison Ward's trials and Benjamin Remington's achievements reveal the contrasting effects that the growth of a national market economy could have on various pioneers. In the 1820s and 1830s turnpikes and canals opened new markets for products from the West, and western farmers increasingly defined their goals less in terms of self-sufficiency and more in terms of cash income. Prospects for profits—whether acquired through the sale of cash crops, land, or stock in canal-building companies—all stimulated speculation in western land and fostered enthusiasm for commercial capitalism. Capitalism had two faces, however, for the other side of optimism and expansion was despair and depression. As all parts of the more nationalized economy grew dependent on each other, a cyclical pattern of boom and bust became characteristic of American economic life. If one caught the cycle right, as Benjamin Remington did in Erie Canal country in the 1820s and early 1830s, all went well. But Addison Ward's story illustrates the misery that could result if one entered the cycle in a different time and place, Indiana, just before the boom collapsed in the late 1830s. To be sure, personal factors—how hard one worked and whether one assiduously avoided speculation—might modify the impact these large cycles had on any given individual, but the economy's unpredictability in an age of commercial capitalism was such that even the wise could come out looking like fools.

OWEN BROWN'S TIME
OF TROUBLES

Like his son John, Owen Brown found the 1830s to be a testing time. The father, however, played a more significant role in the decade's events than the son, famous though John later became. Until the mid-1830s John lived in a backwater Pennsylvania township, the citizens of which, John included, made only the most marginal contribution to the national debate over such issues as Antimasonry and abolitionism. By contrast, Squire Owen's hometown of Hudson, itself but a small village, was thrust into the national limelight by extraordinary events in the 1830s somewhat in the way that an incident in nearby Kent in 1970 placed the words "Kent State" on many Americans' lips. Moreover, Owen Brown became a spokesman for several of the era's most controversial new political and religious causes, even though, as we will see, his activism threatened to undermine two things he held dear: the harmony of communal life in Hudson and his own secure membership in that community.

At the time Owen Brown turned fifty-nine, in February 1830, he had, however, every reason to be optimistic about what the new decade might hold for him. In business all his wide-ranging enterprises—stock raising, tanning, farming, and construction work—were prospering. The carefully kept pages of his leather-bound account book indicate that his income was at its all-time peak between 1825 and 1835. Moreover, the ledger reveals that, whatever problems he may have had with spelling, he had no difficulties with business arithmetic. His largest single source of income in these years was from contracts for the construction of buildings at Western Reserve College, but he also made every effort to increase his farm's productivity. In 1830, for example, he bought one of the earliest threshing machines developed in the United States; soon thereafter he acquired a mower and a reaper. These purchases indicate his forward-looking cast of mind, a readiness to adopt modernized agricultural methods at a time when mechanized equipment was just beginning to replace hand tools. The prosperity that enabled him to buy such farm machines also permitted him in 1830 to make his largest-ever single purchase of land, a 250-acre farm he bought from his old friend Benjamin Whedon. On this property Owen built what he later called his "favorite house," a plain but comfortable two-story frame structure to which he moved with his wife, Sally, and their six young children.[6] Located two miles northeast of Hudson center on Aurora Road, the new Brown farm seemed perfectly situated, a happy expression of Owen Brown's success in the material sphere.

In religious and political matters, Owen held strong and abiding convictions. He sincerely wanted to live a Christian life in preparation for eternity and worried that he would fail in that endeavor. "My earthly cares were too many for the good of my family, and for my own comfort in religion," he once wrote. Similarly, he fretted about his children's souls. When his son Watson, not yet ten years old, died in January 1832, Owen lamented, "He had not given evidence of being a Christian in health but was in great anxiety of mind in his sickness, [and] we sometimes hope he died in Christ." Religious principles also shaped Owen's feelings about what was the right thing to do regarding social and political problems. Often, as when he argued that intemperance was in opposition to the law of God because overindulgence harmed individuals and families, he was taking a position that nearly all his respectable neighbors endorsed. But sometimes his convictions led him to adopt more-controversial views. For instance, he believed that Indians were children of God no less than whites were and that they should be dealt with fairly under the law rather than driven away or exterminated. Slavery, too, in his opinion, was "a great sin," a conclusion he had reached early in life, while living with a minister who introduced him to the writings of several early Congregationalist critics of slavery.[7]

Owen Brown's staunch commitment to his principles, a quality that had generally won his neighbors' approbation prior to 1830, often had quite the opposite effect in the 1830s, when debates over new currents of religious and reform thought sharply divided Hudson residents. The first such controversy among townspeople was caused by Antimasonry. The presence of many old-time Federalists and opponents of President Jackson in Ohio's Western Reserve made the region a natural breeding ground for Antimason sentiment, as a result of which the Antimason crusade briefly became a successful political force there. In Portage County (where Hudson was located) the chief Antimason newspaper, the *Ohio Star*, hammered away at the order, emphasizing the now-familiar charges that Masonry promoted the interests of the few against the many, that Masons concealed the crimes of fellow members, and that such conduct made membership in the lodge "incompatible with Christian character."[8] Two of Owen Brown's sons, Frederick and Oliver Owen, were among the many Portage County Masons who resigned from local lodges. Meanwhile, their

[NUMBER SIX.]

ANTI MASONIC ALMANAC,

FOR THE YEAR

1833:

BY EDWARD GIDDINS.

THE FIRST STEP TO GREATNESS IS TO BE HONEST.

THE BEST COURT OF EQUITY IS A GOOD CONSCIENCE.

UTICA:

WILLIAM WILLIAMS, PUBLISHER.

SOLD ALSO BY MOST OF THE BOOKSELLERS IN THE UNITED STATES.

Orders, where the makers are known, or satisfactory references are given, will be promptly attended to, and the horizon adapted to the meridian, as nearly as practicable, for which they are wanted.

THE SPIRIT OF TRUTH DWELLETH IN MEEKNESS.

father aided the cause by becoming a subscription agent for the *Star* and by serving as a delegate to county-level Antimason conventions in 1830 and 1832. With such strong grass-roots support, Antimason candidates won big electoral majorities throughout much of Portage County in the midterm elections of 1830. In Hudson, however, voters split almost fifty-fifty over the movement, in large part because David Hudson, the town's founder, retained his membership in the order and opposed Antimasonry. The initial conflict between the town's moderates (led by David Hudson) and come-outers like the Browns thus ended without either faction gaining a decisive edge, a stalemate that all parties to the dispute seem to have accepted relatively amicably.

More-divisive controversies soon followed, however. The most injurious of them was presaged by a brief editorial in the *Ohio Star* for July 21, 1831. The editor urged readers to study the prospectus for William Lloyd Garrison's journal, the *Liberator,* which appeared elsewhere in the issue. In praising the *Liberator,* the *Star*'s editor came close to endorsing one of Garrison's central points: that it made no sense to say one opposed slavery while one continued to accept the right of whites to own slave property. Programs of gradual emancipation, Garrison contended, tacitly recognized that right and were therefore morally repugnant. Only the immediate abolition of slavery passed the test of moral rectitude. By implication, though not yet directly, Garrison was questioning the morality of the moderate's antislavery program, colonization, under which American slaves would be gradually freed and deported to Africa.

Knowledge of Garrison's ideas and the *Liberator* had reached Hudson several months before they surfaced in the *Ohio Star.* A Western Reserve College student who had spent his winter vacation in Massachusetts had obtained copies of the *Liberator*'s first few issues and passed them on to Charles B. Storrs, professor of Christian theology and president of the college. By late 1832 President Storrs, Elizur Wright Jr., and Beriah Green, three of Western Reserve's four faculty members, had been converted to the Garrisonian perspective. Then, inspired by Garrison's latest call to arms (his book *Thoughts on African Colonization,* in which he had for the first time openly attacked the colonization idea), these three strong-willed men resolved to oppose not just slavery but colonization too.

Anti-Masonic Almanac picture satirizing the secret initiation ceremony of the Masonic Lodge.

Only one member of the college's board of trustees shared the abolitionist views now advocated by Storrs, Wright, and Green. The remaining trustees, among them such pillars of Hudson society as David Hudson and Caleb Pitkin, were gradualists. Colonizationists were also in the majority in the college student body. Undaunted, Professor Wright challenged the majority view in August 1832 by sending the *Hudson Observer and Telegram* a series of articles in which he charged that those who rejected immediate emancipation were not men of conscience. A prominent local colonizationist wrote a rebuttal, and the dispute raged on for months. Soon the controversy spilled over into the college itself. Professor Beriah Green was in charge of organizing a program of monthly debates among the students, and he chose abolition versus colonization as a topic for fall 1832. After the debate period was over, Green declared himself shocked by some of the arguments advanced by the colonizationists.

Green now plunged into the controversy personally, making the pulpit of the college church his public platform. It was a fateful decision. Many Hudson residents had been annoyed earlier when Green had insisted that the college church be separate from the First Congregational Church, a separation that served little purpose except to provide him with a pulpit all to himself. Already irritated by Green's pushiness, the venerable trustees and their gradualist allies were infuriated when during November and December 1832 Green delivered four sermons in which he declared, among other things, that gradual emancipation was founded on expediency, that expediency was in "opposition to naked rectitude," and that those who did not work to eliminate totally and immediately the evil of slavery loved neither their neighbors nor God.[9] Publication of the sermons in pamphlet form with an endorsement of Green's views by Professor Wright and President Storrs, together with the growth of abolitionist activism among the college undergraduates over the winter of 1832–33, exacerbated the bitterness gradualists felt toward the advocates of immediate emancipation.

The controversy's denouement came with unexpected suddenness. In May 1833 President Storrs suffered a pulmonary hemorrhage, and four months later he died. An abolitionist admirer, the poet John Greenleaf Whittier, wrote of Storrs, "Thou hast fallen in thine armour, Thou martyr of the Lord!"[10] But there was no disguising the fact that the cause for which Storrs had fought was defeated at Western Reserve College. Professors Wright and Green avoided being fired only by resigning first. The college, having lost three-fourths of its faculty, including its president, opened for the 1833–34 academic year in disarray, its very survival in doubt, but with gradualists firmly in control. Local abolitionists like Owen Brown, an early subscriber to Garrison's *Liberator* and a founder of the Western Reserve Anti-Slavery Society (which favored immediate emancipation), were clearly losers, left without a college to which they could give their wholehearted support.

Fortuitously, events soon conspired to create just such an institution at Oberlin, Ohio, only fifty miles west of Hudson. In October 1834, students who advocated immediate emancipation withdrew from Lane Seminary (Cincinnati) after the school's trustees voted to dissolve the college's antislavery society and to fire John Morgan, an abolitionist on the Lane faculty. Meanwhile, several hundred miles to the north, the founder of Oberlin College, the Reverend John Jay Shipherd, was searching for a way to keep his new and struggling school afloat. He struck on the idea of bringing the Lane rebels to Oberlin. The students would fill Oberlin's classrooms. Professor Morgan would teach, and the Reverend Asa Mahan, a Lane trustee who had aided the rebels, would become Oberlin's president.

In search of money to implement his plan, Shipherd made a trip to New York to talk with two of the era's wealthiest abolitionists, Arthur and Lewis Tappan. The Tappans agreed to aid Oberlin, but only if the college admitted blacks and appointed the noted antislavery evangelist Charles Finney to its faculty. Shipherd was willing, but his trustees had doubts. They pointed out that the college had already adopted two highly innovative ideas, admitting women and making the so-called manual-labor system (under which students spent four hours daily in physical labor) a required part of an Oberlin education. Now Shipherd was asking them to endorse an even more advanced notion, the open admission of students without regard to race. After extensive discussion, however, the trustees reluctantly assented. By May 1835 the Lane rebels began arriving in Oberlin.

Owen Brown was pleased. A college that opened its gates to the Lane rebels was an institution after his own heart. He, too, embraced the goal of educating blacks, believing that to "elevate the colored people of our land" it was necessary to give them educational opportunities.[11] As a father who wanted his daughters to receive a good education, he also found the idea of coeducation appealing. Once Oberlin's commitment to these new directions was clear, therefore, Brown made his approval known. In the spring of 1835 he entered his sixteen-year-old son, Jeremiah, in the school's preparatory program, and the following October he enrolled his daughter Florella in Oberlin's Ladies' Course. Oberlin's trustees were delighted to have Brown as an ally, and on November 24, 1835, they elected him to their ranks. He served in that capacity from 1836 to 1844, rarely missing a board meeting in the years before 1841. During his tenure on the board he actively solicited donations for the college, served as its financial agent on a number of occasions, and made frequent donations himself—sometimes of cash, but more frequently of goods, as in 1839 when he gave the college a yoke of oxen and a cow.

Although Owen Brown shifted his support from Western Reserve College to Oberlin in 1835, he did not cease to labor on behalf of antislavery principles in Hudson. A case in point was the meeting called in November 1837 after word reached Hudson that Elijah P. Lovejoy, the radical abolitionist editor, had been murdered in Illinois by a mob of proslavery men. Angered by the news, many Hudson citizens gathered at the Congregational church to hear speeches of protest and to pass resolutions condemning Lovejoy's murderers. Owen Brown was one of the speakers, and although he stammered during his address proper, he closed with a fervent and eloquent prayer delivered without hesitation. According to one eyewitness account, Brown had just finished when an intense young man rose in the back of the room. It was Owen's son John, aged thirty-seven. John affirmed his father's message, declaring, "I pledge myself with God's help that I will devote my life to increasing hostility to slavery"—portentous words whose full significance would not be evident until twenty-two years later, when John led his fateful raid on Harpers Ferry.[12]

Owen's close ties with his children were evident both in positive moments (as when John followed his father's lead into the abolitionist camp) and in unhappy times like the late 1830s when Owen and his sons, particularly John, suffered severe financial setbacks. The value of the Portage County land that John had bought on speculation declined sharply in the second half of 1836, but it was the panic of 1837 and subsequent depression that finally ruined him. His father and brothers (mainly Frederick) from whom he had borrowed money or received aid as guarantors of loans also lost significant amounts of money. The Browns, of course, were not the only investors to fail. More-grandiose projects than John Brown's went under no less decisively than did his Brown and Thompson's Addition scheme. In Michigan, for example, a development that included a hotel that cost in excess of $30,000 was worth so little after the panic that "the hotel and thirty lots were sold for less than the cost of the glass and paint" used for the hotel.[13] But one did not need to look so far afield to find symptoms of the economic malaise that wrecked the Browns' dreams. In 1837 a majority of the merchants in Akron, a city not far from the Browns' homes, went bankrupt, and lots suddenly brought only a tenth of the price they had commanded less than a year before. Ohio banks also failed right and left, more than a third of them closing their doors in the first few years after the panic.

Given the breadth of the depression's impact, a good case could be made that the Browns, like many other Americans, were simply victims of bad luck, caught by an unfortunate turn of events of the sort that quite commonly ruined investors at the end of an expansive era. Some people in Hudson, however, put the blame on the Browns themselves. Owen summarized his neighbors' reaction as follows: "My property was in jeopardy; I expected all to be lost. I had some to pity me, but very few to help me . . . [and] I had many to inform me that I had brought my troubles upon myself."[14] Without knowing the names of those who chided Owen, we cannot be certain of their motives, but it is possible that some Hudsonians relished the discomfort of a man who had switched his allegiance from Hudson's college to the upstart institution at Oberlin. Perhaps, too, there was some jealousy at work. In 1816 Owen had ranked eleventh among fifty-seven taxpayers in town (not counting partnerships), but by 1834 he had moved up to third place, on the basis of the assessed value of his real estate. Some of his better-educated and more conservative neighbors very likely were glad to see Squire Brown put in his place.

Neither Owen Brown nor his eldest son, John, ever fully recovered from the losses they sustained during the depression of the 1830s, but of the two men, John suffered greater losses and was forced into involuntary bankruptcy. In an effort to help his son, Owen urged him to apply for a job as Oberlin's agent in western Virginia, where the college owned a large tract of land donated by a wealthy patron. In 1840 John spent part of the spring in Virginia surveying Oberlin's land under a provisional arrangement. Then, at its August 11 meeting, the college's prudential committee voted to offer him a long-term contract. Although Owen Brown's wife, Sally, died the very day the committee made its decision, Owen nevertheless attended a trustees meeting at Oberlin less than two weeks later, apparently not wanting to miss a chance to twist a few arms on his son's behalf. John, however, waited five months before accepting the college's proposal, by which time the prudential committee, to the great dismay of both Owen and John, had second thoughts and voted to rescind its offer.

Owen Brown became less active as an Oberlin trustee between 1841 and 1844, the year he resigned his position. Perhaps his relative inactivity was due in part to disappointment over Oberlin's treatment of his son. Nevertheless, he had not lost his enthusiasm for the theological and educational ideals that Oberlin represented, as he forcefully demonstrated in 1842 when, at the age of seventy-one, he led a small band of antislavery radicals out of Hudson's First Congregational Church and helped organize these come-outers into a new Oberlinite church.

The danger of some sort of split had long been present in the Hudson church. By background and conviction most of its members were Congregationalists restive with the early compromise that had placed the church under Presbyterian jurisdiction. Although a partial resolution of this issue was achieved when the congregation withdrew from the Portage Presbytery in 1835, the old split between the Presbyterians and the Congregationalists was perpetuated in a broad way by a division over new issues between moderates (most of whom had been content under Presbyterian control) and radicals (who had generally favored Congregational ties). During the antislavery debate at Western Reserve College in the early 1830s, the moderates advocated colonization, while the radicals argued for abolitionism. Then, in the late 1830s, Owen Brown and perhaps half a dozen radical antislavery men in the church went beyond arguments to actions by turning their houses into stations on the so-called underground railroad, which helped runaway slaves make their way to freedom in Canada. This defiance of state and federal laws requiring the return of fugitive slaves to their owners deeply offended the more conservative church members. They were no less upset, however, by the interest Brown and others showed in Oberlin theology, especially as espoused by Oberlin's president, the Reverend Asa Mahan. Mahan rejected such traditional Calvinist doctrines as predestination and the imperfectibility of human nature, arguing instead that human beings had the capacity to perfect themselves and to achieve freedom from sin (sanctification) through the exercise of free will. To the conventional Congregationalists of Hudson, Oberlin theology was dangerously heretical. By 1839, factional divisions among the town's Congregationalists had become so serious that Owen Brown wrote an Oberlin correspondent, "We are in a bad state in our Church, and . . . we have reason to fear a separation."[15]

The separation between moderates and radicals did take place, but not until September 1842. During the fourteen months before the break, Oberlin theologians and their followers had been campaigning throughout western New York and northern Ohio to establish perfectionist churches and to demonstrate, in Mahan's words, "That entire sanctification in this life is attainable."[16] This movement reached Hudson when Mahan came to town and addressed a series of meetings in the fall of 1842. At the conclusion of Mahan's lectures twenty-one men and women, all but two of whom had been members of Hudson's First Congregational Church, organized the Free Congregational Church, or Oberlin Church, as it was also known. Notably, the Free Church's members were drawn almost exclusively from the families of Hudson residents who ran stations on the underground railroad: Owen Brown, George Kilbourne, Jesse Dickinson, and Gerry Sanford. Their faith in the perfectibility of society through the freeing of slaves went hand in hand with a belief in the capacity of Christians to free their souls from sin.

The Oberlin Church of Hudson proved to be a short-lived experiment. Although committed to practicing mutual Christian watchfulness as a way of ensuring that every member constantly sought sanctification, the Free Congregationalists were not, as a group, particularly receptive to collective discipline. Most were, after all, the come-outers of Hudson, strong-minded individuals ready to invoke the name of Oberlin despite its association with many ideas not yet considered respectable: biracial education, immediate emancipation, coeducation, the Reverend Asa Mahan's brand of perfectionism, and Sylvester Graham's vegetarian dietary program. The Oberlin Congregationalists were also independent spirits ready to undertake illegal missions of mercy on behalf of fugitive slaves. Little wonder, then, that the church had been organized less than a year before Jesse Dickinson, who had objected to several of the church's rules, was suspended from membership for the "unchristian" act of absenting himself from worship services. Disputes over church discipline soon led the Sanford family and then the Kilbournes to drop out, until by the end of 1847 Owen Brown was one of the few original members still active. In July 1849 Brown, as clerk of the congregation, had the sad duty of recording in its minutes that the remaining members agreed it would "be more for the glory of God" to disband than to continue.[17]

The 1840s were dark times for Owen Brown, not just in matters of business and religion but also in his family. In 1840 his wife, Sally, died, and doubly grieved by this tragic reminder of his past losses, he wrote,

"My wounds were broken open anew." Feeling keenly the need for a helpmate, Owen did not long remain a widower. His son Jeremiah Root Brown had married a next-door neighbor, Abi Hinsdale, early in 1840, and in April 1841 Owen married his son's mother-in-law, the widow Lucy Hinsdale. Two years later he moved his family from the Aurora Road place into Hudson. Financial problems influenced his decision to move, but in his autobiography he gave another reason as well: "April, 1843: about this time my family had so scattered—some by marriage and other ways—that I thought best to leave my favorite house and farm, and to build now at the centre of Hudson."[18]

In the thirteen years between his move back to Hudson center and his death there on May 8, 1856, Owen Brown continued his efforts to recover from his financial setbacks of the late 1830s, but without great success. In his old age he remained a devoted father who worried about his sons' difficulties in establishing themselves in stable careers and who was unstinting in his efforts on behalf of all his children. Even a cursory reading of his letters to John when the latter was active in the free-state movement in Kansas in the mid-1850s reveals the warmth of the father's concern and support. Thus, although Owen's troubles continued in these later years, it would be a mistake to dwell too long on his trials at the expense of recalling his many accomplishments. In the personal sphere Brown's integrity, idealism, and fatherly devotion were exemplary. In public life he had made significant contributions to two distinct phases of the history of Hudson, Ohio: the town's pioneer era and its period of adjustment to the tumultuous 1830s and 1840s. With regard to the latter period, it is important to remember that Hudson, though only a small Ohio town, was for a time in the vanguard of national events, responsive to the newest and most radical currents of thought and action in America —abolitionism, the underground railroad, and religious perfectionism. Of those who helped place Hudson in the forefront, no one played a larger role than Owen Brown.

GEORGE AND ANN ELIZA ADAIR: THEY STAYED HOME

Most Americans were not as close as Owen Brown to the eye of the political and religious storms that raged throughout the 1830s. A decade of almost-constant turmoil left Brown weary, but he at least could take satisfaction in knowing that he had made positive contributions to important causes. Not so with George Adair and his oldest daughter, Ann Eliza. They were simple country people whose vantage point during the 1830s, a farm in south central Ohio, was far removed from such storm centers as Hudson and Oberlin. Yet, like people caught by the passing edge of a great whirlwind, they did not escape the storm's destructive power. Indeed, by the end of the decade, George and Ann Eliza Adair, no less than Owen Brown, found that much of what had once been familiar in their social environment—their church, their family, and their neighbors—had been greatly altered, some of it almost beyond recognition.

The social structure of early-day Paint Township has long since vanished completely. Its disappearance was presaged by the fate of the Rocky Spring Presbyterian Church, once the cornerstone of local spiritual and social life. After a long period of declining membership, the church was dealt a final blow in 1876, when a storm damaged the church building beyond the capacity of the few remaining members to repair it. Even the physical sites of the farms once occupied by early Paint Valley pioneers have become largely inaccessible since the mid-1970s, as the rising waters of Paint Creek Lake, backed up by a new Corps of Engineers dam downstream, covered property like the Adairs' that was located along the river. Nevertheless, old family letters enable us to reconstruct the scene that would have greeted a visitor to the Adair farm around 1830.

After passing through rural countryside to a point five miles south of Greenfield, the nearest village of any consequence, the traveler turns west on a dirt lane. Soon the visitor catches a first glimpse of the Adairs' modest, two-story frame house and, a moment later, hears the family's dog barking an alarm. The Adairs keep a few cows as sources of milk and cheese, and workhorses—Jack, Fly, and Ball—help with the heavy labor.

There, too, scratching in the dirt near the barn, is old Cheeppe, the mother hen that once started a brood of thirty-one chicks, of which the old sow ate six. Wheat and corn are the chief crops here, although the Adairs supplement their income by the sale of hogs and of a very thick syrup made from the sap of maple trees.

The Adair farm, roughly 150 acres in size, runs from the low bluff above the valley down a fairly steep slope to Paint Creek. The best field, albeit one that is rocky in places, is in the narrow strip of bottomland beside the river. A branch or creek, with a wooden bridge across it, separates the main field from a smaller one on the southwest corner of the Adair property. George Adair, who is often asked to ferry folks across to the Paint's west, or Highland County, bank, has left his canoe near the water's edge, ready for service.

The Adairs also use the boat, especially on Sundays when they cross the river to attend Rocky Spring Presbyterian Church, nearly two miles away in Highland County. On a typical Sabbath they listen to one or two and occasionally three lengthy sermons. Sometimes, too, they participate in special protracted meetings, as they call the three- and four-day sessions of preaching and praying. Throughout the congregation the Adairs see the familiar faces of their neighbors, people from the farms that spread thinly across the Paint Valley: the Taylors and the Wilsons from

George Adair (1783–1867) when he was about seventy years old.

the Ross County side of the river, and the Strain, Hollyday, Rogers, and Lunbeck families from the Paint's west side above its junction with Rattlesnake Creek. In time, the Adairs will intermarry with all these families except the Strains and Hollydays. Marriages, indeed, figure prominently in Paint Valley social life, and the festivities are often accompanied by such pranks as scaring off the wedding party's horses while the bride, groom, and their friends are at dinner. Quilting bees, apple-paring sessions, prayer meetings, and singing practice are other occasions on which neighbors gather.

The attitudes early-day Paint Valley settlers held on moral issues were strict, but not excessively so. Most local residents had previously lived in slave states and had no quarrel with the morality of slaveholding, although many, such as the Adairs, had never held slaves themselves and apparently would not have been comfortable doing so. In sexual matters these earnest Presbyterian farmers clearly understood the difference between a child born seven or eight months after the parents married and one born nine or more months later. While they shook their heads over occurrences of the former sort, few treated the responsible parties as social outcasts. Similarly, Paint Valley pioneers did not rigidly condemn the use of tobacco and liquor. Tobacco chewing, a custom with strong regional roots, was widespread. Drunkenness was disapproved of, at least

Ann Eliza Adair (1809–1872).

by church-going folk, but light-to-moderate drinking was generally accepted. As late as 1829, when temperance sentiment was growing, locals still regarded a crusade run in Greenfield by hard-line advocates of total abstinence as a product of misguided and newfangled notions. God, the pioneer generation believed, judged people not by what they used but by what they abused.

The times were changing, however, and a major source of the changes that disrupted Paint Valley life was outward migration. The Adairs provide a good illustration of how emigration to the West broke up families. When Benjamin Adair, the family's patriarch, died in 1829, nine of his sons and daughters still lived in Highland or Ross County. Less than four years later only his oldest sons, Philip and George, remained in the Paint Valley, and even they had at least one son apiece who had gone west or planned to do so. Of Benjamin's sons and daughters who emigrated, five moved to north central Indiana and settled near Logansport in Cass County. The lure was the rich Wabash River valley farmland, which had been opened for settlement in 1830 and which one Indiana Adair said was "the best land" that he had ever seen.[19] By clustering together in the southern part of a single township (Noble Township), these Adairs managed to maintain considerable continuity in family ties. However, from the perspective of George Adair, one of the brothers who stayed home, their departure from Ohio was jarring. He had inherited his father's farm on the banks of the Paint but had lost most of his brothers and sisters to the lure of the Indiana frontier.

Whether they stayed in Ohio or went west, the Adairs had to come to grips with the newer ideas that flourished in the 1830s. Most of the Indiana Adairs, for example, helped organize a church aligned with the so-called New School Presbyterians. In practice this meant that they were more liberal than traditional Presbyterians on such subjects as original sin, infant damnation, communion with other denominations, and a believer's ability to merit salvation. When James Harper, one of George Adair's brothers-in-law, arrived in Indiana in 1833 with George's teenage son Benjamin in tow, both uncle and nephew were scandalized by their relatives' membership in a New School congregation that they considered an "abominable, corrupt church . . . [that] did not deserve the name of a Presbyterian church."[20] Harper subsequently took his traditionalism one step further and led a splinter group of Noble Township Presbyterians in founding what they called the Old School Church. These conflicts, of course, were simply part and parcel of the contemporary challenges to traditional ways that affected many individuals and churches, including Owen Brown and Hudson's Congregationalists. But for George Adair, a man for whom Presbyterianism had long been synonymous with eternal verities, these disagreements between his Old and New School relatives were very confusing.

In the 1830s Paint Valley people felt the influence of yet another kind of stirring, the younger generation's increased eagerness for educational advancement. Training at the grammar-school level had once been thought adequate for farmers' sons. But in the early 1830s nearly every family that belonged to the Rocky Spring Presbyterian Church saw at least one son leave the Paint Valley to attend an academy or college. In George Adair's family it was Samuel, his oldest son, who caught college fever in 1832 and enrolled in Western Reserve Academy in Hudson. Most Rocky Spring boys who entered college around this time chose institutions closer to home, but Samuel believed he would receive scholarship aid at Western Reserve and hoped to meet any remaining expenses by working under the college's manual-labor system. In addition, he had received favorable reports on the school from his boyhood chum and cousin Joseph Wilson, a member of the class of 1833.

George Adair endorsed his son's educational aspirations, but mainly for traditional reasons. A good education, George Adair believed, was in keeping with the Presbyterian tradition of an educated laity. Moreover, he assumed not that Samuel was leaving home permanently but that he would return home and teach school once he had completed his studies. George Adair would have been happier had his son chosen a college in southern Ohio, and he hoped Samuel would transfer to one of them after Joseph Wilson graduated from Western Reserve. By attending Ohio University in Athens or Miami University in Oxford, the father argued, Samuel would be able to come home more often. Prompted by George Adair's entreaties, several Rocky Spring boys at other colleges wrote Samuel and urged him, unsuccessfully, to switch to their schools.

Hudson's distance from Paint Township was not the only thing that bothered George Adair. He was an old-fashioned Presbyterian, and although he had increasing doubts about some Old School doctrines, he had even greater doubts about the sort of religious environment Samuel would encounter in Hudson, a town full of people with Yankee and Congregationalist antecedents. "Well son," he wrote in 1833, "you say you want to see a few lines from your father at the bottom of the page. The rest has not quite filled it to the bottom. All the sermon has been rote and

I have but little to say. You say that the people at Hudson is most all Congregationalists but I would say that I cant like there form of Government. It is some better than the Methodist for they are governed by a bishop, the rest by the Congregation and if they are [wrong] there is no higher power of men [to] correct them and I would only be cautious how you imbrace every wind that flies and so no more."[21]

Such direct expressions of George Adair's anxieties about his son are rare, for he usually left the responsibility for family correspondence to Ann Eliza. This spinster daughter of his was a lively observer of people and events who devoted considerable energy to trying to keep Adair family bonds strong. When differences arose among her loved ones, she did her best to mediate between them, but more typically she filled page after page with topics of the sort that she enjoyed sharing: Paint Valley gossip, comments on events of the day, and news of Adair relatives in Virginia, Ohio, and Indiana. Her simple, homespun narratives are often vivid and affecting, as in her account of a crisis that involved old Jack, one of the family's workhorses. "We are all well," she began, "except Father has a cold and has been sick with it. But is better and is gathering his corn in the bottom field ———— Since writing the above I have had a fright and my hand trembles and I feel week; Father in crosing the bridge across the branch in the bottom field with his waggon it empty, one side of the bridge gave way and fell and old Jack fell down between the rock and the bridge, there he was in a bad fix. Father called several times before I heard. We then went to help get old Jack out, the waggon was to lift out before we could get to him, he was lying on one side withe his feet under the bridge and in getting out left his harness in the branch except the collar. He is not as we can see much hurt, both hind legs are cut one pretty smartly, no bones broken that we can see as yet; Had it been some horses they would have strugled and strained until they would have killed or cripled themselves. Whenever Father would speak to him he would lie still apealingly for us to help him and would groan pitously ————"[22]

During Samuel's student years, Ann Eliza's best efforts to maintain family unity were sorely tested by her brother's acceptance of a variety of new ideas advocated by his teachers and friends in northern Ohio. His younger brother, Benjamin R. Adair, was a conservative Presbyterian who expressed alarm at the thought that Samuel was "about to be led off" by New School liberalism. For her part, Ann Eliza fussed about Samuel socializing with "Yankey ladies," especially as she had heard it said that **the more modern** ones "cease to lace." She also rebelled at the notion, which she asserted could only have come from a "Yankey" preacher, that "all that would not join the Temperance Society was in the way to distruction." And Ann Eliza's replies to a long list of Samuel's questions made it plain that the home folks wanted nothing to do with other forms of abstinence being advocated by Yankee reformers:

40. Father chews tobacco yet and has no notion of quiting [*sic*].
41. We still use tea and coffee and not any notion of quitting.
42. And we do not think it wrong to do so.
43. I'll tell you plainly I like it very well.[23]

Interestingly enough, one of Samuel's new views that did not perturb his father and sisters was his conversion to the abolitionist cause. Not only did they support his decision, but in 1833, when their local minister urged women to join the Paint Valley Abolition Society (a somewhat daring proposal in an era when there was a very strong bias against women participating in public affairs), Ann Eliza signed up and proudly wrote Samuel, "There my name stands with numbers of others I could name to you."[24] Apparently, some combination of long-standing doubts about the morality of slavery and a distaste for the social pretensions of the slaveholding class overcame any lingering influence the family's southern background may have had.

If Samuel's being at Western Reserve College had been worrisome to his family, the prospect of his going to the even more unorthodox Oberlin proved altogether alarming. When Samuel wrote in 1837 that he intended to take his senior year (1837–38) at Oberlin, his father did his best to say some positive things about the decision; however, he then added a line regarding his overall reaction: "I felt sorry to hear that you had got to Oberlin . . . on account of the new schools doctrin[e]s." George Adair was even more upset in 1838 when Samuel announced that he wanted to continue at Oberlin for an advanced degree in theology. It was Samuel's "duty," his father replied, to come home after graduation and find a job as a schoolteacher. As for Samuel's idea of "studdiing five or six years more," especially studying theology at Oberlin, George Adair was adamantly opposed: "I have a strong desire you would not," he wrote. The conflict between her father and brother left Ann Eliza in a gloomy mood. Instead of her usual two- or three-page letter, she added only a brief note below her father's. "I do not feel," she explained, "in the spirit of wrighting at this time. I have got the *blues* or some thing not much better."[25]

Samuel's decision to study for the ministry at Oberlin in spite of his father's opposition was a hard blow to George Adair's sense of how things ought to be. It might have been less hard, however, had the news not come so close on the heels of his wife's death in February 1838, after a protracted illness.

The narrative of Peggy Adair's troubles, drawn mostly from Ann Eliza's letters, reveals the trials of a sick woman, the stoicism of her family, and the limitations of contemporary medicine. In June 1833, when Peggy Adair was fifty-three years old, she developed what one physician called a carbuncle on her right hand, an infection that over the next few weeks spread until her arm was "inflamed almost to her shoulder." A doctor came from a nearby town and lanced the infected hand. There was no improvement, however, so he was sent for again. The doctor being unavailable, George Adair lanced the hand himself, and, as Ann Eliza reported, "an abundance of matter come." The swelling diminished, but the pain did not, so another physician, "Doc Mccollem," was summoned. He "maid a cooling wash with milk and watter putting something else in it and bathed her hand with it." Later he "laid open the inside of her wrist" and inserted a "tent" (i.e., "a gauze pad or sponge inserted into a wound to promote drainage and absorb pus and blood"). Serious infections of this sort would also be treated surgically today, but the availability of antibiotics gives modern physicians an enormous advantage over their predecessors. Even so, under Doc Mccollem's care, Peggy Adair gradually improved. Nevertheless, as late as mid-September the fingers of her right hand were still "very crooked and bent," and she was rubbing her hand two or three times a day with "opossum grease" in hopes of restoring its use. By January she was able to knit again, but still unable to straighten her fingers.[26]

In December 1835 Peggy Adair suffered a stroke that left her unable to speak and partly paralyzed on the right side. Over the next year she lost weight, had trouble sleeping, and often failed to recognize friends and relatives. In 1837, the year before her death, she frequently awoke at night, restless and confused, sometimes bursting out with what Ann Eliza called "curious notions" about herself. Her right foot, side, and even face were badly swollen, apparently a sign of edema due to the nonuse of her limbs, a typical poststroke symptom better understood and more frequently minimized by modern treatment. Peggy Adair's discomfort, physical and mental, led her to cry out a good deal, and Ann Eliza resignedly wrote, "It is the most trying thing to sit in the room with her and be obliged to listen to her when we can do nothing of consequence . . . for her." Finally, only opium doses nearly every night permitted the failing mother to rest at all. The long-delayed end came on the morning of January 27, 1838. "Oh Brother," Ann Eliza wrote Samuel, "I cannot tell how much we miss her here; she is not oftain absent long at a time from my mind in my wakeing hours."[27]

The events of the 1830s and early 1840s hit George Adair hard. It was ironic that he, as the family man who had stayed home, found himself stripped of close contact with many of his nearest kin. All but one of his eight brothers and sisters who had come to Ohio left the Paint Valley area, and his two oldest boys, Samuel and Benjamin, also moved away. Even Addison, his third son, was talking about going west. His wife's death was yet another blow. He remarried in 1839, but his second marriage produced difficulties of its own, largely because his new wife, Nancy Swan, did not get along well with his three daughters. Of the conflict between the three and their stepmother, Ann Eliza had this to say: "The girls have tough enough times to get along with the Old Lady. I cant tell what she means by her talk and actions. I sometimes think she would like to clear the house of us all and I think Father has not the happiness he promised himself when he brought her there."[28]

Developments outside his family gave George Adair little solace either. Locally, the Rocky Spring Presbyterian Church underwent a discouraging decline of membership during the late 1830s. Nationally, the fact that the Presbyterian church's governing body, the general assembly, "ran wild if not mad" (in George Adair's words) in expelling local synods it considered tainted by New School and abolitionist ideas left him feeling more disenchanted than ever with his old denomination.[29] To top everything off, the economic depression that began in 1837 dragged on well into the early 1840s. Even though the downturn's effect was a bit milder in the Paint Valley than in areas where agriculture was more commercialized, the decline in farm prices to approximately one-third of what they had been in 1836 meant that the households of farmers like George Adair lacked virtually everything but the bare necessities.

George Adair responded more with puzzlement than with anger. As Ann Eliza, who knew him best, put it, he was caught "on the fence" regarding the many options that had emerged in a time of change.[30] He understood the lure that good land in the West had for farmers, but he wished his closest kin had not followed that rainbow; he sympathized with some of the reasons for Samuel's New School leanings, but he felt more

affinity with his second son, Benjamin, who stuck by Old School traditions. Like old Jack, the workhorse that had been trapped under the
bridge when it collapsed as he was crossing it, George Adair knew he
would only hurt himself if he struggled too hard. So he lay still. In the
1840s he seldom attended services at the Rocky Spring Presbyterian
Church. He said little to his daughters about their conflicts with his
second wife, and he stopped writing to his absent sons, Samuel and Benjamin, leaving it to Ann Eliza to fill them in on news from home.

In time, however, George Adair began to emerge from his withdrawn
state. An important step in this direction was reported by his daughter
Martha late in 1849 when she wrote Samuel to thank him for having sent
a daguerreotype of himself, his wife, and their two children. "Father
received your portraits & letter today," she began. "It would be needless
to tell you how happy we were to see those loved faces again or a represen-
tation of them. . . . Father & E [Ann Eliza] are talking about Mothers age

The photograph that got
George Adair to talking
about "past times." Left to
right: Samuel Adair,
Charles Storrs Adair,
Florella Brown Adair,
Emma Florilla Adair.

& her sister. I have not heard him say a word about Mother for a long time. I dont know what . . . to hope[.] He seem to like to talk this morning more than usual about past times. Your portraits seem to have called up those tender feelings of a Father's love. You have done *us* a great kindness for which we thank you heartily."[31]

In the early 1850s George Adair resumed his practice of adding an occasional brief note to Ann Eliza's letters from home, and he also attended church at Rocky Spring with greater frequency. Perhaps the passage of time alone was sufficient to explain his changed behavior, although signs of progress outside his family circle—economic conditions were improving and the railroad had come to Greenfield—contributed too. It is interesting to note, however, that a picture of his absent loved ones was instrumental in renewing George Adair's spirits. The new age, which had brought so many geographical and ideological separations, also provided a new bridge over those separations—the daguerreotype.

Chapter   Four

IN THE

SHADOW OF

CONFLICT

1850 - 1865

I
n November 1831, about the time Owen and Sally Brown moved to their new house and farm on Aurora Road, their daughter Florella* was admitted to membership in Hudson's First Congregational Church. She was fifteen at the time and was taking her first step into adulthood on the eve of dramatic events that would unfold in Hudson and the United States over the next three decades. In the early 1830s her hometown of Hudson was rocked by a bitter debate over William Lloyd Garrison's proposal that all American slaves be freed immediately. A few

---

*Although her father and many friends and relatives spelled her name Florilla (leading most historians to do the same), she signed her name Florella.

years later Florella entered Oberlin College, an institution that was attracting national attention because of both its radical antislavery stance and its introduction of coeducation and biracial education at the college level. Then, in the 1850s, as Americans became increasingly polarized over the question of whether slavery should be allowed into the newer territories and states of the West, Florella, now married, went with her husband and children to Kansas in hopes of helping to prevent that territory from becoming a slave state. Finally, in 1861, the Civil War broke out, and the national struggle that had been so long in the making became a war of such gigantic proportions that it lasted four years and left more than 600,000 Americans dead. Each of these events shaped Florella's life in significant ways, for although she was a woman and could not vote or bear arms, as an abolitionist, an Oberlin student, and a free-state pioneer to Kansas in the 1850s she lived all her adult years in the shadow of the conflict over slavery.

Owen Brown was one of the first residents of Hudson to subscribe to Garrison's newspaper, the *Liberator,* and during the 1832–33 debate at Western Reserve College over the relative merits of abolition and colonization, his house became a meeting place for many of the college's leading advocates of immediate emancipation. Elizur Wright Sr., the only college trustee to favor abolitionism, was Owen's friend and a frequent visitor to the Brown house. Wright's son Elizur Jr. was one of three faculty members who forcefully promoted Garrison's ideas and whom the conservative trustees bent every effort to silence. Two of Elizur Jr.'s brothers, James and William, were Western Reserve students and participants in the memorable burst of student activism during the winter of 1832–33, when undergraduates made a door-to-door canvass of many Ohio towns, urging residents to support abolitionist principles. With most respectable Hudsonians opposing such activities, abolitionist students such as the Wright boys took inspiration from the example of Owen Brown, a member of the older generation who was not only with them but often ahead of them, and they eagerly sought his company. By modern standards the meetings these antislavery radicals held in Owen's drawing room were tame affairs: they featured a warm fire, apples to munch on, lots of talk about antislavery, and periods of prayer for God's guidance. But the undergraduates were ready to back their words with actions. After Elizur Wright Jr. was forced to resign his faculty position, his brothers James and William abandoned Western Reserve for Oberlin College. Sometime before they left in 1834, however, James introduced his roommate, George Adair's son

Samuel, to the Browns. A special friendship soon developed between Florella Brown and Samuel Adair, or Sister Brown and Brother Adair, as the etiquette of that time and place required them to address each other.

In October 1835, at the age of nineteen, Florella entered the Ladies' Course of Oberlin Collegiate Institute. She thus became one of the very first participants in Oberlin's experiment with the joint education of men and women at the college level. In fact, only one woman completed the Ladies' Course before 1839, the year that Florella and four others finished it. To understand the significance of her achievement, however, one needs to know both what it meant and what it did not mean. To be sure, Florella was one of the first women to complete postsecondary training in the United States or anywhere, but that accomplishment was not viewed by her or her contemporaries as making her or any other Oberlin woman equal to Oberlin men or even to less-educated American males.

The innovative side of Oberlin's decision to admit women can be best understood by contrasting it with the prevailing view in early-nineteenth-century America that regarded women as creatures without the mental faculties necessary to engage in academic work much beyond the elementary-school level. According to this view, pushing women beyond their natural intellectual limits would injure them mentally and physically. Worse yet, it would unsex them, that is, make them competitors with men, their natural superiors and to whom they were meant to defer.

In the 1820s and 1830s the part of this sexist ideology that denied women the right to higher education came under challenge from a variety of sources. Evangelists, notably Charles Finney, urged women to take active roles in Christian social reform, and education would enhance their ability to do so effectively. Westward expansion was also an indirect influence. The need for new schools in the West created a demand for more teachers, and since teaching was the only profession thought suitable for women in the pre–Civil War era, the case for more and better teacher training also became a case for expanded educational opportunities for women. Finally, a small band of such educational innovators as Joseph Emerson, Emma Willard, and Catharine Beecher began to develop a theoretical and institutional base for female higher education. Several of Emerson's protégées, among them Mary Lyon, who in 1837 founded a single-sex institution, Mount Holyoke Female Seminary (now Mount Holyoke College), and Alice Welch Cowles, who became head of the Female Department of a coeducational school, Oberlin, made important contributions to this cause.

Traditionalists were sure that Oberlin's experiment in the joint education of the sexes would be a moral and educational disaster. But such critics ignored the fact that a very conventional view of women was implicit in the rationale that Oberlin's leaders gave for endorsing coeducation. For example, in 1834 the founder, the Reverend John Jay Shipherd, described the goal of joint education as "the elevation of female character, bringing within the reach of the misjudged and neglected sex, all the instructive privileges which hitherto have unreasonably distinguished the leading sex from theirs." In referring to males as "the leading sex," Shipherd took as a given the idea that women were men's inferiors. Thus, although Oberlin did admit women to its regular collegiate program, the so-called Classical Course, which emphasized the study of Hebrew, Latin, and Greek, most women were, like Florella Brown, encouraged to enter the Ladies' Course, in which there was no required foreign-language study and no mathematics beyond geometry. Moreover, the commingling of men and women in classes and at mealtime was justified with traditional arguments. Women's presence would make the college more like a "well-regulated family" in which the rowdiness and disorderly conduct so prevalent among students at all-male institutions would be reduced. It was also hoped that daily contact with members of the opposite sex would prevent male students from forming idealized images of women and thus inhibit the practice of masturbation, which was encouraged, or so Oberlin's early leaders believed, by men's obsessive fantasies about absent women. Sylvester Graham's vegetarian scheme was introduced for much the same reason, in the hope that abstinence from meat would subdue the male students' carnal appetites and redirect their energies to intellectual and spiritual pursuits.[1]

Many of Oberlin's practical arrangements reinforced the notion that women were to devote themselves to serving the leading sex. Under the college's manual-labor system men in all departments—preparatory, college, and theological—did farm labor, construction work, and office jobs. The women, regardless of their course of study, did domestic labor: washing, ironing, sewing, cooking, and housecleaning chores. In the spring of 1836, for example, Florella Brown earned three cents per hour (a typical wage for Oberlin women in the 1830s) working in the college boardinghouse. Domestic labor, according to Oberlin's administrators, would prevent women students from thinking that being feminine meant being decorative and idle. Monday, therefore, was a half holiday from classes during which women students did laundry for all the undergraduates.

Lest anyone not know immediately that the needs of the leading sex were to come first, Mrs. Cowles, the lady principal, placed the following injunction at the top of her list of instructions to women students working in the washing department: "Never carry your own articles into the wash room until the gentlemen's are finished."[2]

Oberlin's early leaders maintained that a major justification for educating women was to make them useful in the world. This was a theme that Florella Brown echoed at the time she entered college in 1835, writing that she was attending Oberlin in order to prepare for "usefulness in whatever field the Lord may see fit to place her." When Oberlin's women students of the 1830s and early 1840s mentioned more-specific professional aspirations, the fields most frequently named were missionary work and teaching. Given the intensity of antislavery sentiment at Oberlin in these years, it is not surprising that some women students were especially interested in teaching in schools for blacks. In 1836 Florella wrote her parents that the student antislavery society to which she belonged had received a letter from "the sisters engaged in the coloured school at Cincinnati," and she expressed frustration at feeling herself not yet well enough educated to go and do likewise. Despite these aspirations, and despite the fact that "many first-decade alumnae taught for a longer or a shorter time," research done by Francis Hosford in the 1920s revealed that, "statistically speaking, . . . the occupation of nearly all of the alumnae of the first decade was marriage." Seventy-eight of the first eighty graduates married, and 60 percent of them married ministers. Many married Oberlin men, a practice that the school's administration and faculty encouraged. No less an authority than the Great Evangelist, Charles Finney, once gave his male students the following advice: "Here in this college is the best material for a minister's wife. Don't leave this town before you are engaged!" The corollary to this doctrine as it applied to women was that nothing they could do would be more useful than to become a helpmate to a graduate of Oberlin's theology department.[3]

Florella Brown and Samuel Adair's courtship and marriage followed Finney's formula. They had met and become friends while both lived in Hudson. After Florella entered Oberlin, Samuel continued to call on her parents, and when he occasionally went to Oberlin to visit old schoolmates, he also called on her. In 1837 he transferred to Oberlin, where his career overlapped hers for two years while Florella was finishing the Ladies' Course and he was completing his bachelor's degree and starting the theology program. Even though Oberlin students were not supposed to become engaged while still in school, the numerous marriage banns published each year around graduation time indicate that a good many engagements were made, but not announced, during the school year. Careful not to transgress the college's rules, Samuel did not pursue the question of engagement in earnest until 1841, when he had only a few months of study left.

Samuel and Florella were living fifty miles apart in early 1841, so they discussed the prospect of marriage entirely through letters. Although they had some sort of earlier understanding, progress toward a formal engagement was not always smooth. Samuel was a methodical person who set schedules for himself and everyone else. When Florella's correspondence fell behind the timetable he expected her to meet, he was quick to express his disappointment. Her response to his complaint does not survive, but apparently it was satisfactory, because in his next letter Samuel wrote that it had been "all for the best," that "Our Heavenly Father saw that we needed something of this kind to try our feelings— test our patience." More tests followed, however. Florella wrote that she needed to be reassured of his affection for her because she had sometimes detected "manifestations of coldness and distance" in him. In his reply he acknowledged that something "a little unfavorable" had been on his mind and possibly caused the behavior she had noted. It seems that a year earlier, during his last visit to Hudson, he had invited her to pray with him and had been upset because she had not joined him in kneeling. "Satan," he admitted, "has tried several times since to use it against your piety." But his deepest fear, he continued, was that she might not stand by him through the hardships he expected his chosen profession to impose. Putting his formal proposal into words he hoped would make Florella understand the extent of commitment he wanted from her, he asked whether she, "come *poverty*, come *persecution*, come *death* . . . [would be] a succour, a comforter, a prop" to his spirits. Despite this formidable approach, perhaps even because of it, Florella said yes, and they were married in November 1841 at her father's home in Hudson.[4]

Florella's dowry from her father provided her with most of the basic goods she needed to set up housekeeping. These included, among other things, a set of silver teaspoons, a gilt mirror frame, three blankets, several quilts and spreads, "Callico" curtains, sheets, pillow cases, table cloths, four towels, one "Fraying pan," one straw bed tick, twenty-two pounds of feathers, a pair of brass candlesticks, a flatiron, a trunk, one old chest, a table, a wash stand, and "1 high post bed sted."[5] It was fortunate that the young couple had Owen Brown's help. Samuel's income from the series of small congregations he served was as paltry as their sometimes unreceptive attitude toward him was ungenerous. The Adairs had to move frequently in these years, living in succession in Sandyville, Ohio (1841–42), Dundee, Michigan (1843–45), Maumee City, Ohio (1845–47 as pastor; 1847–49 as a schoolteacher), and Lafayette, Ohio (1849–54).

The first decade of marriage brought Florella at least as many sorrows as joys. Her greatest anguish was occasioned by the loss of three of the five babies born in these years. The Adairs' first child, a son they named Charles Storrs Adair in memory of the martyred president of Western Reserve College, was born in 1842 and lived to a ripe old age. But a second son, Henry, born in 1844, died in 1848, five months after the birth of a sister, Emma Florilla. Emma thrived; however, the Adairs' twin daughters, born in November 1851, died soon after birth. The first twin lived less than three weeks, the second just under two months.

Florella's thoughts on national political issues in the 1840s and early 1850s are not known explicitly, but some of them can be inferred with confidence. As abolitionists, she and her husband must have been profoundly troubled by President Franklin Pierce's aggressive foreign policy. Not only did his election in 1844 ensure the annexation of Texas, another slave state, but he unhesitatingly advocated further territorial acquisitions under the doctrine of Manifest Destiny, which justified American expansion across the continent as divinely ordained. In the war with Mexico (1846–48), Pierce's policies led to the conquest of vast new western territories, at least some of which might eventually enter the Union as slave states. Antislavery leaders countered with the so-called Wilmot Proviso, which would have excluded slavery from the newly acquired territories. In the bitter national debate that followed, the older generation of political leaders, among them Henry Clay and Daniel Webster, eventually succeeded in winning congressional approval of a series of measures known collectively as the Compromise of 1850. The Adairs were in all likelihood pleased with the provisions that admitted California as a free state and abolished the slave trade in the District of Columbia. But they were undoubtedly appalled by the new federal Fugitive Slave Act, a major concession granted to southern slave interests. Under this law even legally free blacks, if accused of being fugitives, were denied the right to have a jury determine their status. The decision was to be rendered either by a federal judge or, worse yet, by special commissioners who would receive ten dollars for every fugitive returned to a slaveholder and

Opponents of the Fugitive Slave Law make their point
in a cartoon by Peter Kramer (early 1850s).

only five dollars for cases decided in the accused black's favor. Moreover, the new law greatly increased penalties for antislavery militants who, like Florella's father, aided fugitives to escape.

The war of words over slavery abated somewhat in the first few years of the 1850s, but it did not cease altogether. Some antislavery radicals in the North attempted, sometimes successfully, to rescue blacks who had been captured and detained by federal authorities under the new Fugitive Slave Act. The publication of Harriet Beecher Stowe's novel *Uncle Tom's Cabin* (1852) also kept the slavery issue in the public eye. But the most damaging blow to national harmony, one that destroyed any faint hope that the slavery issue would go away, came in the aftermath of the passage of the Kansas-Nebraska Act in 1854. The Kansas-Nebraska legislation, sponsored by Senator Stephen A. Douglas of Illinois, incorporated the principle of popular sovereignty, under which the people of a territory, not Congress, would determine whether their state entered the Union slave or free. To abolitionists like Florella and Samuel Adair this was a highly pernicious doctrine. It not only swept aside congressional authority to bar slavery from the territories but also repealed the Missouri Compromise of 1820. Under the older law slavery was prohibited north of the line 36°30' in the area that had been part of the Louisiana Purchase of 1803, land that included Kansas. Now, as the Adairs immediately recognized, there was a grave danger that settlers from the relatively populous slave state of Missouri, which bordered Kansas on the east, would pour into the newly organized territory and turn it into a slave state.

The plight of Kansas had a profound impact on Florella's thinking. Her husband had long dreamed of becoming a missionary, but he had set that ambition aside after his marriage because Florella had resisted any suggestion that they move far away from Ohio, where her Brown relatives lived. But Kansas changed all that. It touched the very heart of Florella's long-standing commitment to abolitionist principles. She had never forsaken the aspiration she had expressed nearly twenty years earlier to be useful, and it now seemed to her that the most useful thing she could do was to support her husband's desire to become a free-state missionary in Kansas. It would not do, she said, "for the slaveholders to take possession of that territory and curse it with slavery."[6] So, in spite of the possible dangers, the almost certain hardships, and the inevitable separation from her loved ones in Ohio, she told Samuel that she was willing to go west. It helped that antislavery people all over the North shared her feelings and that some were preparing to join the free-state migration to Kansas. But many proslavery settlers were headed for the new territory too. As these different Americans with their seemingly irreconcilable goals converged on Kansas, the risk of armed conflict over slavery increased. Indeed, by 1854 the momentum toward war was already almost too strong to be reversed.

THE ADAIRS AND
BLEEDING KANSAS

On June 24, 1854, less than a month after President Franklin Pierce
signed the Kansas-Nebraska Act into law, the Reverend Samuel
Adair wrote the American Missionary Association to apply for a
position as a missionary in the newly organized Kansas Territory. By way
of explaining his request, he wrote, "[F]or many years my heart has
rather been with the West; but my wife has been rather disinclined to go
to the new settlements. But since the 'Nebraska Iniquity' has been perpe-
trated she has entirely changed her mind & thinks now is the time to
strike."[7] Toward the end of August the AMA's board approved Samuel's
application, and by mid-September he, his wife, and their two children
were on their way to Kansas. Although swiftly taken, these actions were
not products of casual whims on Samuel's part. Like the desire to aid the
antislavery cause that made Florella willing to go west, Samuel's zeal to
be a missionary had burned for fully twenty years. His decision to head
for Kansas was therefore simply the last in a series of steps that he had
begun to take in the early 1830s and that had ultimately removed him
very far, culturally and even temperamentally, from his Paint Valley
origins.

Samuel's journey began in 1832 when he left home for Hudson, Ohio,
to prepare for college. The odds for success were by no means all in his
favor. For one thing, he was off to a late start, for he was nearly twenty-
one and thus several years older than most of his classmates. In addition,
he was an unsophisticated country youth who had for the last five years
been an apprentice in a Paint Valley blacksmith shop where day-to-day
discourse was mainly small talk, the "many dry jokes and neighborhood
tales" (as one boyhood chum of Adair's put it) that country people relished. Lastly, though this did not worry him the way it did his Paint
Valley kin, there was no telling what might happen once he was exposed
to Yankee culture in Hudson, especially in the early 1830s when the town
was aflame with talk of all sorts of newfangled reform ideas. Samuel's
sister Ann Eliza, in reading between the lines of his letters, soon sensed
changes in him and expressed her fear that he might "be taken in too
much with the Yankes [sic] and the Eastern people and begin to think and
do like them."[8]

The home folks' fears grew over the years and were in large part confirmed in 1837 when Samuel transferred to Oberlin. But Samuel's move to Oberlin, the second long step in his spiritual journey, was not made precipitously. Whereas nearly all his classmates had abandoned Western Reserve College earlier, he did not leave until the end of his junior year, a full four years after the institution had been thrown into turmoil by the debate over slavery. Even so, his caution could not disguise the fact that in switching to Oberlin he was moving yet further away from his Old School Presbyterian beginnings and closer to the New School (or, worse yet, perfectionist) ideas then dominant at Oberlin. When, despite his father's outspoken disapproval, he decided in his senior year to stay at Oberlin to pursue a degree in theology, it was another choice in a direction that led away from his roots.

The same was also to some extent true of his marriage to Florella Brown. Although her earnest piety and Oberlin education made her (by the standards of Samuel's student friends) a perfect mate for him, she nevertheless was a "Yanky Girl" of the sort his sisters had worried that he might find attractive.[9] Whether he feared that Florella and his family might not get along well, or simply lacked the money for the trip home (a journey of nearly two hundred miles and four or five days by canal boat and stagecoach), Samuel did not take his wife to meet his Paint Valley kin until 1845, four years after they had married.

The final factor that put Samuel on the road for Kansas was his conviction that he had failed in his career between 1841 and 1854. For all but two of those years he had labored as a minister to tiny congregations in small Michigan and Ohio towns. The experience had not been rewarding, either spiritually or financially. He was unsuccessful at drawing members to his churches, in part (as some parishioners were quick to point out) because he was not sufficiently "Buckeyed," that is, folksy and emotional in his preaching style. By 1854 Samuel was close to despair. He confided to his journal that the last five years, during which he had preached at Lafayette, Ohio, had seemed "remarkably barren." And the Lafayette years had been difficult ones for Florella also, not only because Samuel's troubles soon became hers too, but because she had lost two infant daughters in that period. Both Adairs therefore desperately wanted to make a change at the very moment when the opportunity to go to Kansas presented itself.[10]

When Samuel and Florella left their native state of Ohio in September 1854, it was an act reminiscent of similar uprooting moves their fathers had made fifty years earlier in coming to Ohio. Half a century, however, had brought some innovations in travel. On the first leg of their trip, the Adairs went from Cleveland to Chicago on the Michigan Central Railroad. From Chicago onward they split into two parties. Samuel and young Charles (who was just a shade shy of twelve years old) drove the family's horse and buggy across Illinois, Iowa, and Missouri. Meanwhile, Florella and little Emma (who would be seven in October) joined a group of settlers bound for Kansas under the auspices of the Massachusetts Emigrant Aid Society, an organization that had been formed in 1854 to promote free-state migration to Kansas. This party went by train to St. Louis. There they boarded a shallow-draft river steamboat, another improved form of transportation that had become popular in recent decades. Although the *Banner State* hit several sandbars and once was stuck for twenty-four hours, Florella and Emma reached Kansas City, Missouri, early in October, two weeks before Samuel and Charles arrived by their overland route.

It was a bit ironic, but also virtually unavoidable, that abolitionists like the Adairs used travel facilities provided by St. Louis and Kansas City, both slave-state towns. These Missouri cities had long served as outfitting and supply depots for migrants heading west. Indeed, economic reasons as well as proslavery sentiment figured in Missourians' determi-

The Reverend Samuel Adair (1811–1898) during Civil War years.

nation to make Kansas into an economic and political adjunct of their state. Any growth of such Kansas settlements as Lawrence and Topeka, where free-staters were in control, was a threat to the economy of the Missouri supply cities.

A combination of strong motivation and Missouri's proximity to Kansas initially enabled Missourians to dominate the new territory. In the first territorial census (March 1855) nearly 50 percent of those enumerated had come from Missouri, and two proslavery settlements, Atchison and Leavenworth, were showing particularly rapid growth. But antislavery leaders were not willing to stand idly by while proslavery interests triumphed in Kansas, and in the first year after the territory opened to settlement the Massachusetts Emigrant Aid Society (soon renamed the New England Emigrant Aid Society) underwrote the immigration of approximately one thousand settlers to Kansas. A similar number of free-state migrants, the Adairs among them, came without the society's direct sponsorship. Nevertheless, for the first few years these committed free-staters were outnumbered at least three to one by Missourians and other proslavery settlers. In addition, many newcomers moved to Kansas out of purely economic motives, and since most of these politically uncommitted settlers were hostile to abolitionism, their presence exacerbated the free-staters' minority position.

Florella Brown Adair (1816–1865) in the early 1860s.

Kansas City, Missouri, as it looked when the Adairs
were there in early 1855.

As the Adairs' experience illustrates, the newer methods of travel—
trains and steamboats—were certainly superior to oxcarts as means of
reaching the frontier. The closer the Adairs came to Kansas, however, the
more they encountered conditions not so very different from those their
parents had faced in early-day Ohio. Even in Kansas City, Missouri, the
Adairs had to endure shortages of some provisions, shockingly high
prices, problems in cashing drafts on eastern banks, and illness. Severe
bouts with dysentery kept them from moving on immediately to the
"promised land," as Florella called Kansas. In January and February
1855, however, Samuel was well enough to make two long tours into the
territory, often riding twenty miles a day in subfreezing temperatures.
Shelter was so rare in the sparsely settled new land that he sometimes
found himself at nightfall near no settlement and was forced to bed down
in the open under a buffalo rug. "The constant, piercing prairie winds,"
he wrote, "penetrated all."[11]

By early March, Samuel had located what he was looking for, the
beginnings of a well-situated community whose population included "a
few warm hearted Christians." This was Osawatomie, a town at the junction of the Pottawatomie and Marais des Cygnes rivers, approximately
fifty miles south of Kansas City and less than twenty miles due west of
the Missouri border. The settlement had been established in October 1854
by a party of ten or twelve free-state families who had come to Kansas
with the backing of the Massachusetts Emigrant Aid Society. The town-

site itself was not surveyed until February 1855, but within a little more than a year after that date Osawatomie had a population of about two hundred (most of them free-staters) and perhaps thirty buildings, including a store, a hotel, a sawmill, and a blacksmith shop. Samuel bought a claim about a mile west of town and brought his family to their new home on March 21, 1855. A rough log house had been built on the property by a squatter in 1854. It was typical of most frontier cabins both in its size (eighteen by twenty feet) and in the crudeness of its construction. Samuel described it as follows:

a chimney built with sticks and mud—jambs and backwall and hearth of stone, two doors—half a floor and that made of puncheons—that is, timber split and hewd. The house is chinked in the cracks, partly daubled with mud on the outside. It has no windows, but in lieu of them the cracks between the logs in the gable end towards the east are left open for the light to shine through.

Need we add to his description that the convenience of having an unmortared gable end to admit light in the summer was offset by the chilling effect this arrangement produced in winter when icy winds and snow came through the cracks?[12]

For the good of the antislavery cause, Florella had accepted the sacrifices that life as a missionary's wife entailed. Nevertheless, the first months in her new home must have borne out all the fears that had earlier led her to veto a move west. Dwellings such as the Adairs' log cabin imposed particular hardships on women. The then-current cult of domesticity promoted the view that middle-class women like Florella were to find fulfillment in home management, a goal that under frontier conditions became, to say the least, challenging. By any measure the Adairs' cabin represented a drastic reduction in material comfort for Florella, who had been accustomed to more-settled town conditions in Ohio. The lack of a stove (standard in Ohio homes) meant that she had to cook over an open fire. Feeding a family adequately was made more difficult by the unavailability of many items, for, as Samuel reported in May 1855, they had "had no vegitables scarcely" since they had left Chicago (the preceding October). All the ordinary labor of sewing the family's clothes, doing laundry, ironing, tending children, cooking, and washing dishes was just that much more taxing in such crude circumstances. For Florella there were also losses in social contacts (the Adairs lived outside of town and had few close neighbors) and of privacy. In her father's house it was

Samuel and Florella Adair's cabin
after a window was added.

possible to offer guests a private room, but in her Kansas home everyone
—whether family, friends, or strangers—had to crowd together in one
room and a loft. Tight family finances led Florella to take in sewing and
washing, something many frontier women did to earn extra money, but
definitely not what a minister's wife would have done in Ohio. Samuel had
to ask the *American Missionary*'s editors (who published his quarterly
reports from Kansas) to omit what he had written about Florella because,
he said, "she would rather not have it come under the eye of some of her
friends" (i.e., relatives in Ohio).[13]

The Adairs at least knew they were no worse off than most settlers.
The nearest neighboring family, the Morgan Chronkhites, numbered six.
Yet the Chronkhites' cabin was smaller by four feet in both dimensions
(only fourteen by sixteen feet) than the Adairs'. Samuel's quarterly reports to the American Missionary Association contained a veritable cata-
log of the local pioneers' sufferings. Illness, especially chills and fevers,
regularly swept the district. There were deaths due to diseases, drowning,
and childbirth. Disputes over land claims, the struggle to find decent
shelter, and even problems with lack of food were endemic in the early
years. Samuel had been sent to Kansas, in part, to establish a mission

church, but he found it nearly impossible to build a stable congregation among people living in scattered locations, particularly when bad weather often made roads impassable and when many early settlers became disheartened and returned to the East.

The negative side of Kansas frontier life is well illustrated by the case of Florella's nephews, sons of her half brother John. Three of them—Owen, Salmon, and Frederick—arrived at the Adairs' door on April 23, 1855. After a brief stay, they left to establish claims on land along the North Middle Creek branch of the Marais des Cygnes River, some ten miles west of Osawatomie. Despite the impression one might get from the names—Brownsville, Brown's Station, and Fairfield—that the Brown brothers gave the area where their claims were located, the place was in no sense a town, but simply a series of undeveloped farms stretched out along the creek. The loneliness of their situation was diminished only slightly when, in May, five more Browns joined them: John's sons Jason and John Jr., their wives, Ellen and Wealthy, and Wealthy and John Jr.'s mentally retarded boy, a youngster named John Brown III but called Tonny. Jason and Ellen were still distraught over the loss en route of their four-year-old son, Austin, who had caught cholera and died.

Over the next six months things went from bad to worse at Brownsville. Steaming heat and heavy rains in late summer spread fevers through the Browns' ranks. Medical aid was not available, and even if it had been, a doctor's intervention would probably have been of little help, given the primitive state of medicine in that era. By October, when John Brown Sr. arrived, accompanied by another son, Oliver, and a son-in-law, Henry Thompson, the previous Brown migrants were in pathetic shape. Only two of Brownsville's residents were in good health (Wealthy and Tonny), and none of them had had the strength to harvest the family's "Hay, Corn, Beans, or Potatoes." Since the Browns' fields were still unfenced, their cattle were wandering about eating crops the family needed to get through the winter. The only shelters built after half a year in Kansas were log-walled shanties with canvas roofs, and all the Browns—sick and healthy alike—were, as John Sr. observed, "exposed to the dreadfully cutting Winds Morning and Evening."[14]

Added to these hardships, which were perhaps no worse than those faced by pioneers on any nineteenth-century American frontier, was an ominous reality peculiar to Kansas: warfare between antislavery and proslavery settlers. Tension ran high because under the principle of popular sovereignty the future of the territory was to be decided by oneself and one's neighbors rather than by legislators in faraway Washington, D.C. When an election was held in late March 1855, the proslavery vote exceeded the free-state vote 5,427 to 797, enabling the proslavery faction to capture most of the seats in the territorial legislature. But since there were fewer than 3,000 voters registered in Kansas, free-staters immediately charged that the much higher proslavery vote had been obtained through widespread fraudulent voting by Missourians who had crossed into Kansas on election day. Antislavery men, therefore, refused to participate in the new legislature, and they set up their own, separate free-state government. In the same period, late 1855, border warfare broke out between antislavery and proslavery settlers, the latter's numbers augmented by Missourians whom the free-staters scornfully called Border Ruffians.

By early 1856 two competing territorial governments existed in Kansas, one favoring and the other opposing slavery. Both legislatures claimed to be legitimate, a fact that sparked a bitter debate nationally over which of the rival governments Congress should recognize. Throughout Kansas there were sporadic outbursts of violence between individual settlers that left six free-staters dead, according to figures compiled by John Brown. During April the proslavery legislature took steps to enforce its laws, including the collection of taxes from all settlers in the Osawato-

John Brown in
Kansas, 1856.

mie area, thus adding legal pressure to the forcible intimidation already being employed to drive free-state sympathizers from their claims. For the Adairs—missionaries to the antislavery settlers and relatives of the Browns who were becoming known as advocates of armed resistance to the proslavery authorities—the tension was almost unbearable. By May 16, 1856, Florella was writing her sister Martha Davis, "You ask in one of your letters if we have any fear for our lives. I think now we are constantly exposed and we have almost no protection."[15]

Less than a week after Florella penned these lines, a chain of events began to unfold that gave terrible meaning to the contemporary epithet "Bleeding Kansas." On May 21, companies of armed proslavery men stormed through Lawrence, a stronghold of free-state sentiment, sacking the town and destroying much property, but taking no lives. Florella's brother John, furious at the failure of free-state resistance and apparently fearful that the raiders' success would embolden them to engage in further depredations, struck back. On the night of May 24–25 he led six men (including three of his sons—Frederick, Owen, and Salmon—and his son-in-law, Henry Thompson) into bottomlands near Pottawatomie Creek. There, over a period of roughly three hours, Brown's party dragged five proslavery men from their cabins and hacked them to death with broadswords. This incident became known as the Pottawatomie Massacre. Early in June proslavery sympathizers retaliated, destroying everything at Brownsville and sacking Osawatomie, taking no lives but looting free-staters' homes and driving off their stock.

The Adair household was kept in a state of turmoil by the events of late May and early June. Two of Florella's nephews, Jason and John Jr., had not participated in the Pottawatomie slayings; nonetheless, as John Brown's sons they became hunted men. For a time, therefore, the two brothers hid out at the Adairs' cabin. Knowing that Brownsville was no longer safe, the brothers' wives, Ellen and Wealthy (with Wealthy's son Tonny in tow), also sought refuge with the Adairs, "the only friends we had in that part of Kansas," as Jason later recalled.[16] Afraid of endangering their loved ones by being under the same roof, Jason and John Jr. soon fled. Both were captured shortly thereafter by proslavery sympathizers who, though tempted to string up old Brown's sons, turned them over to the authorities.

Despite widely circulated reports that the Browns were responsible for the Pottawatomie murders, their closest relatives were not sure what to believe. Immediately after the incident, Samuel Adair wrote to Brown in-laws in Ohio, "There is much reason to believe that John B. Sen. & sons —J-jun. & Jason excepted— . . . were with the company that did the deed." Florella, however, resisted this conclusion. According to oral tradition among her descendants, Florella asked her brother whether he had murdered the men, and John denied it—true enough in the narrow sense that he had not personally struck any of the fatal blows. Perhaps the words he used in answering Florella's question were like those he used when his son Jason had asked, "Did you have anything to do with the killing of those men on Pottawatomie Creek?" John had replied, "I did not do it, but I approved of it."[17]

Many free-staters in the Osawatomie area, Samuel Adair included, had mixed feelings about the Pottawatomie Massacre. In writing to the AMA's officers (who often published excerpts from his reports in their journal, *American Missionary*), Adair began by condemning the incident as "base, barbarous, and horrible murder." But he immediately went on to argue that the slain men were the worst type of proslaveryites, vicious individuals who had threatened to burn down free-staters' cabins with the occupants inside, if necessary, to fulfill a boast that they would "clear the entire region of the d——d abolitionists." Stories of this sort led James Hanway, a militant free-state homesteader from the Pottawatomie area, to describe the massacre as a much-needed warning that free-staters would defend themselves. Samuel Adair, on hearing that proslavery hardliners had put his name on a "hanging list" of free-state settlers to be killed or driven out of the territory, came close to saying the same thing. "That gun they [proslavery men] have been firing is beginning to kick." Kansas, he concluded, was in a state of war in which "as many pro-slavery men must die as free men are killed by them."[18]

Full-scale civil war raged throughout southeastern Kansas during the summer and fall of 1856, raising repeated alarms in the Adairs' neighborhood. The violence reached a peak late in August. On the twenty-sixth, a large force of armed Missourians crossed into Kansas. Over the next few days John Brown and other free-staters made preparations to defend themselves against the invaders. On the morning of the thirtieth, Frederick Brown, one of John's sons, was coming down the road to the Adairs' cabin when he encountered a band of proslavery men. At the cabin the Adairs heard a shot, and Samuel and an Adair cousin, David Garrison, ran down the road and found Frederick dead from a bullet through the heart. Fearing for their lives, the two cousins fled, Garrison taking off into nearby fields, where he was soon hunted down, shot, and killed. Samuel headed in the opposite direction (into the brushy woods along the Marais des Cygnes), stopping at his cabin just long enough to tell his son Charles to take the family's horse and warn Uncle John and the free-staters in town.

What is known as the Battle of Osawatomie took place later that morning. A contingent of free-staters more or less under John Brown's command clashed with a much larger force of proslavery raiders near Osawatomie. Driven back by superior numbers, Brown's men were unable to prevent the Missourians from burning every building in the central townsite. At this point the Adairs' cabin, located about a mile west of the burning village, remained unscathed. Soon, however, it was approached by a band of mounted Border Ruffians. Florella, seven months pregnant, stepped trembling to the door. Later, in a letter to her sister, she described what happened.

Fifteen or twenty came dashing down to our house and up to the door yelling out who lives here, and where is the man. A sick woman and three little children having fled to us for protection commenced screaming and crying don't kill us, don't burn the house down over us while I stood in the door and begged they would spare our lives and they might have all they could find in the house or on the place. Seeing us frightened almost to death, the Captain said hold on boys there is nobody here but women and children and we are Gentlemen we never abuse women and children, don't be frightened Ladies we won't hurt you, "but if we get the men we will put the rope over their heads mighty quick."[19]

Fearing that she might never see her husband and son alive again, Florella spent the day agonizing over whether they would return. To her great joy, they slipped back to the house that night. The day's toll had been severe, however. Samuel and a neighbor went to gather up Frederick's corpse and brought it back to the Adair cabin. Charles located David Garrison's body in a field where howling wolves were skulking nearby. Three other free-state men had died that day, including George Partridge, a member of Samuel's missionary church.

In the months after the Battle of Osawatomie, the Adairs lived in fear that Border Ruffians would return and do them harm. And these fears were well founded, since the Adairs were not only free-staters but also known to be John Brown's kin. Samuel and Florella took special precautions about their correspondence in this period, for the mails, in their opinion, were unsafe because the postal service was controlled by appointees of a Democratic administration with proslavery sympathies. Such apprehensions led Florella to leave unsigned a letter to her sister that contained a detailed description of the events of August 30. Samuel exercised even greater care. For most of the summer, whenever referring to Brown relatives in his letters, he had used initials rather than complete names: "H.T." for Henry Thompson, "F" for Frederick, "J-sen" for Florella's brother John, and so forth. Now he instructed one regular correspondent, "Please drop my last name & address [letters to] *Mr. Samuel Lyle.*"[20] (Lyle was his middle name.) Moreover, in signing letters written in September and October, he used his middle initial only.

Although the Adairs and Osawatomie's other free-state pioneers were spared further armed attacks, their troubles were not over. The late 1850s brought recurrent epidemics, a ruinous depression (the aftermath of the panic of 1857), and a searing drought. The economic and political turmoil affected all aspects of Kansas life, including Samuel's work as a missionary. He had organized a small Christian congregation locally in April 1856 and hoped to build a meetinghouse for his scattered flock. But the odds against the completion of any such building were great. His church never had more than seventeen members, few of whom had any spare cash to contribute to the meetinghouse project. At times Samuel seemed to be building his stone church single-handed. He raised money, supplied walnut lumber from his homestead, and, with Charles's aid, did much of the actual construction work himself, at least before 1860–61, when funds from eastern philanthropists enabled him to hire local craftsmen to help complete the building.

Although Samuel at times felt "crushed down" by events, the meetinghouse project at least gave him a positive outward focus, a solace his wife did not always have. Happily, the child that Florella was carrying the day she faced the proslavery raiders was born safely. Ada (or Addie, as she was nicknamed) thrived, but another daughter, Marion, born in 1859, died in July 1860. Florella was extremely distraught. She blamed herself, since the baby died from a puncture wound it received when, while sitting on Florella's lap, it threw its head against her bosom and struck a needle that Florella (who had been sewing) had pinned in her lapel. That she continued to mourn her little one for many years is apparent from her letters, in which she tells Samuel what Addie said ("she was a very sweet baby and had laughing eyes") or sees a niece who "looks much like our little one . . . except her eyes aren't black," or speaks four years after Marion died of planning to have the hired man plow "near the little grave."[21]

Her baby's death was only the latest of many losses Florella had sustained over the past four years. Her father died on May 8, 1856. Her nephew Frederick was murdered in August 1856. Her brother John's raid on Harpers Ferry ended in his capture (October 18, 1859), trial, and execution (December 2, 1859). Relations between the Adairs and John Brown had not always been easy, especially given John's tendency to consider his needs more important than theirs. In 1856, for example, John had questioned whether Samuel had "distributed *righteously*" the $49.50 that Samuel had received "for the aid of free State men in Kansas." After defending himself against John's complaints, Samuel, who had kept only $7.25 and given the rest to John and John's sons, tartly observed that in financial matters it had often appeared to him "more difficult to give satisfaction where the parties are relatives." Where the antislavery cause was involved, however, Adairs and Browns almost always presented a united front to the world. Florella was fiercely loyal to her brother, and her closest siblings, to judge from statements they made in 1856, were no less supportive of their Kansas kin. Marian Hand: "We all deeply sympathize with you and J and the boys." Martha Davis: "I suppose Brother Adair would say that I had better pray for them [proslavery politicians], but I think with *Beecher* that one *Sharps* Riffel is better than a half dozen *Bibles* for such men." Jeremiah Brown: "My heart and that of my wife & family are full of sympathy for all of you. . . . Oliver says that Brother John went on purpose to fight and it would be a pity to be obliged to come away without having a good chance." No details of Florella's response to John's fate after Harpers Ferry are known, but when she remarked, in a letter to Samuel, "how sad and trying have been these years" (1855–60), John's death was certainly one of the "trials and afflictions" she had in mind. After she had expressed similar feelings to her sister, Marian replied, "I presume you have felt some as I do often, which is a disposition to retire within myself if I could; the family has so often been held up before the public in every form for, and against, that I have felt like shutting myself up at home and not being known."[22]

In August 1860, less than a month after her baby's death, Florella took Charles and her younger daughter (Addie) east to visit Brown relatives. Much that she wrote Samuel while on this trip expressed the reasons why she and many other nineteenth-century women were loath to go west. The day after Florella arrived in Ohio she received an invitation to attend a large gathering at Oberlin, but the prospect of going made her apprehensive. "I feel," she told Samuel, "that with my weak nerves & broken health I am incompetent for the task. I have been so long away from such refined & stilish society that I feel a shrinking from it. Marian thinks I have grown old very fast." A month in the East, however, enabled her to repair some of the damage that living on the frontier had done to her. "My own health," she reported, "is very good now & they say I am beginning to look more as I used to; they are trying to make me look more like civilized folks than we did in Kansas." After two months more in Ohio she wrote Samuel, "You speak as though you thought I ought to be tired of visiting long ago but I have enjoyed myself so well that I hardly recall how the time flys. . . . I came hoping to enjoy the society of my friends once more after so long being shut up in Kansas."[23]

The longer Florella stayed, however, the more it became clear that Samuel was unhappy because she had gone east and even unhappier because she was still there. From Ohio, Florella poured out her heartfelt feelings about Kansas. What had life there done for them? she asked. She had aged rapidly, Charles was "five years behind" boys his age in school, and Samuel was exhausting himself to build a meetinghouse even though drought and border warfare had driven most of his parishioners from town. "The Territory is cursed of the Lord," she exclaimed. ". . . I cannot help feeling perfect disgust for Kansas life, & most of Kansas people." Under these circumstances she found it "very strange" that he wanted her to come back right away. Why, she wondered, "go back to Kansas together & drag out the rest of our days and lay our bones with the rest of our friends on the schorching prairie." But he must not imagine, as he seemed to, that her reluctance to return to Kansas meant that she no longer loved him. She wrote emphatically, "I have never loved my family each member of it, or *my Husband* any better than I do now."[24]

But Samuel, left in Osawatomie with only Emma to keep house for him, could not understand. He had to complete the church building. It was the Lord's work. And how could he explain Florella's absence to neighbors? How could he explain it to himself? All his training at Oberlin—indeed, all conventional thinking about family relations, which put the husband's needs first—dictated that it was Florella's duty to be at home. Besides, her absence awakened old doubts, deep fears he had expressed before they were married, that when the times were darkest, she would abandon him. "Was awake much last night," he wrote in his journal; "thought much about my wife who has been long absent on a visit to her relatives. Expected her back in the fall; but she has not come. I have suffered much on her account."[25]

Florella, Charles, and Addie returned home on the evening of April 26, 1861. Samuel noted in his journal, "All well." While in Ohio, Florella had devoted considerable time and energy to collecting donations for Samuel's church and for needy pioneers in drought-stricken Kansas. She seems not to have made public addresses; it would have been unusual for a woman to have done so in 1861. Even her personal appeals for aid to Kansas placed her in a role that many conventional women of the time would have shunned. Each "calling and begging trip," as she referred to them, consisted of going—often in the company of a female relative (e.g., David Garrison's widow, Rachel, in Yellow Springs, Ohio; Samuel's sister Martha Wallace in the Paint Valley area)—to visit relatives, friends, former neighbors, and even strangers to ask for contributions. Bit by bit —five dollars from a Metcalf relative, forty dollars in Marian Brown Hand's hometown, and more than two hundred dollars in another village —she collected enough to enable Samuel to finish the Osawatomie church building. It was dedicated on July 14, 1861, and stands there yet. Known now as the Old Stone Church, it has a placid limestone facade that belies the difficulties its founders went through to build it.[26]

Any triumph the Adairs felt at completing the meetinghouse was short-lived. The outbreak of the Civil War in 1861 brought many changes, most of them unfavorable, to their lives. During the war years, organizations like the American Missionary Association either faded out or redirected their efforts toward war-related causes. Samuel's stipend as a missionary was cut off, and since his Osawatomie parishioners were too few and too poor to support a minister, he sought work as a military chaplain, first at Fort Scott and later at Fort Leavenworth. Both posts kept him far from Osawatomie, except for occasional brief visits home. Charles enlisted in the army as soon as he was old enough and went off to war. Emma, meanwhile, at her father's insistence, was sent to school in Ohio, entering Oberlin's preparatory department in early 1863. Her departure left Florella back in Osawatomie trying to run the family's small farm. The task proved formidable for Florella because of a variety of problems: her frequent illnesses, the unavailability of hired hands during the war years, and the extra burden of having both indoor and outdoor chores to do. Her only constant companion was Addie, a high-spirited youngster who constantly tried her mother's patience by refusing to mind or do her studies.

The winter of 1864 proved particularly hard for Florella. Although the Adairs had made some improvements in their cabin, it was not the healthiest place to be in cold weather. In January she wrote, "I have never suffered with cold as I have thus far this winter; everything is frozen up hard even to bread & milk in the safe & with a large fire; we keep up large fires all day & night, but every thing freezes up solid from one meal to another. We are all huddled in to my room & eat together and then sleep on the floor before the fire at night."[27] In March, Florella reported that she was very tired and suffering from chills. The chills were soon accompanied by a hard cough. Worried about his wife's health, Samuel rented a small house in Leavenworth, and Florella and Addie joined him there around the first of May. The Adairs had been together in Leavenworth less than a year, however, when Florella's health declined further. Worn down by an arduous life, she died on February 6, 1865, at the age of forty-eight, a casualty (no less than her brother John) of an era of sectional conflict.

JERRY REMINGTON JOINS MR. LINCOLN'S ARMY

The Civil War was America's costliest war. More than 600,000 soldiers (out of a population of approximately 31 million Americans) lost their lives, the largest total of any war before or after. The proportion of casualties to participants was also the highest ever. Moreover, it was one of the country's longest wars; only the American Revolution and the Vietnam War lasted longer. Given the intensity and duration of the struggle between the Union and the Confederacy, it would be a mistake to claim too much for a view of the war years as seen through the

Jerry Remington (1838–1912) formally posing
in his Union Army uniform.

eyes of a single combatant. Still, Benjamin and Sarah Remington's son Jeremiah, a Union officer who served from 1861 to 1865 in the war's eastern theater, was a witness to many of the era's most important events, and his career was profoundly influenced by changes that were taking place in race relations and in methods of mobilization and warfare. But Jerry Remington's experience of the Civil War years involved more than these large matters. At the same time that he was learning a great deal about his country, he was, as we will see, learning still more about himself, his ambitions, his love of taking risks, and his capacity for command.

When the war broke out in April 1861, Jerry Remington was a twenty-year-old senior at Union College in Schenectady, New York. In anticipation of armed conflict, Jerry and about eighty fellow students had already banded together to drill, calling themselves the Union College Zouaves, after the colorfully clad Algerian infantrymen in the French army. Following his graduation, Jerry went home to his family's Genesee Valley farm and kept a close watch on news from the front. Only a few weeks later, after the Confederate victory at Bull Run (July 21) made it plain that the war would not end quickly, Jerry decided it was time to answer President Lincoln's call to arms and enlisted in the Eighty-ninth Regiment of New York Volunteers. In his readiness to go to war, he exemplified the martial spirit of many young Northerners who, during the early phase of mobilization, volunteered enthusiastically and without the incentives (high enlistment bounties) or pressure (fear of the draft) later needed to fill the army's ranks. By mid-October many members of Jerry's unit began to drill together, and toward the end of November they were mustered into service for three-year terms. A week later Jerry received his commission as first lieutenant, Company D, the part of the regiment composed of Rochester men. The very next day the Eighty-ninth entrained for points south.

In January 1862 Remington and his comrades were assigned to an expedition led by General Ambrose E. Burnside, the object of which was to tighten the North's blockade of Confederate overseas trade by capturing portions of the North Carolina coastline. A sixteen-day voyage aboard troop transports brought the Eighty-ninth to Hatteras Inlet, a strategic point on the sandy cape off North Carolina. After several weeks of drill and guard duty, the New Yorkers were transferred to Roanoke Island, where the chief diversions proved to be coping with wood ticks, sand fleas, and gnats and counting the hundreds of black refugees, former slaves, who sought freedom behind Union lines. "One day," Jerry wrote, "there

Now is the time for those who would serve their Country.

THE
CLINTON RIFLES

Having been accepted, as the FIRST REGIMENT, under the new call,

A FEW RECRUITS ARE WANTED
TO FILL UP VACANCIES.

Rations commence as soon as Roll is signed.

The pay of a Soldier is $15 a month, on a discharge $100 Bounty, besides a Land Warrant.

The Uniform is Handsome, well made, and will not drop off after two week's wear.

Come all who would RESCUE our Glorious Union from Rebels and Traitors, and remember the Government needs every Man at the present time.

THE REGIMENT IS ENCAMPED AT THE

FIRST LANDING, STATEN ISLAND,
THE FINEST CAMP GROUND IN THE STATE.

For the whole Union, and may God Speed the Right.

Union recruiting poster, 1861.

came 154 all in one boat; what is to become of them I cant see. Some of them are quite bright and smart. . . ." Whatever else might be said of this flood of refugees, it certainly gives the lie to the southern myth that blacks were happy in the role of slaves. By mid-March, however, Lieutenant Remington was bored with nonmilitary diversions and spoiling for a fight. He finally got his chance on April 19, when the Eighty-ninth participated in a quick raid on South Mills and Camden, North Carolina. Jerry apparently relished his first taste of combat, for afterward he was in high spirits and boastful about his regiment's performance. "We whipped them," he wrote, ". . . routing them completely."[28]

Burnside's expedition made a useful contribution to the Union war effort, but it was a mere sideshow compared with the major Virginia campaigns of early 1862. Union forces under General George B. McClellan were engaged in the so-called Peninsula Campaign, which by mid-May had reached a point only twenty miles east of Richmond, Virginia, the Confederate capital. By early July, however, the Union advance had lost momentum, prompting Lincoln to consider alternative strategies in the East. The eventual result was a massive realignment of Federal forces, including Jerry Remington's Eighty-ninth New York Volunteers. In early July, Jerry and his comrades, together with the rest of Burnside's troops, were shipped out of Roanoke to Newport News, Virginia. There they spent a month poised almost midway between McClellan's Army of the Potomac (camped on the James) and General John Pope's newly formed Army of Virginia on the Rappahannock. On August 1 Lincoln effectively ended the Peninsula Campaign by ordering all the Union armies of the East to concentrate under Pope. But before the consolidation was complete, Confederate forces under Robert E. Lee launched an attack on Pope's army, dealing it a stunning defeat at the Second Battle of Bull Run (August 29–30). Lieutenant Remington, who had not seen action because the Eighty-ninth had been guarding a ford far from the battle site, remained unshaken in his faith that the Union would eventually emerge victorious. A bit flippantly (considering that the North's losses at Bull Run numbered 16,000), he closed a letter written to his parents just after the battle by quoting an old saying: "The darker [the clouds] close over us the brighter must be their breaking."[29]

Events soon thrust Jerry Remington and his comrades into the forefront of Union campaigns in the East. While the Confederates under Lee sought to capitalize on their recent victory by invading Maryland, McClellan, who had once again been placed in command of the Union forces, moved his army in cautious pursuit. At South Mountain and Crampton's Gap (September 14), advance units of McClellan's troops clashed with segments of the Confederate army and emerged victorious. The Eighty-ninth New York, now part of the Ninth Corps, encountered its fiercest action to date while fighting on the Union's left wing. Lieutenant Remington loved every minute of it. Afterward he was ecstatic about his men's "complete success," which was accomplished with "comparatively very slight" losses. "We piled them up in heaps," he crowed, "literally blockading the narrow pass with their dead over which they struggled again and again to pass, each time only to add to the huge pile of mangled bodies."[30]

South Mountain was but a prelude to the battle of Antietam (September 17, 1862). Lee decided to take a stand against McClellan's forces at Sharpsburg, Maryland, along the banks of Antietam Creek. In broad outline, Lee's armies were initially divided, offering the Union command an opportunity for a major victory, but McClellan at first delayed and then attacked in an uncoordinated way, permitting Lee to use his tiny reserves to stave off successive assaults. The battle commenced on the Union right at daybreak, subsiding around eleven in that sector. From midmorning to early afternoon, there was furious, albeit indecisive, fighting in the center. At that point the battle's focus shifted to the Union left.

The Union left was composed of the Ninth Corps, ordinarily Burnside's troops, but with General Jacob D. Cox serving as field commander at Antietam. Jerry Remington and the Eighty-ninth New York were members of the corps' Third Division, under General Isaac P. Rodman. Although these troops had been in assault positions at 7 A.M., it was not until around 10 A.M. that McClellan's attack orders arrived, sending Rodman's division (and the Eighty-ninth New York) to the far left, where they were to ford Antietam Creek and outflank the Confederate right. Inadequate reconnaissance resulted in endless delays, and it was not until around 1 P.M. that Jerry Remington and the rest of the Third Division began wading through the Antietam's waist-high waters at Snavely's Ford. At approximately the same hour, other units of the Ninth Corps finally forced their way across the creek at a point later known as Burnside's Bridge.

The Southerners and Federals now faced each other in very confusing terrain, "a maze of knolls and cornfields."[31] Before they clashed head on, however, there was another delay of nearly two hours because one of the attacking Union divisions had run out of ammunition. The pause was a welcome gift for the Confederates, who were in a desperate position as a result of their having weakened this section of their front earlier to bolster others. Finally, around 3 P.M., the Federal advance resumed.

The next two hours produced some of the hardest fighting Jerry Remington and the Eighty-ninth would ever see. A Confederate private from a unit opposite the New Yorkers when the attack began described its progress:

The Yankees, finding no batteries opposing them, approach closer and closer, cowering down as near the ground as possible, while we keep up a pretty warm fire by file on them. Now they are at the last elevation of rising ground and whenever a head is raised we fire. Now they rise up and make a charge for our fence. Hastily emptying our muskets into their lines, we fled back through the cornfields.

The sights and sounds were frightful, and in the raw terror of the moment a member of Remington's brigade literally saw the scene in red: "As we rose and started, all the fire that had been held back so long was loosed. In a second the air was full of the hiss of bullets and the hurtle of grape-shot. The mental strain was so great that I saw . . . the whole landscape for an instant turned slightly red."

In spite of the heavy fire, the brigade moved forward steadily. Just as the Union advance threatened to rout the Confederates, however, the cumulative effect of delays by the Union command conspired to deprive their troops of victory. Shortly after 4 P.M., Lee's right was reinforced by A. P. Hill's division, which, having made a forced march from Harpers Ferry, now slammed into the Union line just to the left of Rodman's division. Green troops of the Fourth Rhode Island and the Sixteenth Connecticut buckled and ran. Rodman, attempting to rally the fleeing soldiers, was mortally wounded. The neighboring Union regiment, Jerry Remington's Eighty-ninth New York, bore the brunt of the resulting chaos. "Nothing . . . ," Remington wrote later, "saved . . . the entire left from a defeat but the obstinate . . . bravery of a few Regts amongst them I name with pride my own." The Yankees fell back to positions along the creek, but, their momentum broken, they called it quits for the day.[32]

Fighting did not resume the next morning, because Lee ordered his troops to withdraw and McClellan chose not to resume the attack. The Confederate retreat, however, gave the Federals a de facto victory and provided Lincoln, who hoped to win support for the Union cause among antislavery people in Europe, with an occasion for issuing his Preliminary Emancipation Proclamation. It was a conservative measure, one that did not immediately free any of the country's three and a half million slaves. Nevertheless, the proclamation had momentous consequences, for from January 1, 1863, onward, whenever Union armies advanced, the slaves in the newly conquered areas were liberated.

In other respects, however, Antietam's aftermath was far from positive for the North. Lincoln's army had suffered heavy casualties. Fully a fifth of Lieutenant Remington's regiment were dead, missing, or wounded. Even more damaging in the long run was the Union command's failure to exploit the opportunity offered by the Confederate retreat. Under McClellan's direction, the Union pursuit of Lee's battered army proceeded at such a snail's pace that an exasperated Lincoln dismissed McClellan and and placed Burnside in overall command. Many rank-and-file soldiers were dismayed. They shared Jerry Remington's belief that McClellan's ouster was "a bitter blow . . . equal to the loss of 30,000 of his army." Remington and others had grave doubts about Burnside's ability to handle large numbers of troops—doubts that proved well founded when he led a huge Union army to disastrous defeat at Fredericksburg (December 13, 1862). This debacle, coming less than two months after a promising

Burying the dead after Antietam.
From *Frank Leslie's Illustrated News,* October 18, 1862.

beginning at Antietam, was especially disheartening. "Twas the first thing," Jerry Remington admitted, "which ever shook my firm conviction of the ultimate and complete success of our arms."[33]

Lieutenant Remington was not at Fredericksburg, having earlier been taken ill and admitted to a hospital in Georgetown, Virginia. His letters contain no details about his illness beyond a few vague allusions to fever and fatigue. Although he had earlier written, "There is more danger of my killing myself through eating than from the enemies bullets," in the course of the strenuous fall 1862 campaign his weight dropped below his normal 170 pounds, leaving his six-foot frame on the gaunt side. During his nearly three-month-long stay in the hospital, Jerry celebrated his twenty-second birthday. Then, in January 1863, he rejoined his regiment at Newport News, Virginia, where it was spending the winter months in barracks. The regimen there was not demanding. "Some days and often weeks," he reported, "[we] do nothing but sleep, eat, talk, laugh, tell stories, and go to sleep again." He gained weight again, and as he neared 180 pounds he wrote his mother (who was forever worrying that he was not getting enough to eat), "I am very well. In fact too fleshy for the comfort of my clothes." But this period of inactivity, he realized, was simply part of the characteristic rhythm of military life, for as he once put it, soldiers have "nothing at all to do for months and then perhaps make it up in two weeks."[34]

In late March 1863 the Eighty-ninth moved to a new position near Suffolk, Virginia, where it remained for four months. The regiment's assignment was to help prepare defenses against a Confederate attempt to capture Norfolk and Portsmouth. The rebel siege materialized as expected and resulted in occasional sharp skirmishes. Remington and the Eighty-ninth, however, were not directly engaged until April 19, when they were ordered to attack Battery Huger, a major Confederate artillery outpost. Years later one of Jerry's comrades described how the young lieutenant led his men through the critical moments of the assault.

We were ferried over the river on the Gunboat "Stepping Stones" jumping off we scrambled ashore and up the bank. Lieut. Remington ahead shouting "come on Eighty ninth" which we did in a hurry running around till we got fairly in the rear of the work then making a rush our Lieut. still in the lead everybody yelling and the boats whistling; just as we were almost in, the rebels got a big gun, a 24 pounder brought to bear on us, when I saw it I was about 15 feet from its muzzle and it looked by all odds bigger than any 300 pound gun ever made especially when

I saw the Johnnie Gunner pulling the lanyard. Remington was directly in front of me a few feet, and if that gun had gone of[f] you would never have had the Major for a citizen or got this letter. . . . It was a tense half minute. We were inside the work in another minute, Lieut. Remington about the very first if not the very first inside.

Jerry's letters home fairly burst with pride at his performance under fire. "Our Regt.," he wrote, "has again done nobly performing one of the brightest acts of this war by capturing a Reb battery of five guns and 130 prisoners. . . . It was *your boy* who led the charge." The Confederates, discouraged by this and other setbacks, withdrew in late April. Back in camp again and on duty only one day in seven, Jerry cheerily wrote his folks that he was leading "a gay old life . . . not having a thing to do only read, sail [small boats on the inlet], eat rations and sleep on the grass beneath these grand old mulberry trees." The only events to interrupt this regimen came in May, when Remington was promoted to Captain, and in June, when his unit made a hard but uneventful march as part of an unsuccessful attempt to cut Confederate rail lines near Richmond.[35]

In August 1863 the Eighty-ninth shipped out aboard troop transports to join the Union siege of Charleston, South Carolina. For the next five months, Jerry was stationed on Folly Island, where he supervised entrenchment operations. The opposing armies bombarded each other's positions day and night. In spite of this incessant artillery fire, however, Captain Remington was seldom in serious danger, and he improved his free moments by writing home about contemporary political and social developments. One of the most dramatic of these was signaled by the presence among the Northern forces in South Carolina of black regiments, some members of which were former slaves. "Who would have prophesied it?" Jerry exclaimed. "Shurely [sic] they would have called him mad!" But Union manpower shortages and the spirit of the Emancipation Proclamation had opened the way to recruiting black soldiers in 1863. Remington, who earlier had been critical of the North's failure to "stop all this nigger slavery," at last got his wish that the government "come out and prove faith by acts." He estimated that from six to eight black regiments were participating in the siege, and he noted approvingly that the Fifty-fourth Massachusetts, the first black troops to see heavy action, "did well."[36]

Captain Remington also had strong words to say about what he regarded as the North's lack of fighting spirit, evidence of which he detected in the dwindling number of volunteer enlistments from late 1862 onward. In March 1863 Congress passed the First Conscription Act, with the initial draft set for July. As a soldier who had volunteered early, Jerry could scarcely decide which type of "false patriot" disgusted him more: the men who demanded large cash bonuses as inducements to enlist or those who said they supported the war effort but had to be drafted into service. As the date approached for the names of the first draftees to be drawn, he wrote to say how much he wished he could be in Rochester to see the "malingerers" and "poor cowards" of the town "quaking" for fear of being selected. It would also have been fun, he added, to watch wealthy citizens who knew they could avoid conscription by paying the controversial $300 commutation fee (the notorious "rich man's out") make "wry faces" when their names were drawn and they realized they would have to part with that much cash.[37]

Jerry got his first chance to visit home on a furlough in early 1864. By the time he returned to his regiment at the beginning of May, major changes were in the works. The Eighty-ninth was now assigned to the Army of the Potomac in Virginia, with General U. S. Grant in overall command. Heretofore fighting in the eastern theater had produced much bloodshed, but major battles had generally been of short duration (two or three days at most), after which both armies paused to regroup for weeks or even months. Grant, however, intended to use the North's superior manpower and material resources to wear the South down by waging a grueling war of attrition against Lee's army in front of Richmond. What followed—almost continuous combat between two large armies entrenched close to each other—foreshadowed modern trench warfare of the type that produced such appalling carnage in World War I. Grant's strategy, initiated at the Battle of the Wilderness (May 5–6), took a dreadful toll among his troops. In the first five weeks of the offensive, the Army of the Potomac suffered nearly sixty thousand casualties, more men than Lee had in his entire command; yet Grant, after almost no pause, ordered renewed attacks in June near Petersburg.

Captain Remington and his comrades reached the front on May 9, 1864, less than a week after Grant launched his spring offensive. Over the next few weeks the Eighty-ninth was engaged three or four times, but it suffered few losses. At the Battle of Cold Harbor (June 1–3), however, the regiment sustained its worst casualties since Antietam. The fighting in front of Petersburg took an even greater toll. Placed on a schedule of forty-eight hours in the trenches alternating with forty-eight hours at rest, the Eighty-ninth lost men every day it was in the front lines. Early in July the regiment was in the trenches, under fire, for six straight days.

A few weeks earlier, on June 18, Captain Remington was for the first time in nearly three years of service struck by a bullet. There are some discrepancies between what he wrote his parents at the time—"I got a ball in my coat the other day (the first one ever received) but it was partially spent and my coat is a thick padded one so that it did not even bruise me" —and a postwar military proof stating that he was wounded "by gunshot in right groin, causing flesh wound." But both reports indicate that the injury was, at worst, slight. He was not so lucky early in August, however, when he received a serious wound in the left arm near the shoulder joint, having been, as he described it, "hit by one of the enemies sharpshooters while standing in the trenches."[38]

During the two months while Jerry was recuperating in the hospital, his three-year term of duty expired. On his release he decided to leave his old regiment to accept a staff position as an aide to the commander of the Eighteenth Army Corps. A War Department reorganization of several corps, the Eighteenth included, followed, and by December 1864 Remington was working as an aide to General Godfrey Weitzel of the Twenty-fifth Army Corps. The rank-and-file soldiers of the new corps were "colored troops." That General Grant, President Lincoln, and Secretary of War Edwin Stanton visited and reviewed the corps in March 1865 testifies to the important contribution these black soldiers were making to the North's military efforts. "So you see we are of some account," Captain Remington drily observed, "[even] if we are niggers."[39] As a staff officer, he was seldom under fire, but he would later speak with particular pride of the time when he was given command of a detachment of troops that entered Richmond in the war's final weeks and took possession of the Confederate presidential mansion. Brevetted to the rank of major, he remained in Richmond after the South's surrender and served as a mustering-out officer for his corps until, the task completed, he was discharged on June 4, 1866.

Jerry Remington's army years both revealed and helped shape his character. Ambitious, energetic, aggressive, he was at times self-righteous in his judgments of people who did not share his standards and egotistical about his own talents and achievements. During the course of the war, he found that he enjoyed a good fight, that the conditions of battle, during which one's very existence was, as he put it, "held merely by the single thread of apparent chance," appealed to him. As he wrote after one skirmish, "There is an excitement at such times that rouses all a mans good nature." He was cocksure, too, proudly reporting his comrades' opinion that he stood "the rough and tough best of any officer in the Regt.," and adding, "I think them pretty near right." Remington's practical realism could, on occasion, border on cynicism, as when he wrote his father (who was a farmer) that "of all kinds of labor that of the hands gets the least pay. . . . Body and sinew the world over are cheap." Moreover, since it was his expressed hope "to always be able to live comfortably," it was apparent that life as an officer had increased his resolve not to follow in his father's footsteps as a farmer after the war.[40]

Of all the lessons Remington derived from his military career, however, none was more important than the enhancement of his leadership capacities. He both enjoyed being in charge and learned that he was good at it. According to one fellow soldier, even as a young lieutenant Jerry Remington drilled his troops nearly as well as a West Pointer. "He was," this comrade reported, "rather a rigid disciplinarian but withall considerate . . . never swore or blustered around and the boys used to say they would sooner have the Captain jaw them till he got tired than have Lieut. Remington look crossways at them."[41] Four years as an officer reinforced Remington's naturally decisive manner, and habits of command acquired in the rough-and-tumble school of military life provided him with tools he put to good use after leaving Mr. Lincoln's army.

JIM WARD:
NO SOLDIER HE

J im Ward lived in Northern states throughout the Civil War years but did not join the army, opting rather to stay home and farm. He was not, in other words, the type of Northern soldier, politician, or businessman honored by Civil War historians for contributing to the preservation of the Union. Yet if one sets aside such nationalist prejudices and examines the Civil War era from the perspective of all Americans, soldiers and noncombatants alike, Jim Ward comes out being much more typical than Jerry Remington or Charlie Adair, the eager volunteers of 1861 and 1862. That is not to say that by avoiding military service Ward managed to escape the war's effects. On the contrary, it appears that he moved from Illinois to Nebraska in 1864 in large part because the war, in the form of the draft, was threatening to catch up with him. But his move also had roots, as we will see, in circumstances that predated the war, principally in his impoverished youth, a crucial formative experience that explains the inner logic behind all his actions from 1850 to 1865.

In 1850 Jim Ward was thirteen years old and a resident of Greene County, Indiana. His mother had been dead for nine years, and his father, Addison Ward, had died recently. The Ward orphans—Jim, his sister Susannah (age fifteen), and his brother David (eleven)—had been placed in the household of Osborne and Rebecca Harrah, their stepmother's relatives. Meanwhile, their stepmother, Sarah (Harrah) Ward, was living nearby with her parents and caring for her three young sons, Jim's step-brothers.

Jim Ward's dependence on the Harrahs continued for several years. Uncle Osborne and Aunt Becky, as the Ward children called their foster parents, had no children of their own, but they liked youngsters and welcomed the contribution that Jim, a strong teenager, made to the farm chores. Jim had a good relationship with the Harrahs; however, he knew that Osborne Harrah felt no obligation to him beyond providing him with shelter, food, clothing, and work until he came of age. At that point Jim could expect no more help from Uncle Osborne. Once Jim reached his late teens, therefore, he looked for paying work and began to hire out as a hand to local farmers. It was probably through such jobs (or possibly through Methodist church meetings) that he met Sarah Jane Steele, a farmer's daughter from Owen County, the next county north from Greene. Jim and Sarah were married in January 1858. She was twenty-three and he not quite twenty-one.

Whatever one can say about Jim Ward's luck in life, one must con-clude that he was lucky in love. Sarah, mild-mannered and respectful of other people's feelings, provided a good balance to her husband's some-times hot-tempered ways. Through the couple's early years she made the best she could of their relative poverty. Her family, in fact, helped the young marrieds get started in life. For two years Jim and Sarah lived with her parents. John Reeves Ward, their first child, was born on the Steele family homestead in Owen County on December 10, 1858. When Sarah's father died in 1859, she received a small legacy of sheep and a cow, plus a thirty-eight-acre parcel of farmland. It was good, improved farmland, but Jim Ward saw in the inheritance a chance to assert himself by moving on. Perhaps with the Steeles, as he had earlier with the Harrahs, he had felt restive about living, literally, on someone else's turf. In September 1860, therefore, the Wards sold Sarah's thirty-eight acres for $400. Later that month they moved about sixty miles west, settling in Douglas County, Illinois, where Andrew, the Wards' second son, was born in October 1860.

The Civil War broke out less than six months after Andrew's birth, but his father did not join the fight. No direct record of Jim's thoughts on the subject survives, but a good deal can be reliably surmised from his actions and circumstances. For one thing, Douglas County was a part of the North in which support for the war was at best lukewarm. Like many counties in central and southern Illinois, Douglas was Democratic politically and its population included many native Southerners, two conditions that encouraged hostility toward a Republican war waged to crush the South's rebellion. Then, when the Lincoln administration introduced conscription in 1863 because voluntary enlistments were lagging, the already-existing antipathy to the Union cause in Douglas County was heightened further. Not only could one be drafted to fight for a cause one disliked but the conscription system itself was atrociously biased. Under the 1863 law, a draftee was permitted to avoid service simply by paying $300—a boon to richer Northerners but not an option for ordinary folk like Jim Ward who predominated in such downstate Illinois counties as Douglas, counties in which agricultural wealth was generally below average.

If there was little in Douglas County's political and cultural milieu to encourage Jim Ward to risk his neck as a soldier, there was apparently no compelling personal reason for him to do so either. His younger brother, David, had enlisted, and perhaps Jim thought one soldier in the family was enough. In any case Jim Ward, like thousands of other fighting-age men, decided that his family obligations argued against his joining up. The $400 he and Sarah had received for her inherited farmland probably seemed like a sizable sum to a man who had always worked for someone else, but it was not much cash if one hoped to set up as an independent farmer. Farming even then required a hefty initial investment of capital for equipment, seeds, and at least one team of draft animals. When Jim and Sarah reached Illinois, therefore, they rented a farm, a sign of of their relative lack of money. Wartime inflation (prices rose 35 percent in the first two years of war) and their family's size further strained the Wards' resources. They already had two sons, and the number of mouths Jim's labors had to feed was increasing fast. A daughter, Laura, was born in September 1862. Another girl, Martha, arrived in May 1864, but lived only a few days. The next child, a daughter named Sarah Stora Tryphosa (nicknamed Phosa), came along sixteen months later (September 1865).

By the time Phosa was born, the Wards were residents of Nebraska, having left Douglas County late in the summer of 1864. After first backtracking eastward to visit their Ward and Harrah relatives in Greene County and their Steele kin in Owen County, they started west on September 1, 1864. Apparently, there had been some talk of their going to Oregon, but September was too late in the overland travel season to permit them to go much beyond the Missouri River, even had they wanted to do so. The logical place to stop, for the winter and possibly longer, was Johnson County, Nebraska, where they could stay with Susannah and Robert Harrah, Jim's sister and her husband.

It may have been purely coincidental, but probably was not, that Jim Ward left Illinois at precisely the right time to avoid the draft. Prior to September 1864 Illinois had always managed to fill its Civil War enlistment quotas with volunteers, who usually received bounties for signing up. As a general rule the greater the resistance to the draft, the more a local district tried to avoid drafting its reluctant citizens, and consequently the higher the bounties that district was willing to pay men to enlist voluntarily. Bounties in Douglas County were among the highest in the nation, reaching an astonishing average figure of $1,055.76 after the July 1864 call. Obviously, these fat bonuses would have provided Jim Ward, a man of limited means, with a handsome reward for his patriotism, had he wished to follow in the footsteps of his brother, David, and join the army. However, it was just at the moment when a draft in Illinois became inevitable (late August 1864) that Jim emigrated from the state. He was not the only potential draftee to opt for migration. As one student of Illinois and Civil War conscription has observed, "Upon the approach of the drafts in 1864 and 1865, large numbers of able-bodied men left the broad prairies of Illinois for western points," and Nebraska was one of the most popular destinations for such men.[42]

The threat of conscription very likely determined the timing of Jim Ward's departure from Illinois, and it may have influenced his choice of Nebraska as a destination, but there were also positive factors that drew him to that particular place. His sister, Susannah, and her husband were already there, having moved to Johnson County in 1863 in order to take advantage of the Homestead Act passed by Congress a year earlier. Under this legislation settlers could acquire up to 160 acres of federal land at virtually no cost, and the ready availability of such parcels in southeastern Nebraska led to a significant influx of homesteaders like Susannah and Robert Harrah in the war years. Shortly after the Harrahs arrived, they entered a claim for the maximum homestead allotment. Their reports of the ease with which one could obtain a large acreage of good farmland must have fed Jim Ward's desire to go to Nebraska and see for himself.

Unfortunately, Jim's sister, Susannah, died late in September, about the time when Jim and Sarah arrived in Johnson County. The cause of Susannah's death is unknown. However, the fact that she was only twenty-nine and that her seven-month-old daughter had died only ten days earlier suggests that both mother and child succumbed to one of the infectious diseases such as typhoid and cholera that claimed so many victims among settlers made vulnerable by poor diets and substandard housing. The Wards spent the winter of 1864–65 with their Harrah relatives, but Jim made no immediate move to file for a homestead. Possibly, he still had some notions about emigrating to Oregon, although by spring, with Sarah well along in another pregnancy and not inclined to move on, it was not practical to go right away. Also, it may have seemed to him that filing for federal land, which meant putting down roots and dealing with the government, was not the best idea while the Civil War continued and the draft remained a threat.

By the autumn of 1865, however, the war was over and any thoughts Jim had entertained of going farther west had been set aside. An opportunity arose to acquire a farm not far from Robert Harrah's claim. John R. Butler, a homesteader who had paid outright for a 120-acre government parcel, had decided to sell out. Butler's homestead was only a mile southeast of the Harrah farm, but this placed it across the line into Pawnee County. Jim Ward, Robert Harrah, and Robert's brother John examined the Butler property and liked what they saw. Most of it was open prairie, but there was also a narrow band of wooded land along Turkey Creek, a sturdy little stream that ran across the homestead's northeast corner. All Butler wanted was to recover the $175 he had paid the federal government. Jim Ward, however, was still too cash-poor to raise even this modest sum, so his sister's brother-in-law, John Harrah, bought the Butler place, apparently promising to sell it to Jim later. Ward, meanwhile, used his rights under the Homestead Act to file for 120 acres of unclaimed government land contiguous to Butler's farm, both parcels in Section 3, Steinauer Township.

Thus, for filing fees of perhaps fifteen dollars, Jim Ward took the first steps toward obtaining 240 acres, a dreamlike prospect for a man who had owned no land whatsoever during the past four years in Illinois. Of course, to fulfill his dream, Ward would have to remain in Pawnee County for at least five years before he would receive title to his "free" land. Meanwhile, he would need to save enough cash to buy the old Butler place from John Harrah. For a young farmer who had started as deep in debt as he had and who had gambled repeatedly in order to get ahead—taking a chance on marriage, on moving to Illinois, and on going to Nebraska—it probably seemed like a pretty good bet. How Jim Ward's latest gamble worked out is a story that properly belongs in the next chapter, however, with our narrative of the years following the Civil War.

C h a p t e r   F i v e

CHANGES
OF MIND
1 8 6 5 - 1 8 9 2

B etween 1865 and the early 1890s many aspects of the American scene were transformed by swift and often profound changes. In 1865 the Plains Indians, notably the Sioux nation, were still successfully resisting white settlement of the northern Great Plains, but with the Battle of Wounded Knee, in December 1890, the last vestiges of Sioux resistance were crushed. In 1865 an overland journey from New York to California (the trans-Mississippi leg of which was by covered wagon) took months to complete, but the transcontinental railroads built after the Civil War cut the cross-country travel time to less than a week. In 1865 most American industrial goods were produced in small shops with, on the average, only half a dozen or so workers each, but by the 1890s mills and factories with hundreds of workers apiece were common. Technological breakthroughs in the 1870s and 1880s enabled Americans to harness electric power for a wide range of uses—illumination of streets and homes, communication via telephone, and transportation on urban trolley systems. In the public sphere the federal government gradually expanded its size and functions to meet the demands of an industrializing society, and in 1890 this growth produced the first billion-dollar federal budget, a magnitude of expenditure that shocked many Americans of the time.

The changed economic and technological conditions of American life were accompanied by a changed national mood. With the collapse of the Confederacy the great struggle over public principles—the morality of slavery and the preservation of the Union—lost its grip on the American mind. In the postwar period the quest for wealth took center stage. A contemporary, the novelist Mark Twain, aptly called the new era the Gilded Age. Fifty years later a literary scholar, Vernon L. Parrington, likened the period to a great barbecue at which Americans pushed and shoved each other in their effort to get the biggest helpings at the feast. Contemporaries and historians alike remarked on how different from the pre-war era things seemed to be. The widespread political corruption of the Grant years, the colossal new fortunes accumulated by the era's leading businessmen, and the abandonment of a short-lived attempt to promote civil rights for blacks all seemed to confirm that Americans now put self-interest ahead of the public interest.

EMMA ADAIR'S
BLACK SILK DRESS

The new age's preoccupation with private and material concerns both reflected and reinforced widespread changes in ideas and in values. The shift from the older focus on reform, idealism, and political ideology to the privatist focus of the postwar period mirrored a broad phenomenon of generational change that expressed itself in matters large and small—including Emma Adair's wish, at age fifteen, for a black silk dress.

Wanting to dress like other girls her age was a normal-enough youthful impulse, but it was one that had no place in the set of values to which Emma's parents, Samuel and Florella Adair, subscribed. The causes to which they had long ago committed their lives—the service of God, community, and abolitionism—required self-sacrifice. From their college days onward they had repudiated wordly dress, interests, and amusements as empty vanities to be avoided and had expressed a readiness—even a desire—to accept personal hardships in order to do God's will.

Their chosen path certainly brought the Adairs many hardships. Shortly after Emma's birth, in 1847, Samuel and Florella moved to Lafayette, Ohio, where from 1849 to 1854 they spent an unhappy sojourn marked by Samuel's frustration over an apparently barren ministry and Florella's grief over the loss of twins born in 1851. In 1854 the Adairs left Ohio for the West; however, unlike many migrants to the Kansas frontier, they were not seeking material advancement for themselves but were going in the service of higher causes: the antislavery crusade and the Christian home-mission movement. Once the Adairs reached Kansas, their ties to the free-state community and their relationship to John Brown exposed them to life-threatening situations. On the morning of the Battle of Osawatomie (August 30, 1856), Emma's cousins Frederick Brown and David Garrison were murdered near the Adair cabin by proslavery raiders. Her father and her brother Charlie were forced to run for their lives, and in the afternoon little Emma stood trembling as her mother stepped to the cabin door to face a party of Border Ruffians and plead with them not to harm the women and children inside. The further sufferings that Emma's family underwent later in the 1850s—the death of her baby sister, Marion, the execution of her uncle John, the drought years, and the failure of her father's pioneer church to thrive—could all be taken as object lessons that those who dedicated themselves to doing the Lord's work were likely to undergo ordeals.

It seems only natural that a child who had shared so many hardships with her family would, in adolescence, display an inclination to seek a few of life's pleasures. Her parents understood this well enough and even tolerated it as a youthful weakness she would outgrow, but they could not help being worried by the thought that any lightness or lack of discipline on Emma's part might become a habit and permanently injure her character. An example of such fears can be found in a letter Florella sent her daughter in December 1860, approximately four months after the mother had gone east to visit her relatives in Ohio. Emma, though only thirteen, had been left in Osawatomie to manage the household for her father. From afar, an anxious mother urged her daughter to beware of two problems that might arise from being so much on her own: backwardness in academic skills and forwardness in social matters. She began by bemoaning the fact that Emma's schooling was already badly behind schedule. "You are now in your fourteenth year," she wrote, "and how very soon you will be what is called a young Lady. It makes me sigh when I think how little disaplin [sic] of mind you seem to have and how backward you are in the most common branches, as well as writing." An even greater concern, however, was that in her absence her daughter's reputation might be compromised by a youthful desire for sociability. Apparently, Emma was sometimes visited by her brother's teenaged boyfriends, most often by Rockwell Brown, the son of one of the town's free-state founders. Although these Browns and the Adairs were not related, they had much in common politically and religiously. Nevertheless, Florella was worried about these unchaperoned visits and urged Emma to discourage Rockwell and his buddies from spending time at the Adair place.

I feel anxious to have you [be] very particular & sircumspect [sic] in your conversation with Rockwell or any young man you may be in company; an[y] thing like familiarity or immodesty in company of boys is always noticed and will lead to remarks or suspicions. It would almost break my heart to have you do any thing, that would lead people to talk about you as they do about Martha Harris.[1]

Her father similarly cautioned Emma against frivolity, warning her against such time-passing activities as "light reading," "foolish talking," and "mere amusement" because they did not nourish true piety. His first concern for her, he once wrote, was for "her soul and spiritual interest." After that came her health and then her education. It was Samuel's cherished hope for Emma to attend Oberlin, where he had experienced his greatest spiritual growth some twenty-five years earlier. In 1863 he took the first step toward that end by sending Emma east to enroll in Oberlin's preparatory department. On the eve of Emma's departure for Ohio, he wrote to advise her to avoid trivial pursuits and to find fulfillment in religion:

There was one thing you said in your letter I have thought about a good deal. In speaking of the surprise party at Mr. Chestnut's you said you did not think so much about parties as you did last winter. Now I am really glad to hear you say so. There is nothing that my soul longs for so much as to see my children become devoted Christians; and I have no hope of their becoming such while they are deeply interested in parties and pleasures. The Spirit of true piety is not nourished or delighted with foolish talking and mere amusement. It wants something better —something pure and wise and good. I would hope too that you have begun to lose the taste you once had for so much light reading, and now begin to look on life as a reality, and endeavor to prepare yourself to perform your part in life in the best possible manner. The first thing is to give your heart wholly [*sic*] to God, and lay your whole plans and aims to do the greatest amount of good in the world you can. This is right, this is wise, and this is the surest, and safest and happiest course any one can take in this world.

As you leave home and go away from your father and mother and brother and sister into a wide and wicked world, and will be exposed to many temptations where you least expect them, remember that while life lasts you will still be borne on the hearts of your father and mother. But what I want you to do more than all is to adopt God as your Father, and Jesus Christ as your Saviour, and the Bible as your guide. And then when far away from home you will always have a Father to come to, a Saviour that can always sympathize with you, succour you, and protect you, and a Guide that will never lead you astray.[2]

Emma enrolled in Oberlin's preparatory course, as her father had wished, in April 1863, but for most of that year she was not very happy. The demands of academy-level subjects, especially algebra and Latin, intimidated her. She also felt pressured by her parents' wish that she make a public profession of her Christian faith, something she did not yet feel ready to do. She was anxious and suffered from headaches. Moreover, she was often lonesome for her family, writing many times to say that she was "very blue and homesick." She was, after all, only fifteen and a shy country girl away from home on her own for the first time. Her mother (writing from Osawatomie to Samuel, who was in Leavenworth) sympathetically observed that their daughter "hardly knows how she is to do all that is expected of her." Samuel did his best to encourage Emma, who was, as he said, "now located in the very school where [he had] long desired to have her." He wrote Florella to say that he had put himself on a schedule of sending Emma a letter every Monday and Thursday. "I think it will pay to do so," he asserted. "She will feel more contented, will study better, [and it will] furnish an opportunity to give her much instruction & advice —strengthen her confidence in me as her friend."[3]

Not wanting Emma to move into an Oberlin College boardinghouse immediately, her father had arranged for her to stay with old friends of his, William and Susan Wright. But Emma found the situation at the Wrights' very unsatisfactory. Her room was small and in poor repair, having a broken window and a stove that did not work well. The Wrights also lived a long way from where her morning classes met, and they were not punctual about rising in time to serve breakfast before she had to leave for school. The food at all meals was plain and uninviting. She could admire people, she wrote, for being economical, especially if the savings went (as some of the Wrights' did) to charitable causes, but cutting corners could be the product of a mean spirit too. She concluded that "Oberlin has certainly changed since Father was here." At another time she burst out, "The people of Oberlin are *very proud* and *conceited,*" a statement probably directed at the Wrights, but one that was sure, regardless of its target, to pain her father, given his affection for the Wrights and for the people of Oberlin as well. Emma soon left the Wrights and found a room in another couple's home. Her aunt, Marian Brown Hand, who lived in a nearby town, defended Emma's decision. The Wrights, she wrote, were kind, but they lived in a "slip shodical and narrow contracted way." Samuel, though initially not very happy about the move, eventually became reconciled to it.[4]

Emma had no sooner settled into her new boarding arrangement than she raised the matter of the silk dress. Actually, her first comment on the subject of clothing was that she had "nothing very nice and good to dress in," to which she immediately added an apology for thinking of spending "the money for dress, when it costs so much to keep me at school." It was not long, however, before she came right out and said that what she wanted was "a black silk dress with a waist as that's the way they're worn a great deal here." Florella, who on her visit to Ohio only three years earlier had felt that her Kansas wardrobe was not adequate for public gatherings at Oberlin, perhaps felt some sympathy for Emma's wish; nevertheless, she and Samuel opposed it. Partly this was a matter of the cost. Given the Adairs' limited financial resources, Emma's desire to buy a new Sunday dress seemed extravagant. As a matter of fact (probably because they were using their own student days at Oberlin as a basis for judging), Samuel and Florella were both shocked at Emma's expenses. But more was involved in the silk dress incident than dollars and cents. To Emma's parents, spiritual and educational considerations always came first, and their daughter's desire for an elegant dress seemed to indicate an inappropriate interest in worldly vanities. Again, however, Emma's aunt Marian rose to her niece's defense. Emma's expenses did not strike her as too high, she wrote, and her desire for something "nice" was natural for girls her age; indeed, Marian cited the example of her daughter Celia, who was, like Emma, "mortified" because she lacked a fashionable dress.[5]

Emma Adair (1848–1924) just before she left for Ohio in 1863.

A. C. Platt,   Oberlin, O.

Despite Emma's complaints about Oberlin and her occasional pursuit of social vanities, she was not in rebellion against her parents' most deeply held values, least of all against their hope that their children become "devoted and sincere Christians." In November 1863 Emma wrote her father that she was thinking daily of "Christ's service." Then, in December, she announced that she was going to "present" herself for membership in Oberlin's Second Congregational Church. In a letter written just before she made her public profession of faith, Emma described her feelings as follows: "I shall not tremble when God is so near, to guide and strengthen those who put their trust in him. O! I can not tell you how happy I am that I have found such a friend; every trial draws me nearer to him, even as sorrow draws earthly friends together. . . ." Emma had been worried that she would have difficulty with questions the minister might raise about her faith, but the actual examination (at which several black women also presented themselves) was rather perfunctory. "None of us said very much, not as much as I supposed we were supposed to," she reported. Her parents, meanwhile, were profoundly pleased by the thought, as Florella put it, that their daughter had found "happiness & peace in trusting Christ as her Saviour."[6]

Things went much better for Emma in 1864. Having been at Oberlin for nearly a year made a world of difference. She was still occasionally homesick and sometimes lapsed into self-pity because she found some academic subjects "distressingly hard," but in general she had gained confidence, friends, and maturity. She proudly wrote her parents, "I have never felt so much energy and determination in getting my lessons and in doing everything else." Her increased self-confidence was evident in March when, after the people with whom she had been boarding left town, she quickly located a new room in the home of the Reverend James H. Fairchild, a theology professor and the very sort of person she would have been shy about approaching a year earlier. Other signs of her growing self-possession worried her parents, however. Her father was disturbed to learn that she had sent a cousin a card game—just the sort of "mere amusement" he had warned her about—for a Christmas gift. "I can releive [sic] your mind on that point," she replied, perhaps a bit too optimistically. It was a "most instructive game" called "Authors" that she had

Emma Adair in Ohio, wearing her much-debated
black silk dress (1864).

learned to play at the Fairchilds'. Samuel, who had inveighed against "foolish talk," quite likely also winced when his daughter used the slang phrase "Aint she a wild cat!" to describe a friend's antics. Moreover, Emma had not lost interest in pretty dresses; indeed, when she reported that her latest acquisition "looks very neat," it was an indication that she was as conscious of clothing styles as ever, if not more so.[7]

Emma's Oberlin sojourn was cut short by her mother's death in February 1865. By the end of the year she and all the surviving members of her family—her father, Charlie, and Addie—were living together again in their log-cabin home on the outskirts of Osawatomie. Thus, at the age of seventeen, Emma was thrust into two demanding new roles: housekeeper for her family and mother substitute for her high-spirited eight-year-old sister, whom even her parents had had trouble handling.

Two years at Oberlin had expanded Emma's universe in small but significant ways, and it was hard to endure the narrower horizons of life in Osawatomie. Under her father's watchful eye she lost her freedom to indulge in an "instructive" game of cards and to tease and romp with girlfriends. Returning to Kansas also meant being back in a log cabin whose deficiencies had led even Emma's long-suffering mother to protest, "[I]t is of no use to try to live year after year without having a comfortable house."[8] But her father had no intention of changing anything. Whenever he managed to save a dollar, he sent it to aid former fugitive slaves living in Canada or some similar cause rather than spending it on his or his family's comfort. Emma had no quarrel with her father's benevolence or his high moral standards or his Christian piety, but she saw no reason why, in an era when the old pre-war causes were fading, her family could not be comfortable as well as pious, pure, and benevolent. After her return to Osawatomie, however, that hope probably seemed beyond reach, and one imagines that Emma sometimes, in one of her few leisure moments, stood at the small window by the cabin's front door and watched people pass by on the road, asking herself whether she was meant to spend the rest of her life in this old log cabin. For a while in the 1860s, it must have seemed that such would be her fate. Then along came Jerry Remington.

JERRY REMINGTON AND EMMA ADAIR: A NEW LIFE TOGETHER

I t in no way diminishes the individuality of such Gilded Age Americans as Jerry Remington and Emma Adair to say that their lives reflected the middle-class ethic of their time. In Jerry Remington's case this was obvious enough from the way he pursued his business career. In Emma's the values of the new age were not so evident until, as we will see, she accepted Jerry's marriage proposal.

At the end of the Civil War two-thirds of the American people, Jerry Remington's father among them, still earned their living as farmers. The percentage of those who, like Jerry, were choosing to enter commerce or industry was growing, however. Many of these new businessmen prospered, in spite of two very severe depressions (1873–77 and 1893–96) and several smaller slumps. By the 1890s the nation's new wealth was most conspicuously concentrated in the hands of two or three thousand millionaires whose names were linked with the era's great growth industries: oil refining (John D. Rockefeller), steel (Andrew Carnegie), railroads (Edward H. Harriman, James J. Hill, and Leland Stanford), and meat-packing (Gustavus Swift and Philip Armour). More numerous and more typical of the Americans who benefited from postwar economic expansion were the middle-class business and professional people like Jerry Remington whose fortunes, while not rivaling those of the great entrepreneurs, certainly enabled them to live very comfortably. In common with most such prosperous businessmen, Remington would have said he was a "self-made man," largely because the phrase implied traits—diligence, initiative, and independence—that he admired. But the term can be misleading, if one fails to keep in mind that Remington and many so-called self-made men received considerable help from friends and relatives in their rise to wealth. Moreover, like many Americans who prospered in the postwar years, Remington benefited both directly and indirectly from the effects of railroad expansion, a building spree that left the nation with four transcontinental lines by the end of 1883 where there had been none in 1865.

Jerry Remington set his sights high. When the Civil War ended, he found for a time that his ambitions were best served by his staying in the army. He had risen to the rank of major, and the pay—nearly $2,000 a year—was, as he observed, "too good a thing for me to leave so long as it lasts." Indeed, by living economically he was able to save $100 nearly every month. Besides, he found being a muster officer responsible for processing discharge papers of Union veterans more appealing than returning home and becoming a farmer. In letters to his family he acknowledged that "farming would no doubt be a safe business," but he had no liking for it or talent at it, at least not according to his wry description of himself as "worthless at milking and husking corn and pretty near as bad at sawing wood."[9]

What Major Remington had in mind for himself became apparent not long after his discharge from the service in the spring of 1866. He wanted to invest his savings, either on his own or in partnership with others, in some business, preferably in such industries as mining or lumbering, where his college engineering training might be useful. During the summer and fall of 1866, he lived with his parents in West Brighton, New York, and investigated the local business scene. By the new year, however, he had decided that good investments, at least those open to a man starting out in the fields that interested him, were more likely to be available in the West. In January 1867, therefore, he left home on a search for business opportunities that took him first to Indianapolis, then to St. Louis, and finally to Kansas City, Missouri, where a Union College classmate of his, H. L. Marvin, was in line to become the city's chief engineer. Marvin was eager to have Remington join his staff, but the appointment could not be made until Marvin took office. Though flattered, Remington was in no mood to wait or to work for anyone else, and he decided to go into business for himself. His best bet, he concluded, was to buy a lumber mill that was for sale in Wyandotte County, Kansas, just a short distance across the state line from Kansas City.

The mill in question was a year-old, steam-driven affair that came complete with seven yoke of work cattle, three new logging wagons, and all the related equipment. The purchase price was set at $4,850, the first $2,000 payable in February 1867. In addition to this sum, Remington also needed at least $600 in ready cash to cover his expenses until his mill started producing income. He was able to meet these demands only because his father sent funds drawn from savings accumulated from the family's farm income and Remington's Civil War army pay. Cash in hand,

Remington closed the deal, confidently expecting that profits from the mill's operation would enable him to pay the balance due ($2,850) over the next twelve months.

Although Remington's confidence in himself almost always proved to be an asset, in this case it was not entirely well founded. He was, after all, a newcomer to the West and to the lumbering business. Moreover, even though he had five years' experience as a military officer, he had none whatsoever in managing a private enterprise, and he underestimated the difficulties ahead. It proved impossible to run the mill continuously. During the 1867–68 season, he had to move his mill three times because the supply of timber at the mill site ran out. Since he had to pay his men and feed his work animals during these shutdowns, each move cost him $500 or more. There were other periods of idleness in July and August when extreme summer heat made work difficult or impossible. He also had to close down operations several times because the wells from which he got water to power his steam machinery dried up. Finally, in both 1867 and 1868 there were weeks when the grasshoppers came in large numbers and threatened to destroy the local farmers' crops. Although the grasshopper problem in the late 1860s was small compared with what happened later, a full-scale locust plague that hit the Plains states in the mid-seventies, the damage to crops was sufficient to force farmers to cut back on building projects and thus to reduce the demand for Remington's lumber.

Remington managed to weather these storms, but only at the cost of subordinating everything to his business. He wrote his parents that he was spending no money on himself. There was no reason, he argued, not to wear his clothes until they were torn and threadbare, since nearly all of his time was spent in the brush at his mill site. As for relaxation, the only diversion he allowed himself was a weekly ride into Kansas City, Missouri, where he picked up his mail and stayed overnight with his friends the Marvins. At the mill itself, he insisted on overseeing every aspect of its operation—setting the daily schedule, purchasing supplies, paying the men, contracting for raw materials, and selling the mill's products. Under constant pressure to keep everything going, he twice literally worked himself sick. In reporting one such illness to Jerry's parents, H. L. Marvin wrote, "You know he is one to take all the responsibilities of his work upon himself which is, of course, a great element of success. [But this time] he had worn himself out at his work. . . . The most he needed was rest."[10]

In the end, Remington prospered. He met his debt payments on time and earned a solid income beyond expenses in 1867 and 1868. The railroad-construction boom of the late 1860s was crucial to his good fortune, as it was more generally to American prosperity in those years. Late in 1867 he received a large order from the Union Pacific, which was buying all the lumber it could get in order to complete the Kansas and Nebraska portions of what was to be the first transcontinental rail line. The following summer another company, the Kansas City and Galveston Railroad, needed materials for a line it was building south from Kansas City to Fort Scott. For just six days' work Remington collected $1,049, and though only a part of that was profit, it showed how fast money could flow in when demand was high. Even in more-ordinary periods, it was not unusual for him to clear $50 daily. This was obviously a huge income compared with that of an ordinary farmer, but cash flow was not the only ingredient of his early success. When things got tight, he knew he could call on his father for extra cash to tide him over, something he did on two occasions during the first year after he bought his mill. Like many self-made men of his time, therefore, he was a beneficiary of fortunate circumstances—a railroad-building boom that was fueled by huge federal government subsidies and support from a family that had the resources to aid him when unforeseen problems threatened his investment.

By the autumn of 1868 Remington's sawmill operation had again exhausted the nearby timber. Faced with the need to make another move,

As the twig is bent: Jerry Remington saved these awards he'd received from his grammar school teacher for diligence and good conduct.

This Certifies, that Jeremiah Remington for diligence and attention to studies, and good conduct in school, merits my approbation and esteem.

G. E. Phillips, Instructor.

he decided to make a big rather than a small change. In January 1869 he purchased a 180-acre parcel (just over half of which was river-bottom property suitable for farming and the rest timberland) on the "upper Osage or Maries [*sic*] Des Cygnes River, about 1 mile above Osawatomie, Kansas." This location was approximately fifty miles south of his old mill site in Wyandotte County. By March 1869 he had moved his mill to his Osawatomie property. In a flurry of activity he had two rough log houses built for himself and his work crews, which by this time consisted of three to six men to cut trees and six others to operate the sawmill. He had also hired a man and a boy to plow and plant his farmland. But his letters from this period—particularly one in which he observed that "this is naturally fine stock country"—indicate that he was considering a completely new line of business. Indeed, he was to act soon after spring floods in 1869 damaged his mill. Typically, he turned a crisis into an opportunity, cutting his losses by selling the mill for less than it had cost him, but in so doing freeing capital for investment in stock raising.[11]

By the time he moved to Osawatomie, Remington was also ready to make major changes in his personal life. He had turned thirty the preceding year (1868), and in the months that followed he had taken a close look at the rough existence he had been leading for nearly eight years. He was not pleased with everything he saw. For one thing, he felt that he had been driving himself too much; after his third bout of illness he concluded that he was working too hard. The pace, he wrote, was "actually killing

This Certifies, that *Jeremiah L. Remington* for diligence and attention to studies, and good conduct in school, merits my approbation and esteem.

G. E. Phillips Instructor.

me by inches." Moreover, he had become "an incessant smoker" of pipes and cigars. Unsure about "how strong a hold the weed had upon" him, he put his willpower to the test and successfully quit smoking early in 1869. Finally, he had become increasingly aware that his rough masculine ways were keeping him "entirely out of the society of ladies."[12]

Remington's phrase "the society of ladies" has a formal ring that reminds us of the drastic differences between mid-nineteenth- and late-twentieth-century attitudes toward male-female relations. The accepted standards of behavior for middle-class adolescents of Remington's time were set forth in the Reverend Harvey Newcomb's popular volumes *How to be a Lady* and *How to be a Man;* like many conscientious parents, Jerry Remington's father gave his preteen son a copy of the latter. In these and other books Newcomb told his youthful audience that relations with members of the opposite sex were to be conducted with "the strictest regard for propriety and delicacy." He admitted that in following this advice one risked seeming "cold," a fault to be avoided, if possible. However, he went on to warn women in particular that giving the opposite impression, that of having "an excessive fondness for the society of gentlemen," was "still more to be avoided."[13]

What was bothering Jerry Remington in 1869 was not the rules for playing this genteel mating game but the fact that he had altogether excluded himself from playing. It had not always been so. Prior to entering Union College in 1859, he had attended the Methodist Seminary and Collegiate Institute in Charlotteville, New York. While there he engaged in at least one quite spirited flirtation, in the course of which he received a Valentine's Day poem composed by his young lady friend, who confessed, "When first I met your lustrous eyes, . . . I felt my heart within me rise." The final verse was no better as poetry, and, more to the point, it definitely would not have won the Reverend Mr. Newcomb's stamp of approval:

> O there's music in that name
> Jerrie Jerrie Remington
> But lovelier, sweeter, dearer far
> Is *Mrs Mrs Remington.*[14]

In the ten years after he left Charlotteville, however, Jerry apparently had little contact with women his age. This was partly the result of his having spent most of that period in all-male settings: Union College, the army, and his logging camp. But it also seems to have been a conscious choice on his part to make financial success his highest priority and to treat finding a wife as a later, perhaps even the last, step in the process of establishing himself as a respected member of the community.

If Jerry's approach seems rather too methodical, it should be remembered that an essential ingredient of manliness, as described in the Reverend Harvey Newcomb's best-selling books, was self-control. Newcomb devoted a full chapter in *How to Be a Man* to the topic "On the Importance of Being Able to Say No." Elsewhere he stated that the will was "the main-spring of the soul" and that putting business before pleasure was the "invariable rule" to be followed. Moreover, although Newcomb emphasized that a good marriage was founded on mutual affection, he asserted that in the earlier stages of courtship, when one was trying to decide whether a given individual would make a suitable mate, one must not let emotions cloud one's thinking. "Keep your feelings entirely under control," he advised. "Suffer them to have no influence upon your judgment." Whether Major Remington's search for a wife met Newcomb's criteria in this respect is unknown, but it is clear that not long after his arrival in Osawatomie he began to seek the society of at least one young woman, even though she was giving him no encouragement. "I am very well," he wrote his sister Maggie, "and a very good boy going to church regularly and often, with all of which the ministers daughter has no interest."[15]

The young woman in question was Emma Adair. In November 1869 it was four years since she had returned from Oberlin and become housekeeper for her family. Even her incomplete course of study gave her an education that was well above average, something Jerry Remington admired. Moreover, she was handsome and capable. We may be sure, therefore, that when Jerry wrote his sister that Samuel Adair's daughter was showing no interest in him he had already set his mind on winning her. Major Remington, not one to fail in a campaign once he knew his objective, soon succeeded. He and Emma were married by her father on May 18, 1870. The bride was twenty-two, the groom thirty-one.

For a couple whose life together was built around the values of family, prosperity, and propriety, it was fitting that they began married life by traveling a thousand miles to West Brighton, New York, to introduce Emma to the major's family. After the newlyweds returned from their eastern trip, they settled into a small frame house Remington had built for his bride on his farm northwest of Osawatomie. Originally, the house had only four rooms: a large dining room with a pantry, a parlor, a small bedroom, and a kitchen. Later, after children had arrived, a two-story wing with more bedrooms was added.

The Remingtons' early years of parenthood brought a mixture of happiness and sorrow. Their first child, Sarah Florilla (always known as Flora), was born in 1872 and would live to an advanced old age, but two years later a second baby, a boy named Bennie for Jerry's father, lived less than two days. Throughout 1874 Emma suffered terribly from facial neuralgia. Then, in the winter of 1875–76, scarlet fever swept through the Osawatomie area, eventually reaching the Remington home. As Flora told the story many years later:

At the first break of day, Papa looked over the side of the bed at me [in a trundle bed] and exclaimed in horror, "she has it." All I remember is that there was a terrible pain in my ears. It seems that the combined wisdom of the elders of the neighborhood said that the only cure would be to apply a freshly killed chicken while it was still warm—which was done. . . . All I can remember was my pity for the chicken, mingled with the pain, and myself crying "Chicky bones, poor chicky bones" till I sobbed myself to sleep.

Major Jeremiah Remington in the early 1890s.

Apparently, Emma's failure to conceive in the two years after Bennie's death convinced the Remingtons that they were not likely to have any more children of their own. They considered adopting a boy and even brought a prospective adoptee home but did not keep him. At about this time, however, Flora's grandfather Remington dreamed that Jerry and Emma would have another child, a daughter. As the family later remembered, the dream went beyond simply prophesying a birth and prescribed future familial obligations for Flora and her younger sister. "She," Flora recalled, "would carry on my father's business, while I would marry and so maintain the family line—a role which each of us has fulfilled." The new baby girl arrived in 1879 and was named Ada. Two more daughters were born in the eighties—Bertha in 1881 and Jessie in 1882.[16]

Not long after Jessie's birth an Ohio relative, Emma's aunt Marian Brown Hand, visited the Remingtons and described her hosts as "seemingly very prosperous." "Mr. Remington," she added, "is engaged largely in stock shipping; [he] owns several large farms from which he is shipping cattle and hogs for the Eastern Market."[17] Jerry Remington was certainly doing well in these years. His real-estate holdings increased from the 180 acres he acquired in January 1869 to approximately 1,100 acres by the early 1890s. Just as his lumber business had been given a timely boost by railroad expansion in the 1860s, the arrival of the Missouri Pacific line at Osawatomie in 1879 enabled him to expand his activities as a stockman and shipper. By 1890 he had built large holding pens on property north of town and was doing a brisk business with ranchers who left their stock at the pens to be fed in preparation for shipment. In 1880 he branched out into finance, helping to found and later becoming president of the Osawatomie State Bank. Finally, toward the end of the 1880s, after almost two decades out of the lumber business, he joined with several partners in opening a retail lumber yard in Osawatomie.

During the 1880s, the decade when Major Remington established himself as a pillar of the community, the town of Osawatomie was still a small village. According to an account written in 1883, the year Aunt Marian stopped by to see the Remingtons, Osawatomie had "two general stores, two groceries, two hardware, one drug and one furniture store, one lumber yard, two hotels, three blacksmith shops, one wagon shop, two churches, and about 600 inhabitants."[18] The population figure was a bit misleading, since it did not include the Remingtons or many other local residents who used Osawatomie as a market town but who lived outside the town limits. Nevertheless, for a man of Major Remington's energy and

Jerry Remington's lumber yard at Osawatomie, Kansas.

talent, it was probably quite easy to become a big fish in such a small pond. An active member of the Grand Army of the Republic (a veterans' group) and of the Republican party, he took an increasing interest in politics. In 1890 he was elected to the Kansas House of Representatives.

Jerry Remington's efforts to promote Osawatomie's economic future through shipping facilities and a new bank were paralleled in the private sphere by his and Emma's efforts to advance their children socially and educationally. Pictures of these youngsters provide indirect testimony to their parents' strong desire that the Remington girls be carefully turned-out young ladies. Moreover, Emma and Jerry were so convinced of the educational value of the 1876 Philadelphia world's fair and its exhibits on art, machinery, foreign countries, and the like that they arranged for Emma to take their four-year-old daughter, Flora, to the fair, although this entailed a round trip of more than two thousand miles. The family subscribed to and greatly enjoyed *Harper's Weekly,* indicating their preference for modern secular publications rather than the missionary journals that Emma's parents had supported so earnestly. Jerry's hand is evident in these choices, but Emma must be credited with playing a crucial role in determining how her daughters dressed, what they read, and where they traveled.

Many aspects of Jerry and Emma Remington's new life together mirrored old patterns from Emma's childhood upbringing. Long prayers

at mealtime, regular church attendance, and prohibitions against dancing and drinking alcohol were the rule in Emma's household just as they
had been in her parents' home. But there was often a subtle shift in the
meaning given these familiar practices. Whereas Emma's parents had
regarded proper social behavior as an expression of one's inner spiritual
goals, an effort to get right with God, Emma viewed propriety as a social
necessity, an effort to get right with one's neighbors. Such distinctions
between Emma's values and her parents' were, however, usually matters
of shades of meaning rather than total contrasts. Moreover, these differences had their origin in the spirit of the 1870s and 1880s, which was vastly
different from the climate of religious and political idealism that had
shaped the thinking of Emma's parents in the 1830s. By placing her faith
in prosperity and propriety, Emma Remington, her husband, and many
other Americans of their generation aligned themselves with the values
of secular progress and middle-class respectability that were triumphant
in post–Civil War America.

THE REVEREND SAMUEL ADAIR'S RELATIVES

D uring his thirty-three years of adult life before 1865, the Reverend
Samuel Adair had repeatedly moved on, geographically and
spiritually. During the next thirty-three years, from his wife's
death in 1865 to his own death in 1898, he remained at a standstill.
Immediately after the Civil War he returned to Osawatomie and resumed
his work as minister to a small Congregational church. That he saw this
phase of his career as largely anticlimactic is strongly suggested by his
failure, after 1865, to make new entries in the journal to which he had
previously confided his innermost thoughts and aspirations. Moreover, it
was all too obvious that the come-outer spirit that had earlier shone so
brightly in himself and his Brown relatives (especially in John Brown and

in John's father, Owen) was nowhere evident in Samuel or his kin after the Civil War. To be sure, the old causes were honored, as in the mid-1870s when Samuel and others raised a monument in memory of free-staters killed at the Battle of Osawatomie in 1856. However, with the exception of helping to establish a state-run insane asylum at Osawatomie in the 1860s, he found no new causes after 1865 to energize his life as political abolitionism and Oberlinite theology had once done. Memories and past events now dominated his life. A man who had been on the cutting edge of things, Samuel Adair now became a bystander.

Samuel's bystander status after 1865 was poignantly reminiscent of the position his father and sister, George and Ann Eliza Adair, had occupied in the 1830s and 1840s. Like his father then, Samuel now stayed home and watched as many of his kinfolk moved on physically or moved away from him ideologically. Like his sister Ann Eliza, Samuel the bystander served as historian and chronicler of changes among his relatives. He collected and saved letters that a century later permit us to reconstruct much that otherwise would have been lost. But in common with his father, Samuel became gradually estranged from some of his relatives, to a degree even from his own children. His daughter Emma chose to put material and social aspirations rather than religious conversion at the center of her married life. His son Charles stayed in Osawatomie and worked the Adair farm, building a frame house adjacent to Samuel's log cabin. On several occasions Charles performed commendable public services (he purchased land for the state asylum in the 1860s and later served as Osawatomie town treasurer), but his life as a simple farmer with little formal education who attended church more dutifully than fervently must have seemed to Samuel a retrogression from the path of high religious and educational purpose he himself had chosen in leaving his Paint Valley home for college. Finally, there was Samuel's youngest, a daughter named Addie, who worried him most of all.

Addie was the child that Florella Brown Adair had been carrying on August 30, 1856, when she stepped to the door of the Adair cabin to face a band of marauding proslavery men. It seems fitting that Addie, born in the midst of tumultuous events, manifested a strong-willed and independent nature from early childhood onward. During the Civil War years the Adairs were scattered—Emma was at Oberlin, Charles in the army, Samuel at Fort Leavenworth, and Addie and her mother at the family's cabin west of Osawatomie. Mother and daughter faced many small hardships, and Addie's resourcefulness in bad times was definitely a comfort to her mother. But Addie's independence had a negative side as well. She was difficult for her mother, or anyone else for that matter, to handle. As a youngster she definitely preferred playing to learning to read. Florella tried to make her daughter sit still and do her lessons, but without much success. Letters from "Pa" at Leavenworth urged Addie to be a good girl and mind her mother, but these injunctions had little effect. Both Samuel and Florella worried that their youngest child would grow up unlettered and undisciplined.

They need not have worried too much about her schooling. As a teenager in the 1870s Addie proved to be a quick learner. Her willfulness, however, remained a problem. Addie was only eight when her mother died and Emma, her seventeen-year-old sister, took charge of her upbringing. In tests of wills between the two Adair girls, Addie generally emerged the winner. That this pattern persisted well into their adult years was evident on the trip they made together to the world's fair in 1876. Emma had her heart set on sight-seeing in New York City, but Addie opposed a stopover there, and so the sisters' party went directly to Philadelphia. Emma was not the only one who had trouble with Addie. In 1870, after Emma's marriage to Jerry Remington left Addie as heir to the housekeep-

The Reverend Samuel Adair in his cabin.

ing chores for her father and brother, a cousin, perhaps foreseeing difficulties, wrote to ask "how Ada enjoys housekeeping." None too well, it seems, for the arrangement did not work out, and Addie was sent off to Miss Emily Metcalf's school in Hudson, Ohio, from which she wrote home an apology. "It seems to me," she observed, "that I am a little better or sweeter tempered than I was when I left home[;] to think now of what I said and did I think I could not have been very pleasant."[19]

In sending his daughter first to Hudson and later to Oberlin, Samuel Adair was vicariously repeating his own educational journeys to those Ohio towns. The prescription seems to have been quite suitable for Addie. Unlike her older sister, who had found her studies very difficult, the high-spirited Addie was not in the least intimidated by such subjects as algebra, geography, and creative writing. Addie liked classical music and studied the piano, a discipline her father approved in hopes that her skills could later be applied to playing church music. And when Addie graduated from Oberlin College in 1877, she fulfilled his cherished dream that one of his children would receive the same Oberlin degree that he and Florella had gotten forty years earlier.

Addie Adair (1856–1906)
about the time she was sent
East.

During the two years when Addie studied at Miss Metcalf's in Hudson, she boarded with her aunt Abi Brown. This aunt was the wife of Jeremiah Root Brown, one of Addie's mother's brothers. In his younger days Jerry Brown had the distinction of being the most financially successful of Owen Brown's sons. Born in 1819, Jerry had attended preparatory school at Oberlin in the mid-1830s, the same years that his sister Florella had been a college student there. Not long after returning to Hudson, Jerry Brown married his next-door neighbor Abi Hinsdale (whose widowed mother soon became Jerry's father's third wife). He built a business as a produce dealer who purchased local agricultural commodities for shipment to the growing urban markets of the time; he was so successful that his brothers, sisters, and even his father turned to him for financial advice and assistance.

Unhappily for Jerry Brown, his fortunes took a turn for the worse in the late 1850s because of a fire that destroyed one of his major investments and because of the "perfect derangement" of financial markets that followed the panic of 1857. He gradually drifted into a feverish and largely unfruitful search for a way to escape the financial instability that had often characterized his brothers' business careers. He first tried, without success, to rebuild his Hudson enterprises. Then, during the Civil War, the Union armies' need for supplies opened fresh opportunities for him. As an agent for the United States Sanitary Commission (a private soldiers-aid society) he ran military commissaries at various locations, including Fort Leavenworth, Kansas, where he and Abi had frequent opportunities to visit his sister and brother-in-law, Samuel and Florella Adair. After the war, however, it was all downhill. Leaving his wife and daughters behind in Hudson, he pursued various businesses, first in northern Ohio and later in Chicago, but met defeat at every turn. He suffered a particularly stunning blow when his outlet for American Fence Company products was destroyed by the Chicago Fire (October 8, 1871), which devastated the Monroe Street district where his offices were located. Although Chicagoans later took great pride in the fact that they swiftly rebuilt their city, Jerry Brown did not benefit from the revival. Hoping to recover his fortunes, he launched a new career as a coal dealer, but he had to abandon this venture when, weary and depressed, he developed tuberculosis. In September 1872, shortly after Addie Adair arrived in Hudson, Jerry left Chicago and returned home.

Neither the homecoming nor the final chapter of Jerry Brown's life was happy. As Abi wrote to Samuel Adair about her husband, "I think he

The Chicago Fire (1871) as it swept through the business district where
Jerry Brown's offices were located.

has been away from home so much that he is weaned, as it were, from us."
Equally unfortunate was Jerry Brown's resentment against Abi because
she refused to let him sell everything, including their Hudson home, and
invest the proceeds in a last-ditch effort to recoup his fortunes. "He is so
anxious to make money that he is almost crazy," she reported, "and every
thing is all my fault." As his tuberculosis grew worse, however, Brown
became convinced that what he needed most of all was to move to a
healthier climate. In the 1870s a growing literature—Charles Nordhoff's
California for Health, Pleasure and Residence (1873) exemplified the
genre—was touting California as an ideal environment for many reasons,
including the climate's beneficial effects on tuberculosis victims. Disre-
garding Abi's protests, Brown went west, arriving in Santa Barbara late
in October 1873. On January 31, 1874, he sent his brother-in-law Samuel
Adair a postcard, written in a shaky hand, in which he asserted, "I am
making a big fight with this rotten old disease, and have the loveliest
Climate in the world to help me." But it was another losing fight. Only
three weeks later, he was dead—a victim of the postwar scramble for
wealth every bit as much as Jerry Remington was a beneficiary of it.[20]

Jerry Brown was not the only or even the first of Adair's in-laws to
reach California. Edward Brown, one of Jerry's younger brothers, had

caught gold fever and gone to California in 1850. Bullheaded, a problem drinker, and a man who spent money he did not have, Edward Brown seemed a living example of the wry nineteenth-century saying that at the place where the Overland Trail divided, the high rollers and treasure seekers turned off for California, while the stable family types took the fork for Oregon. Edward certainly was not a stable family man. He left Ohio for the West only a few months after his marriage, leaving his bride behind but taking the money a brother had given the couple to establish a new home. Over the next four years Edward spent his entire bankroll, and in April 1854, when the prodigal at last decided to come home, he lacked the funds to pay for the return trip. With a helping hand from Brown relatives in Ohio, however, he finally made it back, poorer and only a little wiser.

The next Browns to go to California crossed the Plains on the Overland Trail in 1864. This party consisted of John Brown's widow, Mary, her three daughters, and her son Salmon and his family. Mary Brown's decision to move had been prompted by Salmon's desire to go west, by the fact that her farm at North Elba, New York, was subject to harsh winters, and by a hope that her daughters might have "a chance to do something for themselves in a new country."[21] As the Browns crossed the Plains, rumors reached antislavery circles that Confederate sympathizers had killed John Brown's kin. Although Mary and her family escaped unharmed, the danger was real. After being threatened by Missourians on the trail, the Browns were given an escort of Union soldiers for part of their journey. On arriving in California, Mary and her children first settled at Red Bluff in the upper Sacramento River valley. In 1870 they moved to Humboldt County along the northern coast. Finally, in 1881, Mary and her two eldest daughters moved again, this time to Saratoga (Santa Clara County) in the San Francisco Bay Area.

In 1882 Mary Brown made a transcontinental trip that became a sentimental journey at every step along the way. On the eastbound segment of the trip she stopped at Chicago and received hearty ovations at a large gathering organized by her husband's friends, both black and white. An Indiana physician, hearing that John Brown's widow was in the Midwest, wrote and offered to give her the skeletal remains of Watson, her first-born son (killed at Harpers Ferry), which had come into his possession. Subsequently, he shipped the skeleton to Put-in-Bay, Ohio, where Mary and her stepchildren—John Jr., Jason, Owen, and Ruth—had agreed to meet. With the skeleton and her stepchildren, Mary continued on to North Elba, New York, where Watson's bones were laid to rest beside his father's. On her return trip she visited many places, among them the western Pennsylvania scenes of her childhood and early married years. At Hudson, Ohio, she stayed overnight with Abi Brown, Jerry Brown's widow. After several other stops, including a pilgrimage to the Richfield, Ohio, grave of four children she and John had lost in 1843, she went to Topeka, Kansas, and attended another large reception held in her honor.

Mary Brown's final stop was Osawatomie, Kansas, to visit the Reverend Adair and his family. Her stay provided an occasion for lengthy conversations about the pre–Civil War struggle against slavery in Kansas and elsewhere. Mary told her Adair and Remington hosts how gratified she had been, while traveling across the country, by the reception given her as John Brown's widow. Her tour, however, evoked past rather than present national goals. Despite the cheers that greeted her en route, she symbolized a commitment to black civil rights that most late-nineteenth-century Americans were in the process of repudiating. Blacks had been made citizens by the Fourteenth Amendment (1868) and given the vote by the Fifteenth Amendment, but in 1877 the federal troops that had backed these measures had been withdrawn from the South. Although blacks continued to vote and even to hold office in significant numbers in the South during the 1880s, their situation was deteriorating. In 1896 the United States Supreme Court handed down a decision, *Plessy* v. *Ferguson,* that affirmed the legality of separate facilities for blacks, in effect making segregation the law of the land until the "separate but equal" rule was overturned by *Brown* v. *Board of Education* (1954). Moreover, in the 1890s southerners passed new state constitutions with provisions meant to exclude blacks from voting, a goal that was largely achieved. In Louisiana alone, for instance, the number of blacks registered to vote dropped from 130,344 in 1896 to 1,342 in 1904. Mary Brown did not live to see these racist measures instituted, which she would certainly have condemned. Indeed, with her death in February 1884, less than a year and a half after she returned home from her tour, one more voice that might have been raised against the tragic trend toward legalized racism in America was silenced.

Mary's death did not, of course, end interest in the John Brown story any more than it halted the westward movement of his descendants. Mary's four children who had come to California with her remained there after her death (though Salmon eventually moved to Oregon). Of her four stepchildren, offspring of John's first marriage, three—Jason and Owen

Brown and Ruth Brown Thompson—moved to California in 1884 and 1885. Ruth, the oldest of John Brown's living daughters, arrived in the Los Angeles area on Thanksgiving Day, 1884, accompanied by her husband, two daughters, a son-in-law, and three granddaughters. The Thompsons settled in Pasadena not far from an orange ranch to which a married daughter, Grace Simmons, had moved earlier in the decade. Ruth's brother Jason came next, reaching southern California just after the Thompsons. He almost immediately contracted to buy eighty acres of mountain land north of Pasadena, although he had scarcely a cent to his name. In late 1885 he was joined at his mountain retreat by his brother Owen.

Southern California was a new destination for these Browns, but the motives of the family's late-nineteenth-century migrants were familiar ones. Ancestors of theirs had moved from Dorchester, Massachusetts, to Windsor, Connecticut, in 1635 in search of better pastureland. In 1805 Owen Brown left Connecticut for Ohio in large part because he hoped to better himself economically. Owen's grandsons went to Kansas in 1855 because, as one put it, they knew "of no country where a poor man endowed with a share of common sense & with health, can get a start so easy." Over and over again one heard the same refrain: that the newest frontier had "the best land" that the enthusiastic migrant had ever seen, and that it was the perfect place for a fresh start. So in 1885 Jason and Owen, two of the Browns who had gone to Kansas thirty years earlier, were on the road again, this time for California.[22]

The search for the best poor man's country kept pioneers moving west, but they had more specific reasons for choosing a particular destination. For the Browns who went to California in 1884 and 1885, railroad expansion was the chief influence on where they moved and when. Prior to 1880 southern California's economic growth had been slow, because the region's products—grapes, olives, and citrus fruits—could not reach distant markets. By the mid-1880s, however, two railroads, the Southern Pacific and the Santa Fe, had run tracks into the area. This set off a fierce competition for passengers and freight, and at the peak of the rate wars in the mid-1880s it was possible to travel from Kansas City to Los Angeles for as little as a dollar. Low fares were used to attract settlers as well as tourists. Like the Virginia land barons of the mid-1700s and the owners of Connecticut Reserve townships in early-nineteenth-century Ohio, the railroads had huge inventories of vacant land (received as construction incentives from the federal government) that they were eager to sell.

Owen and Jason Brown in 1887 or 1888 in front of the cabin they built
in the mountains north of Pasadena.

Thousands of easterners were lured west by bargain fares and promotional literature published by the railroads. New towns, many of them
creations of the railroad companies, sprang up everywhere, and old towns
like Los Angeles, which grew from 11,000 inhabitants in 1880 to 50,000 by
1890, were swept along by the boom.

Samuel Adair's Brown relatives arrived in southern California just
as economic growth was gaining momentum. All of these Brown migrants
traveled west by train, their move facilitated by low fares. In addition, at
least one relative, Ruth Thompson's son-in-law John Simmons, benefited
directly from the boom's positive effect on his orange-ranching business.
Simmons's wife's uncles, Jason and Owen Brown, probably went west
with some hopes of profiting from rising land values, but that dream came
to nothing.

Jason and Owen ended up devoting themselves to a project that
celebrated their family's past. When their uncle Samuel Adair had known
them, the brothers had been young freedom fighters in Kansas. Now they
were in their sixties, white-bearded old men bent on establishing a memorial to their father on the mountains north of Pasadena. To this end the
brothers entered a claim under the Timber Culture Act (a federal law

that, like the better-known Homestead Act, permitted individuals to obtain federal land virtually free), and in June 1886 they named a mountain spur east of their claim John Brown's Peak and held a ceremony to dedicate the spot. Over the next two years, Jason and Owen labored to build an access road to the place, but their project was halted, unfinished, by Owen's death from pneumonia in January 1889. Owen was buried on the mountain spur, which today is called simply Brown's Peak. An aunt, Marian Brown Hand, visited the site and wrote her brother-in-law Samuel Adair that it was "a beautiful place."[23] It is worth adding, however, that Marian Brown Hand had also recently taken note of the tendency of the Browns to disperse themselves through migration, a propensity to which her nephew's grave on Brown's Peak bears silent testimony.

While his Brown in-laws and correspondents roamed the country, Samuel Adair stayed home. Indeed, on only one occasion in the post–Civil War period did he venture more than a few miles away from Osawatomie. In 1888 he traveled to Ohio to attend the fiftieth reunion of his Oberlin undergraduate class. This first visit to his home state in more than thirty years apparently agreed with him. He stopped to see Marian Brown Hand, his sister-in-law, in Wellington, Ohio, and told her that he had enjoyed himself more than he had expected. For her part, she observed that "he surely had grown young in a week."[24]

At the age of seventy-seven Adair was no longer a young man, and most of his closest Adair relatives had died since he left Ohio. His father, George Adair, had passed on in 1867. Ann Eliza Adair, his spinster sister and most faithful correspondent, had died in 1872, followed by another sister, Sarah Adair Dick, in 1886. All these Adair kin and yet another sister, Nancy Adair Wallace (who was still living when Samuel visited Ohio in 1888), had continued to live in or near Paint Valley until the day they died. Most of Samuel's closest Adair relatives, therefore, did not share the Brown family's wanderlust. But two exceptions must be noted: Samuel's daughter Addie (a Brown on her mother's side) and his brother Addison.

Addison was fourteen years Samuel's junior and but a little boy when Samuel left home in 1832, with the result that the two were not close in childhood. Both brothers, however, lived well into the 1890s, and for twenty-two of those years they lived only a few hundred miles apart, Samuel in Kansas and Addison in Nebraska. Although they laid eyes on each other only once (1888) in more than forty years, they corresponded regularly from the early 1860s onward.

The first of Addison Adair's four moves came in 1863. For some time he had felt burdened by debts, the $2,100 he owed and on which he occasionally had trouble meeting the annual interest due of 10 percent. He began to dream of selling out and buying cheaper land in the West, a maneuver he rather too optimistically hoped would leave him some cash even after he paid for a new farm. In the early 1860s his wife's father moved to Illinois, and when Mary returned from a visit there with a report that it was "the most butifull [sic] place she ever saw," Addison determined to move. By October he had sold his Paint Valley farm. His father, George Adair, now eighty years old, was inclined to go along if his wife was willing, but according to Ann Eliza, the "Old Lady . . . put down a No Never to that"—another striking instance of a man's being ready to head west, but his wife's not finding the prospect at all attractive.[25]

Over the next three decades the lives of Addison and Mary were a bit like a dance, the back-and-forth movement of their fortunes dictated by various railroad companies. In 1863 Addison bought from the Illinois Central Railroad what he considered a choice piece of land near Odin, Illinois. He was delighted with the deal: good prairie land at only $13 an acre, interest of 6 percent, and the principal not due for six to seven years. In an optimistic mood, Addison wrote his brother Samuel, "I do not want to work so hard here after as I have done here to fore."[26] But it was not to be. As good deals have a way of doing for poor men, Addison's bargain with the Illinois Central turned sour. The usual catalog of frontier problems—sickness, the high cost of getting started, and debts that would not go away—kept him from making his final payment on time, and when, in 1870, the railroad's agent refused to give the Adairs an extension, Addison and Mary sold out and moved with their six children to Nebraska. After renting a farm outside of Columbus for a year, Addison bought a place near Madison (one hundred miles northwest of Omaha) in 1871. The arduous task of breaking the thick prairie sod that covered his half section, lack of capital, bad times caused by the depression of the 1870s, and the locust plagues of the mid-1870s all contributed to keeping the Adair family on poverty row for most of the decade.

In 1879, however, with the Union Pacific plan to build a line into Madison, a railroad again dominated the Adairs' fortunes, only this time

Illinois Central advertisement for land like that purchased by Addison and Mary Adair. From the *Tribune Almanac* (1867).

THE FINEST FARMING LANDS

CORN — COTTON — FRUITS & VEGETABLES

EQUAL TO ANY IN THE WORLD!!!

MAY BE PROCURED

AT FROM $6 TO $12 PER ACRE,

Near Markets, Schools, Railroads, Churches, and all the blessings of Civilization.

1,200,000 Acres in Farms of 40, 80, 120, 160 Acres and upwards, in ILLINOIS, the Garden State of America.

The Illinois Central Railroad Company offer, on LONG CREDIT, the beautiful and fertile PRAIRIE LANDS lying along the whole line of their Railroad, 700 MILES IN LENGTH, upon the most Favorable Terms for enabling Farmers, Manufacturers, Mechanics, and Workingmen, to make for themselves and their families a competency, and a home they can call Their Own.

ILLINOIS

Is about equal in extent to England, with a population of 1,722,666, and a soil capable of supporting 20,000,000. No State in the valley of the Mississippi offers so great an inducement to the settler as the State of Illinois. There is no part of the world where all the conditions of climate and soil so admirably combine to produce those two great staples, CORN and WHEAT.

CLIMATE.

Nowhere can the industrious farmer secure such immediate results from his labor as on these deep, rich, loamy soils, cultivated with so much ease. The climate from the extreme southern part of the State to the Terre Haute, Alton and St. Louis Railroad, a distance of nearly 200 miles, is well adapted to Winter

WHEAT, CORN, COTTON, TOBACCO,

Peaches, Pears, Tomatoes, and every variety of fruit and vegetables are grown in great abundance, from which Chicago and other Northern markets are furnished from four to six weeks earlier than their immediate vicinity.

THE ORDINARY YIELD

of Corn is from 50 to 80 bushels per acre. Cattle, Horses, Mules, Sheep and Hogs are raised here at a small cost, and yield large profits. It is believed that no section of country presents greater inducements for Dairy Farming than the Prairies of Illinois, a branch of farming to which but little attention has been paid, and which must yield sure profitable results.

AGRICULTURAL PRODUCTS.

The Agricultural products of Illinois are greater than those of any other State. The Wheat crop of 1861 was estimated at 35,000,000 bushels, while the Corn crop yields not less than 140,000,000 bushels, besides the crop of Oats, Barley, Rye, Buckwheat, Potatoes, Sweet Potatoes, Pump-

kins, Squashes, Flax, Hemp, Peas, Clover, Cabbage, Beets, Tobacco, Sorghum, Grapes, Peaches, Apples, &c., which go to swell the vast aggregate of production in this fertile region. Over Four Million tons of produce were sent out of Illinois during the past year.

CULTIVATION OF COTTON.

The experiments in Cotton culture are of very great promise. Commencing in latitude 39 deg. 30 min. (see Mattoon on the Branch, and Assumption on the Main Line), the Company owns thousands of acres well adapted to the perfection of this fibre. A settler having a family of young children can turn their youthful labor to a most profitable account in the growth and perfection of this plant.

THE ILLINOIS CENTRAL RAILROAD

Traverses the whole length of the State, from the banks of the Mississippi and Lake Michigan to the Ohio. As its name imports, the Railroad runs through the centre of the State, and on either side of the road along its whole length lie the lands offered for sale.

CITIES, TOWNS, MARKETS, DEPOTS.

There are ninety-eight Depots on the Company's Railway, giving about one every seven miles. Cities, Towns, and Villages are situated at convenient distances throughout the whole route, where every desirable commodity may be found as readily as in the oldest cities of the Union, and where buyers are to be met for all kinds of farm produce.

EDUCATION.

Mechanics and working men will find the free school system encouraged by the State, and endowed with a large revenue for the support of the schools. Children can live in sight of the school, the college, the church, and grow up with the prosperity of the leading State of the Great Western Empire.

For Prices and Terms of Payment,
ADDRESS LAND COMMISSIONER, Ill. Central R. R. Co., Chicago, Ill.

to good effect. Addison and Mary's older boys, now teenagers, earned good wages as members of railroad construction crews, while Addison worked as a carpenter on local projects that had been spurred by the railroad's approach. By 1882 the Adairs were out of debt for the first time in more than two decades, thanks not to farm income but to railroad-related work. Addison and the boys apparently would have been content to continue living in a sod house, as they had been doing since 1872, but Mary had had enough. "Mary thinks," Addison reported, "she cant live in our old house another winter."[27] Addison therefore built Mary the first decent house— a frame dwelling that measured sixteen by twenty feet and had four rooms and a loft—that she had had in at least twenty years. The Adairs' troubles were not entirely over, largely because of bad years caused by the record-breaking winter of 1886–87 and the agricultural depression that followed. By the late 1880s, however, the older Adair boys had given up on farming and had moved to Colorado to work on railroad construction. At their urging, Addison and Mary sold their Madison property in 1892 and headed west again. Addison Adair died five years later at Cripple Creek, Colorado.

In search of professional opportunities, Samuel Adair's daughter Addie took an even more meandering course than her uncle Addison. When she received her degree from Oberlin College in 1877 (thirty-eight years after her mother had received hers), Addie was, for her era, in the rather remarkable position of being a second-generation female college graduate. But this did not solve her problem of what to do after graduation. Traditionally, most American women had been farmers' daughters who were expected to become housekeepers for their fathers and husbands. But Addie belonged to a new generation of better-educated women, many of them town-bred. During the nineteenth century daughters of middle-class families entered the teaching profession in growing numbers, with the result that by the mid-1880s more than 60 percent of the country's schoolteachers were women. Although this trend opened professional careers outside the home to women, the increasing identification of teaching as women's work had serious drawbacks. Women teachers received wages only one-third to one-half as high as those that men got for comparable duties. Moreover, men continued to control the profession administratively. Even in districts where all the teachers were women, the principals were men. Other emerging fields in which most practitioners were women, notably nursing and librarianship, carried a similar stigma of inferiority to the male professions of law and medicine. Nevertheless, what was an intelligent and energetic unmarried woman like Addie Adair to do? Soon after returning to Kansas from Oberlin she applied for and obtained a teaching certificate, and set out on a new career.

For several years thereafter Addie taught in country schools near Osawatomie, but she was a venturesome spirit who soon found home and Kansas too confining. Railroads provided her an avenue of escape. In 1882 she took the Sante Fe west to Las Vegas, New Mexico, a town at the foot of the eastern face of the rugged Sangre de Cristo Mountains. After a year at the Las Vegas school, she returned to Kansas and worked for several terms in Osage City. In the mid-1880s, however, she headed west again, this time via the Southern Pacific Railroad, to take a teaching position at York's Ranch, a remote spot near Clifton in the ranching and copper-mining region of southeastern Arizona. Addie developed a particular fondness for Mrs. York, the ranch owner's wife, and she had great fun playing the piano at sing-alongs in which real-live cowboys were participants. The area's wildness also appealed to her. Still sparsely populated and a territory rather than a state, Arizona was the last American frontier of unsettled land in the lower forty-eight states. Though Addie often left, she kept coming back. After her year at York's Ranch, she went east to teach in Kansas, but in 1890–91 she returned to teach in Clifton (near York's Ranch). Again she went away, this time to a school job at a town near Knoxville, Tennessee. By the end of 1892, however, she was back in Arizona, where, having married, she lived with her husband in a tough railroad and lumber town named Williams.

Addie's father, Samuel Adair, preserved the letters that document the moves his daughter, brother, and Brown relatives made in the post–Civil War years, but his own relation to the new age was ambiguous. Railroads and material progress rather than religion and antislavery politics now commanded the younger generation's attention, as was obvious enough in his own family. The young people were good people in their way, but their way was not his. From his position on the sidelines, Adair must have felt a nagging sense of loss, perhaps even of failure, as he observed the emergence of a new age and ethic that so clearly marked the decline of his own.

JIM WARD AND
HIS SONS

I n 1892, the same year when Addie Adair moved to Williams, Arizona,
three of Jim Ward's sons also arrived in town. How they made their
way there is a story of the brothers' relations with their father and
of their transformation from farm boys into mill hands and railroad men.

When we last spoke of Jim Ward, it was late 1864, and he and his wife,
Sarah, had just reached Nebraska with their three small children. With
help from his sister Susannah's Harrah in-laws, Jim obtained a homestead on Turkey Creek in Pawnee County. There the Wards' household
expanded swiftly, for six more children were born to them between 1865
and 1876. The frame house that Jim and Sarah shared with this large
brood consisted of one twelve-by-fourteen-foot room with a loft, dimensions typical of many frontier cabins. Even after a small shed was added,
living space remained minimal.

Jim Ward rode his sons hard and was not easy to please. Tempers
sometimes flared. Sarah, a self-effacing helpmate and mother, tried to
smooth things over, but her love was not always enough. By the time

Jim and Sarah Ward's
tiny homestead in Pawnee
County, Nebraska.

Andrew, her second son, was fifteen he was restive. One day, after a big row with his father, Andrew stalked off down the road. As he was about to disappear from view, he turned to look back, and seeing his mother beside the house, he waved to her. The watching mother's heart sank, or so she always said later, because she knew then that he had no intention of coming back.

Two family anecdotes provide glimpses of Jim Ward's efforts to develop his Turkey Creek homestead during the family's early years in Nebraska. We know he raised beef cattle because it was a standing joke in the family that he had once brought home a herd that was later found to include a buffalo calf. But relatives also liked to repeat his sister Susannah's statement: "If Jim grew only weeds on his land, he would somehow make money."[28] In 1868 he acquired a 240-acre farm, half of it obtained free from the federal government and the other 120 acres purchased from his sister's brother-in-law, John Harrah. Although county records indicate that Ward remained in debt for most of the 1870s, his mortgage liens were generally small ones, and there was no denying that he had made good progress toward accumulating substantial assets.

Ironically, Ward came through the depression of the 1870s quite well, only to run into financial difficulty when the economy was on the upswing in the early 1880s. According to family reminiscences, he cosigned a note

Jim Ward (1837–1928).

for a neighbor who later defaulted on the loan. Forced to meet a settlement date, Ward had to sell his cattle when the price for beef was low. His subsequent struggle to recoup his losses may be deduced from county records, which show that within an eighteen-month period he made deals that left him with one-third less land and more than twice as much debt as before.

Several factors now came together to convince Ward that his best option was to leave Pawnee County altogether. In the early 1880s huge numbers of new emigrants came pouring into Kansas and Nebraska, especially into the less populous central and western sections. The results of this Kansas-Nebraska fever were readily apparent to Jim Ward and his neighbors. The *Tecumseh Chieftain,* published in nearby Johnson County, reported in October 1882, "Competent judges assert that 50 or more covered emigrant wagons passed through the town yesterday going west. Some idea may be gathered of the immense tide of immigration."[29] A side effect of the boom was rising land values in Pawnee County. The quarter section Jim Ward had bought for $2,100 in 1880 sold for $3,000 only two years later, more than enough to pay Ward's debts and leave him with a tidy profit besides.

Family connections also figured in Ward's decision to sell out. In March 1882 his eldest son, John Reeves Ward, had married a neighbor, Frances (Fannie) Dancy. Later in the year his daughter Phosa married Emmet Baughn. Besides acquiring new in-laws, Jim Ward found himself surrounded by people who shared his itch to move west. John and Fannie wanted to go. Fannie's father, William Dancy, was eager to relocate and so was Phosa's husband, Emmet. These families therefore sold their Pawnee County farms in 1882 and moved west over the winter of 1882–83. Emmet and Phosa Baughn migrated to Lincoln County, Kansas, but the rest of their relatives went to Republic County, just south of the Nebraska border.

The timing was good for a move to Republic County. Although it was barely one hundred miles west of Pawnee, Republic County had only recently begun to fill up with settlers. Republic City, near which the Wards and Dancys settled, was an example of the instant communities that sprang up when railroad construction pushed into new areas. Repub-

John and Fannie Ward:
their wedding picture (1882).

Residence of J. O. Ward in 1886, near Republic City, Kansas.

lic City had not even existed before 1878, when the approach of the Missouri Pacific started a boom. In order to promote the locale, Republic City's founders laid out the town and set aside a twelve-block district where lots were to be given free to anyone who would build on them. The Missouri Pacific's tracks reached the town in 1879, and the community grew swiftly, adding many stores, churches, schools, and houses in the next few years. Jim Ward did his part, using some of his profits from the sale of his Pawnee farm to build a two-story, eight-room house on his land just south of Republic City. For all the house's deficiencies—its second-story porch door opened into space; inside only three downstairs rooms had plaster; and the parlor (ordinarily the focus of Victorian-era material display) was a bare, unfinished room—it must have seemed like a castle to the Wards, and its construction was undoubtedly a proud moment in Jim and Sarah Ward's life.

Railroad-inspired land rushes could provide golden opportunities, but they could also become a town's curse, as Jim Ward's oldest son, John, found out to his regret. The Missouri Pacific line that passed through

Republic City followed the Republican River in a generally northwestward direction. About six miles up the line was a depot at Warwick, a town of about three hundred. In the mid-1880s, the Burlington Railroad began building its east–west line, most of which was to run north of the Kansas-Nebraska border. But when the Burlington surveyors reached a point just above Republic County, they encountered hills. In order to bypass this low range, the Burlington planners decided to dip into Kansas. One logical location for the Kansas bypass was Warwick.

This was the stuff of which dreams of civic greatness were built. Nearby White Rock had languished and Republic City had prospered when the Missouri Pacific bypassed the one and ran through the other. Warwick already had one rail connection, and if one railroad brought good times, two assured a spectacular future, or so the reasoning went. John Ward was so impressed by the possibilities that he quit his job as a rural schoolteacher and moved his family to Warwick in early 1887, taking a job as editor of the town's newspaper, the *Warwick Leader*. The Wards lived in the back of the building that housed the newspaper's office and presses, but this was an improvement in housing quality over the "dugout" where they had been living. John soon was elected to the city council. Suddenly, at age twenty-nine, he was one of Warwick's leading citizens. Excited by the Burlington's approach, many property owners in town took a look at land values and began to hike prices. Perhaps they overdid it; at least some observers thought so when the Burlington's planners chose to ignore Warwick and to establish a depot at Hardy, Nebraska, less than a mile to the north and in plain view of the disappointed Kansans. After only six months as editor of the *Warwick Leader*, John Ward decided he was better off teaching and took a job at Dry Lake School near Republic City.

By early 1889, after two years at Dry Lake, John was restless. His income from teaching was sufficient to support himself, his wife, and four young children, but nearly every payday his father would show up and ask for part of his son's salary. This left John feeling that he would neither get ahead nor get out from under Jim Ward's parental claims as long as he stayed near home. About this time, however, John and Fannie heard glowing reports from friends who had moved to newly opened federal lands near Gordon in northwestern Nebraska. Also, one of John's younger brothers, Joe, had recently turned twenty-one and was talking about leaving home. The brothers therefore decided to emigrate to Gordon and enter claims under the Homestead Act.

John and Fannie Ward's house near Gordon, Nebraska, was a combination of these two typical home types from the treeless West—the dugout and the soddy.

The Wards left Republic City on March 1, 1889, a party of seven: John and Fannie, their four children, and Joe. Bertha, the oldest Ward girl, was only five, but years later she still remembered precisely how the overland trip had begun:

We left Grandfather Dancy's on the morning of March first. There were two wagons, the first was a covered wagon, drawn by a pair of oxen, with two cows tied behind. The second wagon was also drawn by a team of oxen and contained most of our worldly belongings. Uncle Joe Ward drove the second wagon while my father drove the first. We got as far as Byron, Nebraska that day where my father wanted to have some blacksmith work done. We left Byron the next afternoon headed northwest.[30]

The journey, roughly 350 miles, was tedious, but not particularly arduous. Traveling six days a week but (good Methodists that they were) resting on Sundays, the Wards made it to Gordon in a month. For the next week or so they camped in their friends' front yard while John and Joe looked for land.

The brothers may not have noticed it immediately, but eventually they realized that they had made an error common among homesteaders:

they had not gotten there first. Early comers had snapped up the choicest parcels locally, and although plenty of federal land remained available, it was generally of inferior quality. The brothers did the best they could, John filing a claim on 160 acres located ten miles directly south of Gordon and Joe picking a site well to the east of John's.

The brothers immediately set to work building the John Wards a house. It combined features of the two most popular prairie-frontier types, the dugout and the sod house. The north and east walls were solid earth, part of a low hill into which the brothers had dug. The south and west walls, each of which had one window, were made from blocks of prairie sod piled one above another. The door was in the south wall. As was typical in such buildings, the roof was made of sod blocks set on beams. Although this type of structure had the advantage of staying cool on summer days and of holding heat well in winter, its grave deficiencies became all too evident in wet weather, when the rain-soaked roof dripped constantly. The floor was dirt, partly covered with a rag carpet. The four-hole wood stove the family had brought from Kansas served for both cooking and heating. Wood that John had hauled two miles from the Niobrara River was used for winter fuel, but for most of the year the Wards burned cow chips. Bedding was equally basic—ticks filled with straw or dried grass. Fannie did her best to give the place a homey touch by raising houseplants in old tin cans and wooden boxes set on the windowsills.

Joe Ward's claim was far enough away that he could not conveniently stay with the John Wards, so he built his own soddy, a very simple affair, windowless and just big enough to crawl into. Essentially, it was a place to sleep and a shelter from rain. Little is known about Joe Ward's life during the summer of 1889, except that he was a frequent and welcome visitor who helped the John Wards harvest their garden crops. Not long thereafter, however, he was gone, off for Arizona to join his brother Andrew, who now lived in Winslow. One season had been sufficient to convince him that farming a Nebraska homestead was not for him. Like nearly two-thirds of the settlers who sought to take advantage of the Homestead Act, he had filed a claim but had failed to obtain title to his piece of federal land.

John Ward stayed in Nebraska and for a time was able to manage because he had no intention of depending on farming for his livelihood. He sold his oxen (but kept the milk cows) and resumed teaching in the fall of 1889. The only problem was that the school was five miles away from his claim. Since he had no horse, he made the round trip daily on foot. The John Wards' fifth child, Grace, was born that winter. The following fall

Wagon train passing through Topeka,
Kansas (1879).

(1890) John continued teaching at the same place but was able to move his family to a two-room dugout close to the school.

The winter of 1890–91 brought Indian trouble. Throughout the fall there had been increasing tension between Indians and whites on the sod-house frontier. Emboldened by a resurgence of a religious revival known as the Ghost Dance, traditionalist Indians had begun to drift away from reservations in large numbers. A few went to war. Although the Wards tried to comfort themselves with the thought that the main scene of these troubles was in South Dakota, the sobering truth was that the Pine Ridge Reservation, where several major incidents occurred, was only twenty-three miles north of the Wards' homestead. The Wards and their neighbors were understandably anxious, therefore. They designated one of the larger houses locally to serve as a fort in case of Indian attack and sent at least one of the local men to Gordon every day to gather news of the Ghost Dance War. Several incidents fed the Wards' apprehensions. On one occasion a small number of Indian braves passed the Wards' place on the road, and on another the Ward children, while standing on their dugout's roof, saw smoke rising from fires on the horizon to the north. By that point, however, the danger was very nearly over. On December 15, Indian police had killed the great Sioux chief Sitting Bull, who was feared

Covered wagon of the type John and Fannie Ward used in moving their family from Kansas to Nebraska.

by the whites as a symbol of Indian resistance. Two weeks later, at a site only thirty miles from the Wards' homestead (and about the time the Ward kids saw the smoke off to the north), members of the Seventh U.S. Cavalry, including some veterans of the Battle of Little Big Horn, massacred more than two hundred Sioux men, women, and children in what the whites later called the Battle of Wounded Knee.

The next fall, 1891, the Wards' sixth child, a daughter named Rose, was born, and John began teaching at a sod schoolhouse that had just been built a mile and a half north of his homestead. His two oldest children, Orie and Bertha, were in his class. Before the term was far advanced, however, an all-too-commonplace frontier tragedy struck. Typhoid fever swept the district. Family after family lost members, and all the Ward children except Rose, the baby, were sick. Bertha and Grace had particularly severe cases but recovered by early November.

About that time John Ward came down with typhoid. His case was so bad that the doctor who was treating him (and who had been taking Fannie's letters to the post office for her) wrote John's and Fannie's fathers, Jim Ward and William Dancy, and urged them to come to Gordon. Toward the end of November they made the trip by train. Fannie saw the doctor's carriage turn in the gate and went to the door. There, to her astonishment, stood Jim Ward with the doctor just behind him. She

The close quarters inside a typical covered wagon.

turned to see her husband's reaction to his father's arrival, having not yet realized that her father was there too. When William Dancy put his hand on her shoulder, she turned and exclaimed "Oh Pa!" and threw her arms around his neck and wept.[31]

Jim Ward stayed only a few days. He apparently feared for his own health and was not completely convinced by the doctor's judgment that his son was fatally ill. Just before Jim Ward left he told his son, "Don't expect any help from me." After his father had gone, John sobbed, "I never asked him for any help."[32]

John Ward lived less than a week longer. On the night of December 7 (Fannie's birthday), the Ward children were awakened by their mother screaming, "Oh, John!" Their father was dead. Thus John Ward's homesteading venture ended, and his wife, Fannie, was forced to accept her father's offer to bring her six children back to live with her parents in Republic, Kansas.[33]

On reaching Republic just before Christmas, Fannie learned that her father-in-law, Jim Ward, was ill. He thought he had caught typhoid in Gordon, but some relatives and neighbors believed the grippe (as flu was called in those days) had laid him low. Fannie felt resentment toward her father-in-law for not having stayed at his son's side to the end, but she and her children remained very fond of Grandma Ward, as they called Sarah Ward. It was a great shock, therefore, when they received word one morning in February 1892 that Grandma Ward had died of a heart attack the preceding night.

His wife's death left Jim Ward practically alone in his eight-room house. All four of his daughters were married. Three of his sons—Andrew, Joe, and Fletcher—had gone to live in Arizona. Only his youngest boy, Burch, then fifteen, was still at home. When Jim at last recovered from his long illness, he discovered that it had left him with lame legs, which hindered his farmwork. In mid-1892, therefore, he made a quick decision to sell his farm in Republic and went to live with his daughter Phosa Baughn in Lincoln County, Kansas. Burch stayed in school about a year before heading off to join his brothers in the Southwest. Like so many farm boys who abandoned agricultural pursuits for industrial jobs in the late nineteenth century, Jim Ward's four surviving sons became mill hands and railroad workers. Of the four only Joe ever returned to farming. More to the point of our story, however, Joe and his brothers were now residents of Williams, Arizona, the railroad town to which Tom Fleming had recently brought his bride, Addie Adair.

C h a p t e r   S i x

JOE AND

FLORA WARD:

ON TO

CALIFORNIA

A s is true of many love stories, there might have been no romance between Joe Ward and Flora Remington had they not met in just the right place at just the right time. Both were midwesterners, but had they met in Flora's hometown of Osawatomie, Kansas, it is unlikely (for reasons we will soon describe) that any attachment would have formed between them. However, their paths crossed instead in Arizona Territory, in circumstances that facilitated the growth of their friendship. Friendship led to marriage, and marriage eventually led to the birth (in Santa Monica, California, in 1900) of a daughter named Marguerite, who was the first descendant of the combined families treated here to be born on the Pacific Coast.

Addie Adair was the intermediary without whom Joe Ward and Flora Remington would not have met. Addie was Flora's aunt, Emma Remington's younger sister. Somewhere in her travels in the Southwest and Midwest, Addie acquired a handsome admirer, Tom Fleming. Tom was thirty-five and Addie just one day short of thirty-six in November 1892 when they were married at the Adair family cabin outside of Osawatomie by Addie's father, the Reverend Samuel Adair. Immediately thereafter the Flemings left for Williams, Arizona, where Tom had recently bought an interest in a general merchandise store.

Williams was a railroad town in north-central Arizona. As was typical of ranching frontiers, the surrounding countryside was sparsely settled. Williams itself was of recent vintage. As late as September 1881 the future townsite probably had only one resident, but the following year, after construction crews for the Atlantic and Pacific Railroad had completed tracks to Williams, the local population began to increase. Even then, however, growth was slow, largely because the townsite lacked a water source that was dependable during the annual nine months of dry weather. By 1884 there were still only thirty-five residents of the town proper, although another two hundred or more people on nearby ranches used Williams as a postal address.

In the decade between the railroad's arrival and Addie Adair Fleming's move to Williams in 1892, the settlement acquired a reputation as an unsavory, wide-open frontier town—a notoriety apparently well deserved. It was not just that civilizing influences like churches were absent prior to 1890 but that a lawless fringe element went largely unchecked. According to the town's historian, "The railroad construction workers were followed by the usual run of gamblers, saloon keepers, and prostitutes." Armed robberies were commonplace, and there were several sensational murders in or near the town. Moreover, some Chinese who had followed the construction crews stayed on to run laundries and, ample evidence indicates, to operate "hop" or opium dens. A paper in a neighboring town, commenting on crime and violence in early-day Williams, judged the place one of the worst examples of its type.

Tom Fleming's store in Williams,
Arizona, about 1900.

From the continued reports of the perpetration of crimes, that come from Williams, we are led to think that our sister town is infested by some very lawless and desperate characters, as for nearly every week during the past few months she has furnished some highly sensational occurrences, and her reputation for arrests and shooting affrays, for so small a place, will exceed that of any town in the Territory.[1]

The restless and transient sorts—railroad construction workers, cowboys, and gamblers—who caused much of the trouble remained a significant factor in Williams well into the 1890s. Their hold locally, however, was eventually challenged, as the town developed institutions and attracted settlers committed to a more orderly community life. The Williams branch of Harvey House, a restaurant chain whose outlets adjoined railroad depots, was established in 1887. The first church in town, a Methodist one, was built in 1891. In the same year Clark and Adams, a big lumber company, opened a mill at Williams. The managers of this and other mills in town soon joined with small businessmen such as Tom Fleming and organized to make Williams a safer, more decent place to live. To that end, the town's respectables sponsored a drive to incorporate Williams in 1895. Tom Fleming backed the move, and when he and his allies prevailed at the ballot box in October, Fleming was named city clerk

Flora Remington (1872–1967) in November 1881, at age nine and a half.

and treasurer of the newly incorporated town. The pro-incorporation forces immediately took steps to consolidate their victory by passing an ordinance that required saloons, gambling houses, traveling salesmen, and the opera house to pay high license fees for the privilege of doing business locally. This was too much, too soon. Defenders of inexpensive fun (drinking, gambling, and vaudeville) counterattacked and successfully blocked incorporation with a court injunction. For a while yet the area north of the railroad tracks remained a saloon and bawdy-house district into which respectable women like Addie Adair Fleming and her niece Flora Remington would not venture.

Flora Remington, as was noted earlier, was born in 1872, the first child of Jerry and Emma Remington. Although she grew up with greater material abundance than did her mother and aunt (there was always plenty of money for pretty dresses for Flora and always an extra horse available to ride to school), the Remingtons' new gentility did not lead to any relaxation in moral principles. On the contrary, their principles were every bit as starchy as the major's dress collars and his daughters' white shirtwaists. Major Remington never joined a church, but he believed in attending one regularly (and in any case his wife, the daughter of a Congregational minister, would not have had it otherwise). Every Sunday, therefore, excepting only those when the Marais des Cygnes was at flood stage, the Remingtons forded the river and attended church and Sunday school in Osawatomie. Major Remington had given up tobacco before he and Emma Adair were married, and they raised their daughters to disdain smoking, drinking, and dancing and to have as little as possible to do with people who indulged in such vices. Emma Remington also instilled in her daughters a respect for telling the truth. When, for example, a neighbor dropped in and excused a white lie with the phrase "but of course we have to live," Emma, as her daughter recalled, "did not urge [the woman] to stay and as soon as she was gone said to us girls, 'Well, WE do not have to live, but we do have to be honest."[2] Consistent with her parents' values, Flora sought to associate herself with good deeds and worthy causes, and we thus find that in the year after her twentieth birthday the local newspaper was reporting that she had attended a young people's Christian education meeting and given a recitation at the local Women's Christian Temperance Union meeting.

Flora had a serious bout with scarlet fever at the age of four. Almost every year thereafter she missed from several days to a week or more of school because of recurrent earaches. In her teens and twenties she was often ill, suffering from (among other things) a delicate stomach and splitting headaches that she called neuralgia. Troubles of this sort continued to plague her throughout her life, leading one neighbor who remembered her from the early 1900s to describe her as an "invalid."[3] Family experiences reinforced her anxieties about health. Her sister Bertha died when in her late teens. Also, their mother had chronic health problems, and in this and many other respects Emma Remington was a role model for her daughter.

Both of Flora's parents valued educational achievements. Even before Flora entered school, her mother had drilled her in the three Rs. However, because Emma herself was not very good in arithmetic, Flora received only limited tutoring in mathematics and never developed much interest in the subject. Her father worried that Flora and her sisters would be shortchanged by the nearby country schools, and, not being one to leave such matters to chance, he lobbied successfully to require that the local county school district hire college-educated teachers.

When Flora was nineteen, she was sent to Washburn College in Topeka, Kansas. Her father, then serving his first term in the state legislature, was near at hand and thus able to keep a close watch on his daughter's progress. Her first year went well. She had always admired her father's artistic abilities and had tried to emulate him. Pencil sketches she did in her high school art class showed promise, and this artistic sense was further reflected in the specimens of common Kansas weeds and flowers that she collected for her college botany class. Mounted on art paper and labeled in careful script—*Viola palmata, Physalis Philadelphia, Galium aparine*—these specimens remain handsome objects today. But during Flora's second year, accidents and illness undermined her work. In returning to school in January 1892 after spending the holidays at home, she sprained her ankle and had to hobble about with a crutch. Then she came down with a severe case of the flu and was more or less ill for months. When she came home for summer vacation in 1892, she was no longer sure that she wanted to return to Washburn for another term.

Like her aunt Addie fifteen years earlier, Flora had a problem deciding what to do. There would perhaps have been no problem if she had had immediate prospects of marrying, but she had none. Again, as Addie had done, Flora assumed that schoolteaching was the most suitable employment for a young woman of good education and respectable background.

As it happened, however, Flora never got beyond applying for a license. Even before she could do so, her father suggested that she spend a summer working in the office at his lumberyard. The office manager taught Flora how to use one of the newfangled mechanical writing machines called typewriters. Flora, however, considered the work temporary and was about to seek a teaching job when her father came up with another alternative. He had been reelected for a third term in the legislature and wanted Flora to come to Topeka as his secretary-assistant. When the legislature opened in 1895, therefore, off they went.

The preceding session had been a stormy one, highlighted in the lower house by the so-called legislative war between Populists, who represented drought-ridden and depressed western counties, and conservative Republicans like Major Remington, many of whom were from eastern Kansas. The Populists initiated the controversy by challenging election returns in several closely contested districts that had provided the GOP

Republican State Representatives looking through the door they smashed through in capturing the House of Chambers during the Kansas legislative war (1893).

with a slim majority in state house seats. This legal and constitutional debate soon escalated into a struggle for actual physical control of the house chambers. Populists deputized rifle-toting supporters who took possession of the hall, but shortly thereafter the Republicans tricked their rivals into leaving the room, smashed the chamber's locked doors, and rushed triumphantly inside. Fear that bloodshed might ensue finally led the Populists to allow the Republicans to organize the house, and among the leaders chosen for the 1893 session was Major Remington, named chairman of the House Ways and Means Committee. Two years later the situation was entirely different, with relative tranquillity assured by the GOP's comfortable majority in the house. This may explain why Flora's memoirs are silent on the subject of political events during her tenure as her father's secretary and legislative assistant. Instead, she simply recorded how excited she was at making her "first big money" and at having her own bank account with several hundred dollars in it.[4]

Flora had still not decided what she would eventually do with herself, but later in 1895 an opportunity arose from another family source. Her Aunt Addie had visited Osawatomie in the fall of 1894 in order to present her father with her first child, a son named George Adair Fleming in honor of her father's father. Apparently, Addie sized up her niece's career problem with a sympathetic eye, and about six months after Addie re-

Flora Remington working behind the postbox barricade her uncle Tom Fleming built for her in his Williams, Arizona store.

turned to Williams she sent Flora the offer of a job. Addie's husband, Tom Fleming, had bought a general store and also acquired a post office franchise. (The previous licensee may have been glad to relinquish the privilege after a January 1895 incident in which burglars, intending to dynamite the post office safe, set too large a charge and blew up most of the building along with the safe.) Flora's uncle needed someone to run the post office for him. Why not Flora?

Flora's trip west in early July 1895 was her first long journey out of state by herself. She enjoyed the train ride, but Williams itself proved something of a shock to Jerry and Emma Remington's very proper daughter. "My first impression of the town," she wrote later, "was [of a street] mostly lined with business houses and hotels, and at least every third one was marked in big letters SALOON. At that time Kansas was under prohibition, and the difference in appearance was most striking."[5] In nearly three years as a Williams resident, Flora never became comfortable with the town's wilder side. On the whole, however, her situation was a protected one. For her first few weeks in Williams, she helped Addie care for a newborn daughter named Marjorie. Even after she began working in the post office, she kept on living with the Flemings on the southernmost (i.e., safest) edge of town. Moreover, her uncle Tom made the post office into something of a sanctuary for her by constructing a floor-to-ceiling wall of post boxes to shield her from customers and others, including drunken cowboys who sometimes wandered in, who might make improper advances.

The label on one box in this protective wall caught Flora's eye because it bore not one but four names: A. J. Ward, J. A. Ward, W. F. Ward, and J. B. Ward. It amused her that there were so many *J* initials in the names. She and her uncle made a practice of taking their lunch hours separately, first Flora and then Tom making a dash to a nearby eating place where customers shared a long table family style. On one such occasion someone happened to introduce Flora to a young man sitting across the table from her, and she "learned that he was the J. A. Ward of the mailbox."[6]

This was Joe Ward, the failed Nebraska homesteader. After abandoning his claim near Gordon, Nebraska, he had returned to Republic, Kansas, for a brief visit with his parents and then joined his brother Andrew in Arizona. During 1890 and 1891 Joe had worked first at a sawmill in Flagstaff and later in the Santa Fe Railroad's roundhouse at Winslow. In the winter of 1891–92 (probably in January 1892) he visited Republic again, and in all likelihood it was at this time that his next-youngest brother

Fletcher (the "W. F. Ward" on the mailbox) had decided to join Andrew and Joe in the Southwest. In any case only Burch ("J. B. Ward") was still at home in February 1892 when the boys' mother, Sarah Jane Ward, died. That spring their father sold his Republic County farm. Burch stayed behind to finish another year of school, but then he, too, headed west to Williams, where his three brothers now lived. Joe was still working at the Clark and Adams sawmill when he was introduced to Flora. Soon thereafter, however, his brother Andrew helped him get a job as a fireman for the Santa Fe.

Had Flora been home in Osawatomie, her parents would probably have discouraged her friendship with Joe Ward. They certainly had not found any of the local suitors good enough for their daughter, and Joe was no more prepossessing than those Kansas boys. He had less education than Flora, was a man of limited means, and held jobs—as mill hand and as railroad fireman—that put him in the class of men Major Remington hired rather than those he would want courting Flora. Joe's family background might have bothered the major too, but it is doubtful that either Joe or Flora gave much thought to the contrasting histories of their families during the Civil War years—how Flora's father had been an eager volunteer, while Joe's had avoided military service. These were bygone distinctions, and any meaning they might have had to the young

Joe Ward and Flora Remington on one of their Sunday walks near Williams, Arizona.

people concerned was far outweighed by the fact that Joe's puritanical prejudices against alcohol and tobacco closely resembled the moral code that had been inculcated into Flora. Also on the positive side, Joe was an engaging young man who loved to sing, a definite social asset in an era when vocalizing at home was such a major form of entertainment that middle-class families were more likely to own a piano than to have indoor plumbing. But Joe's greatest contribution to Flora's life was companionship, which helped mitigate her loneliness in a rough frontier town. After asking her to a railroad party and being turned down because it was a dance, Joe invited her to a church social and was accepted. From that time on, as Flora wrote:

it was never very long after Sunday dinner till he would appear with an invitation to a good long walk. You can scarcely realize how much I appreciated those Sunday walks after being shut up in the house six days a week from before sunup till long after dark.[7]

Joe and Flora loved to stroll along the logging roads that crisscrossed the slopes of Bill Williams Mountain south of town. Twice, however, Joe brought horses from the Clark and Adams mill and he and Flora went for long rides, on one occasion going as far as Challendar (the next railroad station east of Williams). By the time Joe left for Winslow in late 1896 to work for the Santa Fe, the romance was well established. When friends of the Flemings invited Flora to join them on a horseback trip into the Grand Canyon via the Havasupai Indian Reservation, they assumed that Joe should also be invited.

Sometime in 1897 Flora accepted Joe's proposal of marriage, and the wedding itself took place at the Flemings' home on February 17, 1898. Two of Joe's brothers, the Fleming family, and four friends were in attendance. The ceremony, which began at 9:30 in the morning, was marked by a particularly memorable moment when, as the minister started to speak, the sun rose over the hills to the east and "lighted up the whole room."[8]

The rising sun's first rays seemed a good omen at the beginning of Joe and Flora's life together; however, it proved a not altogether accurate indicator of what was ahead for them, particularly in the years after they reached California in 1900. Let us for a moment set aside our narrative of the first two years of Joe and Flora's married life—the time from their wedding in 1898 to the birth of their daughter Marguerite in August 1900 —and jump ahead to see how things worked out for them in the early decades of the twentieth century.

At the time Marguerite was born, Joe Ward was still working for the railroad. In the weeks that followed, however, he made up his mind to change jobs. Mr. Hubbard, the man who owned the Santa Monica house in which the Wards were renting rooms, also owned a lemon ranch in Glendora (a small village forty miles east of Santa Monica) and urged Joe to try his hand at raising lemons. Mr. Hubbard asserted that if Joe could make a down payment on the Hubbard place in Glendora, profits from the first year's harvest would enable him to finish paying for the land.

Joe went to Glendora to investigate Mr. Hubbard's proposition and returned convinced that it was, as Flora later bitterly put it, "the chance of a lifetime."[9] So Joe, Flora, and their two children moved to Hubbard's lemon ranch, only to find that the reality did not match the dream. For the next six years, despite frequent infusions of cash from Flora's parents, the Wards struggled to make ends meet. Finding that his property pro-

The Flemings' house in Williams, Arizona, and (left to right) Joe Ward, George and Addie (with Marjorie on her lap) Fleming, and Flora Ward.

Jerry and Emma Remington in front of their newly built home in Osawatomie, Kansas, with their two younger daughters and their granddaughter, Christine Ward.

duced more rocks than profits, Joe tried to supplement his income with a succession of other livelihoods—running a grocery, selling soft drinks from an ice wagon, butchering stock for neighbors, and distributing coal —none of which proved especially rewarding. Four times in five years, Joe and Flora moved from one rented house to another. Meanwhile, Flora gave birth to three more children—Christine in 1903 and twins, Chester and Esther, in 1905—and went through a period of bad health. Again, her parents came to the rescue, taking some pressure off her by bringing Christine back to Kansas to live with them.

In 1906 the Wards achieved some stability of place, at least for a while. Major Remington had just completed a handsome three-story Victorian house in Osawatomie and moved his family into it. He wanted Joe and Flora to have a permanent home also, and he sent money and two workmen west to build the Wards a house in Glendora. The family occupied this house, which was one mile east of town, from 1906 to 1914. Joe developed an orange grove on the property and also built a barn and corrals. But his efforts to get an adequate water supply proved both expensive and fruitless, and by 1914 he was again dreaming of greener pastures. Flora doubted the wisdom of Joe's plan to move yet again, but he went ahead and traded their Glendora property (house, orange grove, and twenty-acre ranch) for a larger but undeveloped acreage near Poplar in Tulare County (north of Bakersfield in the San Joaquin River valley).

The Wards moved to Tulare County in August 1914, and it quickly became clear that Joe had struck a bad bargain. Soon the land near Poplar was exchanged for mountain property near Porterville with a mineral spring from which Joe hoped to bottle and sell water. This did not work out either. Meanwhile, the Wards rented houses in Lindsay, and Joe pursued various ventures, one of which was a newspaper dealership for the *Fresno Republican*. Later he opened a gasoline station, only to have it burn down. In spite of the financial misfortunes that dogged him, Joe was able, in 1920, to buy a house and orange grove in Lindsay, where he and Flora lived until he died in 1944. She went north to live with her daughter Esther in the San Francisco Bay Area, where she died in 1967.

Even as brief an account as this of the Wards' life in the early 1900s plainly shows how from 1900 onward they were caught in a difficult and often losing struggle for economic well-being. They moved repeatedly, living in no fewer than nine different houses between 1900 (when they rented rooms in Santa Monica) and 1920 (when they moved into their Lindsay home). What, one may ask, was the harvest of all this moving and striving? Moreover, how, if at all, were Joe and Flora's experiences similar to or different from those of their ancestors who had also been on the move for so many years—Flora's since they left England for Massachusetts in 1630 and Joe's since their coming from Ireland to Pennsylvania in the 1730s? Finally, and most broadly, what does the story of Joe and Flora Ward and their forebears tell us about the American dream, especially as dreamed by Americans who moved west?

The American dream came in more than one variety. Among Joe and Flora's ancestors at least two broad variations were evident, one of which we will call dreams of purity, the other dreams of plenty. The pursuit of plenty was obviously a formidable force, undoubtedly the preeminent one, in spurring westward expansion. The desire to get a fresh start on better land in a new place and the expectation that this would improve one's

Joe Ward and his gas station before
it burned down in 1920.

fortunes was the principal reason many Americans had for moving west. Among Joe's and Flora's ancestors, Joe's father (Jim Ward) and grandfather (Addison Ward), and among Flora's forebears her father (Jerry Remington), grandfather (Benjamin Remington), and great-great-grandfather (Jeremiah Root), come immediately to mind as men who went west mainly in search of economic opportunity. It is worth noting in passing, however, that men were apparently more susceptible to the West's siren call than women were; at least it was women—Huldah Root, Florella Adair, Nancy Adair, and Flora Ward—who expressed doubt about the idea that moving on was such a good thing.

A second version of the American dream involved aspirations to purity—purity of conduct, purification of society through reform, and pure obedience to God's will. Flora's grandparents Samuel and Florella Adair provide perhaps the clearest examples of ancestors who placed the quest for purity above the pursuit of plenty, but others—Owen Brown of Hudson, his son John, and (much earlier) Margaret Greenfield's Baptist forebears—shared this dream in some measure. It is also clear that this dream influenced their decisions to migrate. Samuel and Florella Adair and John Brown and his sons went to Kansas in an effort to save the new

Joe Ward (1867–1944), around 1898.

territory from what they regarded as the corrupting influence of slavery. Owen Brown moved from Connecticut to Ohio in 1805 partly out of a desire to find a more perfect community. Margaret Greenfield's Baptist forebears migrated to the Little Hoosick Valley of New York in order to preserve their religious practices.

Whether they pursued dreams of purity or dreams of plenty (or, more often, some combination of the two), Joe's and Flora's ancestors were reflecting aspirations held widely by nineteenth-century Americans. To pursue these dreams, with real hope of fulfillment, was the promise of American life. To judge from what happened in most cases, however, the promise was larger than the vast majority of Americans had the power to accomplish. Joe and Flora Ward, for instance, both fell far short of achieving what they most wanted. To oversimplify a bit, Flora was an inheritor of the aspiration to purity. Raised in relatively prosperous circumstances, she set her sights on the pursuit of artistic accomplishment and the promotion of social purity (the latter through her Women's Christian Temperance Union work). Joe, less privileged in his economic background, dreamed of getting ahead financially. But Joe achieved only marginal economic security and had to live with the knowledge that he

Flora Ward (1872–1967).

had not provided for his wife as well as her father would have. Flora had her disappointments too. Although she belonged to the third generation of women in her family to receive some college training, marriage cut off the possibility of an independent career. Like Florella Adair and Addie Fleming in earlier generations, she had to subordinate any thought she may have had of continuing to work to the claims of raising a family. She and Joe nevertheless valued education and were proud that one of their daughters, Marguerite, received a college degree and became an elementary-school teacher, and another daughter, Esther, completed nurse's training. Moreover, the members of this younger generation, Flora's daughters, broke with tradition and worked in their respective fields after they married.

The kinds of disappointments that Joe and Flora suffered were by no means unique to them. Dreams of wealth and economic security fired the imaginations of many Americans in the 1800s, but few actually rose from rags to riches. Although some gigantic fortunes were made, most were acquired by individuals who started the race for wealth with significant advantages. As for the vast majority of Americans, even those who, like Benjamin Adair, Jim Ward, Owen Brown, and Benjamin Remington, moved up the social ladder from their parents' positions, did so in very small increments. Moreover, these successful middle-class Americans remained vulnerable to circumstances that were largely out of their control. Among Joe's and Flora's ancestors, the fragility of economic success is well illustrated by the examples of Owen Brown (who prospered until 1836) and Jim Ward (who built his big house in 1886), both of whom got a little ahead, only to suffer severe financial setbacks soon thereafter. Many things could conspire to keep or put an ordinary man down: bad health (Jim Ward), a national depression (Owen Brown and Addison Ward), limited resources (George Adair and Jason Brown), or bad investments (Joe Ward). To be sure, several of Joe's and Flora's ancestors, notably Jeremiah Root and Jerry Remington, were able to leave their heirs better off than they themselves had been at birth, but Jerry Remington was the only one who came close to achieving a substantial rise in social status, and even he, as we have observed, was little more than a big fish in a small pond.

Despite their financial problems in the early 1900s, Joe and Flora Ward were better off materially than their forebears had been a hundred years earlier. It is important to recognize, however, that the difference between the Wards' standard of living and their ancestors' depended not so much on whether they or a given forebear had gone west and worked hard as on the advent of the industrial era and such conveniences as railroads, electricity, gas lighting, central heating, and telephones. It was possible to enjoy the overall rise in the standard of living that accompanied industrialization without making any relative social gains. Joe Ward, for example, eventually acquired a farm (and was therefore definitely better off in later life than he had been as a young homesteader in Nebraska thirty years earlier), but he and Flora still ranked relatively lower on the social ladder than several ancestors like Owen Brown and Jeremiah Root and no higher than most others. All the moving and striving associated with westward migration had not produced consistent upward social and economic mobility among Joe's and Flora's ancestors. Benjamin Remington and his son Jerry had certainly enhanced their fortunes by heading west, but others such as Addison Ward and Joe Ward seem to have gained little from frequent moves. Indeed, as a general rule, those of Joe's and Flora's forebears who went west did not do significantly better overall than those who remained where they were born.

Like their ancestors, Joe and Flora did not dream only of material gains. However, in some respects the latter-day versions of community, social reform, and godliness to which Joe and Flora attached themselves seem rather weak forms of commitments that their forebears had held. This was partly a matter of different circumstances. The meaning of community, for example, had undergone a significant change between 1805, when Owen Brown moved west to Hudson, and 1900, when Joe and Flora settled in southern California. In the early 1800s a spirit of community based on mutual assistance was to some degree compulsory, imposed by the physical demands of oxcart travel and the needs of pioneers who were in the process of establishing new settlements in frontier environments. Even in 1889, when John Ward enlisted his brother Joe's assistance in driving wagons from Kansas to northwestern Nebraska, cross-country travel could still require a certain amount of togetherness. By the second half of the century, however, the conditions that had once necessitated close mutual assistance had changed. Since the advent of the railroad it had become perfectly possible for men and women alike—as the travels of Jason Brown, Addie Adair, and Flora Remington in the 1880s and 1890s exemplified—to cover long distances by train without direct assistance from family or friends. Of course, the new modes of transportation could be and were used to maintain ties with friends and loved ones separated by many miles, but such bonds were now maintained in a voluntary and sporadic way rather than as matters of daily necessity.

Something that had also been present in their ancestors' efforts to achieve social reform was missing from Joe and Flora's. There were plenty of causes to choose from in the early twentieth century—socialism, feminism, unionism, and civil rights—but the Wards were drawn to none of these, least of all to the more radical and unconventional causes. The come-outer stance, that spirited rejection of conventional wisdom that had characterized some family members in the pre–Civil War period (most notably the abolitionists in the Adair and Brown lines), was lacking in Joe and Flora's generation. The point at which the balance shifted from the come-outer spirit to a more conventional and conservative outlook came, we suggested earlier, about the time when Flora's mother married Jerry Remington. Jerry and Emma Remington's daughters still contributed money to small black churches and supported (as their grandparents Samuel and Florella Adair had done) the cause of temperance, but these were very attenuated forms of the abolitionist and perfectionist views that the older family members had held.

In religion, too, Joe and Flora's generation seemed to have lost much of the intensity that had characterized their ancestors' pursuit of godliness. To be sure, the Wards and most other younger family members continued to join and attend churches. It seems likely, however, that many of their ancestors—especially Margaret Greenfield's Baptist grandparents, Owen and Sally Brown, and Samuel and Florella Adair—would have found this a rather lukewarm commitment compared with what had been expected of professed Christians in 1800. Whereas the old believers had focused on the eternal (with all the life-and-death comprehensiveness that word connotes), the Wards and their relatives in the early twentieth century, though churchgoing Christians, were motivated more by secular piety, the desire for respectability and fellowship, than by profound spiritual seeking.

To speak of what was lost between 1800 and 1900 with regard to family ties, causes, and Christianity is, of course, to approach Joe and Flora's story from their ancestors' perspective. To Joe and Flora, the more important fact would have been that the two of them had so much in common. They agreed that family ties were to be maintained no matter how scattered relatives were geographically, that causes such as temperance needed their support, and that churchgoing was an essential part of Sundays in their lives. Moreover, in common with many Americans who joined the westward migration movement, Joe and Flora always hoped that, no matter what problems they might have financially, they would be able to give their children the wherewithal to achieve a better life— an aspiration that, as we have suggested, was largely fulfilled by the Ward children in their parent's lifetimes. Indeed, it was such shared assumptions that drew Joe and Flora to each other in 1898 and kept them together through forty-six years of married life.

On the morning of February 17, 1898, after a brief wedding ceremony and a small party, Joe and Flora left the Flemings' to catch the eleven o'clock eastbound train for Winslow, Arizona. There they were to share a house with friends.

Flora soon took advantage of the fact that Joe, as a railroad employee, could get a free pass for his wife. Not having seen her parents and sisters for nearly three years, Flora was eager to visit them. Toward the end of May, she left Winslow for Kansas. Once at her parents' place, she found that she "was not very well," perhaps a veiled reference to morning sickness, for she was pregnant. About this time Joe, who was wont to change jobs frequently in search of a better living, left the Santa Fe and hired on with the Southern Pacific. The SP sent him to El Paso, Texas, from which some of his runs took him into Mexico. "My folks," Flora recalled, "shivered at the thought of my going into that wild country." With only a little coaxing she was induced to remain with them on the family farm. She was well along in her pregnancy now, and it was not unusual in rural areas and small towns without hospitals for women to have their babies at their parents' houses in order to be taken care of by close relatives.[10]

Flora's baby was born on December 4, 1898, and named Wallace Remington Ward. This was the male heir that her father had always wanted, and Flora was amused (and doubtless delighted too) when a neighbor said, "O, he looks just like Major Remington."[11] The child's significance within his family circle was further emphasized by the fact that he was always called Remington rather than Wallace, his given name. The only shadow to darken this happy event was the death of the Reverend Samuel Adair on December 26, just three weeks after the birth of his first great-grandchild.

Flora stayed on with her parents and sisters into 1899. Meanwhile, Joe got a new assignment on a run out of Tucson. That sounded safer to

Pictures from Joe, Flora, and W. Remington Ward's scrapbook of their stay
(July–August 1900) by the Pacific in Santa Monica, California.

Flora than El Paso, so when Joe came east with a pass for himself and his wife and baby, she was ready to return to the Southwest with him. The Wards lived in two places in Tucson. The first was a house they shared with acquaintances; then they got a place of their own. It was not in a very safe neighborhood, however, and Flora took the precaution of buying a revolver, just in case.

Early the following winter Joe again became restless and applied to get his old job back with the Santa Fe Railroad. The company was glad to rehire him, but instead of sending him to Albuquerque, New Mexico, as he had expected, they assigned him to Needles, California, a railroad town in the middle of the Mojave Desert. He and Flora rented a house that was rather isolated from the main part of town, and because Joe was frequently given overnight runs in the first months of 1900, Flora was often left alone with her baby. Strangers who came to the door caused her a couple of bad scares, and at times she found the desert heat almost unbearable. Moreover, she was pregnant again, and that clinched her determination to leave Needles. Mindful of her aunt Addie's example of going to cooler locations in July and August, Flora proposed that they move to some place along the California coast.

Joe applied for a transfer and was reassigned to a Los Angeles run. The Wards left Needles one day and arrived in Los Angeles the next. While strolling through the city's downtown section, they were thrilled at the sight of the first automobile they had ever seen; its occupants (or so Flora recalled) "both looked as though they expected to be blown up." Later in the day the Wards boarded an interurban trolley for Santa Monica, where they hoped to rent rooms. Much of the countryside between Los Angeles and Santa Monica was open fields, and Flora remembered the trolley passing through large stretches of what she, as a Kansan, called prairies. It was while they were crossing just such a field that she caught her first glimpse of their destination. "Suddenly," Flora recalled, "I saw in the distance, a shimmer of brilliant blue, and could scarcely realize that it was the Pacific Ocean." The date was July 4, 1900.[12]

Flora enjoyed the next few weeks better than almost any others of her early married life. She and little Remington—and Joe, too, when he was not working—took frequent walks on the beach. Then, on August 17, her second child, a daughter she and Joe called Marguerite, was born, the great-great-grandchild of George Adair, Owen Brown, Margaret Greenfield, Sally Root, and David Ward, Jr. One journey was over; another had begun.

Sources

W hat follows is a highly selective listing, by chapters and titled subdivisions, of source materials; it draws almost exclusively on published items. I have used three other kinds of sources that I believe anyone doing a study of this kind will find valuable.

A close reader of my text will recognize many places where I am depending on unpublished local sources, especially official records: land records, probate files, court transcripts, tax lists, census materials, cemetery records, and church documents.

No amount of work in documents can entirely substitute for visits to the sites where these families lived. Over a ten-year period I managed to visit nearly every place where an episode in my text had taken place. Just getting a sense of the lay of the land was extremely useful, but I sometimes also made a discovery (for example, locating and photographing Jim and Sarah Ward's house in Pawnee County, Nebraska) that I could not have made in any other way.

In the course of my travels I benefited enormously from conversations with descendants of the families studied here, both their direct relatives and their former neighbors. I was repeatedly astonished and delighted by the readiness of people I had never met before to respond helpfully when I asked them questions about people and events from the distant past.

In addition to these three general categories of source material, I benefited from (and was inspired by) a personal confrontation with ancestral lore that took place when I was very young. In the summer before I entered the sixth grade, my grandmother Flora Ward took me for a visit to her birthplace, Osawatomie, Kansas. For nearly a year we stayed in the three-story Victorian house that her father, Jeremiah Remington, had built in the early 1900s. We also visited the cabin her grandparents Samuel and Florella Adair occupied when they arrived in Osawatomie in 1855. Many dinner table conversations during that year (and during other, later visits to Osawatomie) focused on pioneer-era memories. As a professional historian, I am now fairly skeptical about the accuracy of some of the stories that passed around the table along with the fried chicken, string beans, and ice cream, but I would be less than candid if I did not acknowledge that this book probably would never have been written (or contained some of the nuances of interpretation found in it) were it not for questions and perceptions about my family that date back to those boyhood experiences of thirty-five years ago.

Introduction

FAMILIES ON THE MOVE

There is a vast literature on westward migration and on American families. Three such sources that I found helpful in the earliest phase of my work were Eric L. McKitrick and Stanley Elkins, "A Meaning for Turner's Frontier," *Political Science Quarterly,* 69 (Sept. and Dec. 1954), 321–53 and 565–602; Daniel J. Boorstin, *The Americans: The National Experience* (New York, 1965); and David J. Russo, *Families and Communities: A New View of American History* (Nashville, 1974).

Sources for the account of the Browns' trip to Ohio in 1805 and of the Wards' sojourn in Santa Monica in 1900 include Owen Brown's "Autobiography" and his son John's letter to Henry L. Stearns (July 15, 1857), both reprinted in F. B. Sanborn, ed., *The Life and Letters of John Brown* (Boston, 1891), 4–10 and 12–17; Stephen B. Oates, *To Purge This Land with Blood: A Biography of John Brown* (New York, 1970), 8–9; Richard O. Boyer, *The Legend of John Brown: A Biography and a History* (New York, 1973), 172–75; and Flora R. Ward, "Autobiography" (Typescript dated "Tuesday, August 4th," probably Aug. 4, 1958, copy in Gerald W. McFarland's files).

Chapter One
BEGINNINGS: THE COLONIAL ERA

Of the many books I consulted on early New England, I found the following particularly useful for this introductory section:

General background. David Grayson Allen, *In English Ways: The Movement of Societies and the Transferal of English Local Law and Custom to Massachusetts Bay in the Seventeenth Century* (Chapel Hill, 1981); Charles E. Banks, *The Winthrop Fleet of 1630* (Baltimore, 1961); William Cronon, *Changes in the Land: Indians, Colonialists, and the Ecology of New England* (New York, 1983); Edmund S. Morgan, *Visible Saints: The History of a Puritan Idea* (Ithaca, N.Y., 1965); Sumner Chilton Powell, *Puritan Village: The Formation of a New England Town* (Middletown, Conn., 1963); Laurel Thatcher Ulrich, *Good Wives: Image and Reality in the Lives of Women in Northern New England, 1650–1750* (New York, 1982); and Alden T. Vaughan, *New England Frontier: Puritans and Indians, 1620–1675* (Boston, 1965).

More specific sources on the English settlers who came from England aboard the *Mary and John* and eventually settled in Windsor, Conn. Linda Auwers Bissell, "Family, Friends, and Neighbors: Social Interaction in Seventeenth-Century Windsor, Connecticut" (Ph.D. diss., Brandeis University, 1973); Maude P. Kuhns, *The "Mary and John": A Story of the Founding of Dorchester, Massachusetts, 1630* (Rutland, Vt., 1971); and Henry R. Stiles, *The History of Ancient Windsor*, 2 vols. (Hartford, Conn., 1892).

THE BROWNS OF ANCIENT WINDSOR

For a sampling of the general sources used here, see Bruce C. Daniels, *The Connecticut Town: Growth and Development, 1635–1790* (Middletown, Conn., 1979); James Deetz, *In Small Things Forgotten: The Archeology of Early American Life* (New York, 1977); John Demos, *A Little Commonwealth: Family Life in Plymouth Colony* (New York, 1970); Philip J. Greven, Jr., *Four Generations: Population, Land, and Family in Colonial Andover, Massachusetts* (Ithaca, N.Y., 1970); Robert A. Gross, *The Minutemen and Their World* (New York, 1976); Kenneth A. Lockridge, *A New England Town: The First Hundred Years* (New York, 1970); Paul R. Lucas, *Valley of Discord: Church and Society along the Connecticut River, 1636–1725* (Hanover, N.H., 1976); Edmund S. Morgan, *The Puritan Family: Religion and Domestic Relations in Seventeenth-Century New England* (New York, 1966); Daniel Scott Smith and Michael S. Hindus, "Premarital Pregnancy in America, 1640–1971: An Overview and Interpretation," *Journal of Interdisciplinary History*, 5 (Spring 1975), 537–70; and Michael Zuckerman, *Peaceable Kingdoms: New England Towns in the Eighteenth Century* (New York, 1970).

More-specific sources on Windsor used in this subsection include the works by L. A. Bissell and H. R. Stiles cited above, as well as Abiel Brown, *Genealogical History of the Early Settlers of West Simsbury now Canton, Connecticut* (Hartford, Conn., 1856); Noah A. Phelps, *History of Simsbury, Granby and Canton, from 1642 to 1845* (Hartford, Conn., 1845); and Connecticut Historical Society, *Some Early Records and Documents of and Relating to the Town of Windsor, Connecticut, 1636–1703* (Hartford, Conn., 1930).

THE ROOTS OF WESTFIELD AND SOUTHWICK

In addition to the previously cited general works by P. J. Greven, R. A. Gross, K. A. Lockridge, and P. R. Lucas, see Roy Hidemichi Akagi, *The Town Proprietors of the New England Colonies* (reprint, Gloucester, Mass., 1963); and Stephen Innes, *Labor in a New Land: Economy and Society in Seventeenth-Century Springfield* (Princeton, 1983). Other sources that deal in more detail with Westfield, Southwick, and the Roots include John H. Lockwood, *Westfield and Its Historic Influences, 1669–1919*, 2 vols. (Springfield, Mass., 1922); Gilbert Arnold's essay in Jean Mason et al., *Southwick Congregational Church History, 1773–1973* (Southwick, Mass., 1973); Susan Jensen Reik, "Genesis of a New England Town; The Growth of Farmington, Connecticut, 1645–1700" (M.A. essay, Columbia University, 1969); and James P. Root, *Root Genealogical Records, 1600–1870* (New York, 1870).

MARGARET GREENFIELD'S BAPTIST HERITAGE

General works. On Baptists and revivalism: Edwin S. Gaustad, *The Great Awakening in New England* (New York, 1957); C. C. Goen, *Revivalism and Separatism in New England, 1740–1800* (New Haven, Conn., 1962); and William G. McLoughlin, *Isaac Backus and the American Pietistic Tradition* (Boston, 1967). On overpopulation: Kenneth A. Lockridge, "Land, Population and the Evolution of New England Society, 1630–1790," *Past and Present*, no. 39 (Apr. 1968), 62–80. And on the manorial system in New York: Sung Bok Kim, *Landlord and Tenant in Colonial New York, Manorial Society, 1664–1775* (Chapel Hill, 1978).

On Greenfield and Rogers family history in various localities, see the following: For Exeter, R.I., Willet H. Arnold, *Historical Sketch of the Baptist Church of Exeter, R.I.* (Central Falls, R.I., 1883); J. R. Cole, *History of Washington and Kent Counties, Rhode Island* (New York, 1889); Edward M. Cook Jr., *The Fathers of the Towns: Leadership and Community Structure in Eighteenth-Century New England* (Baltimore, 1976); and Mary K. Huling, *Historical Sketch of the Baptist Church in Exeter, R.I.* (Lafayette, R.I., 1939). For Montville, Conn., Henry A. Baker, *History of Montville, Connecticut* (Hartford, Conn., 1896). And for Rensselaer, N.Y., S. B. Kim, as cited above, and Nathaniel B. Sylvester, *History of Rensselaer County, New York* (Philadelphia, 1880).

DAVID WARD AND TAZEWELL COUNTY'S HEROIC AGE

For general background, see Rhys Isaac, *The Transformation of Virginia, 1740–1790* (Chapel Hill, 1982). The standard sources on the battles of Point Pleasant and King's Mountain are Rueben G. Thwaites and Louise P. Kellogg, eds., *Documentary History of Dunmore's War* (Madison, Wis., 1905); and Lyman C. Draper, *King's Mountain and Its Heroes: History of the*

Battle of King's Mountain, October 7th 1780, and the Events Which Led to It (Cincinnati, 1881); but see also Randolph C. Downes, "Dunmore's War: An Interpretation," *Mississippi Valley Historical Review,* 21 (Dec. 1934), 311–30; and Hank Messick, *King's Mountain* (Boston, 1976).

On Tazewell County history, see Nellie White Bundy, *Sketches of Tazewell County Virginia's Early History* (Tazewell, 1976); David E. Johnston, *A History of Middle New River Settlements and Contiguous Territory* (Bluefield, Va., 1906); W. C. Pendleton, *History of Tazewell County and Southwest Virginia* (Richmond, Va., 1920); Netti Schreiner-Yantis, *Archives of the Pioneers of Tazewell County, Virginia* (Springfield, Va., 1973); and Lewis P. Summers, *History of Southwest Virginia, 1776–1786, and Washington County, 1777–1870* (Richmond, Va., 1903). The Pendleton volume also reprints large sections of an older source, George W. L. Bickley, *History of the Settlement and Indian Wars of Tazewell County, Virginia* (Cincinnati, 1852).

BENJAMIN ADAIR: A NEW AMERICAN

For general background, see Robert D. Mitchell, *Commercialism and Frontier: Perspectives on the Early Shenandoah Valley* (Charlottesville, Va., 1977). On the Scotch-Irish, I used Charles K. Bolton, *Scotch Irish Pioneers in Ulster and America* (Boston, 1910); R. J. Dickson, *Ulster Emigration to Colonial America, 1718–1775* (London, 1966); and James G. Leyburn, *The Scotch-Irish: A Social History* (Chapel Hill, 1962).

Many details about the Adairs and Lyles and their relatives in Augusta and Rockbridge counties can be gleaned from Lyman Chalkley, *Chronicles of the Scotch-Irish Settlement in Virginia,* 3 vols. (reprint, Baltimore, 1965); F. B. Kegley, *Kegley's Virginia Frontier* (Roanoke, Va., 1938); Oscar K. Lyle, *The Lyle Family: The Ancestry and Posterity of Matthew, John, Daniel, and Samuel Lyle, Pioneer Settlers in Virginia* (New York, 1912); and Joseph A. Waddell, *Annals of Augusta County, Virginia, from 1726 to 1871,* 2d ed. (reprint, Bridgewater, Va., 1958).

Chapter Two

TRANS-APPALACHIAN PIONEERS, 1805–1829

An excellent introduction to the social history of nineteenth-century frontier life is Richard A. Bartlett, *The New Country: A Social History of the American Frontier, 1776–1890* (New York, 1974). Daniel J. Boorstin, *The Americans: The National Experience* (New York, 1965), uses the Ohio frontier to illustrate his point that the pioneer spirit was often more communal than individualistic.

BENJAMIN ADAIR'S COUNTY FULL OF COUSINS

There is a wealth of material on the Paint Valley frontier. See, in particular, Daniel Scott, Esq., *A History of the Early Settlement of Highland County, Ohio* (Hillsboro, Ohio, 1890);

Isaac J. Finley and Rufus Putnam, *Pioneer Record and Reminiscences of the Early Settlers of Ross County, Ohio* (Cincinnati, 1871); Williams Brothers, *History of Ross and Highland Counties, Ohio* (Cleveland, 1880); J. W. Klise, *The County of Highland* (Madison, Wis., 1902); and Violet Morgan, *Folklore of Highland County* (Greenfield, Ohio, 1946).

JEREMIAH ROOT'S OHIO GAMBLE

Four published sources on Jeremiah Root's Ohio are R. C. Brown and J. E. Norris, *History of Portage County* (Chicago, 1885); *Combination Atlas Map of Portage County* (Chicago, 1874); William J. Dawson, *The Aurora Story* (n.p., 1949); and *Pioneer and General History of Geauga County* (Chardon, Ohio, 1880).

SQUIRE BROWN OF HUDSON, OHIO

In addition to sources cited in the notes, see L. V. Bierce, *Historical Reminiscences of Summit County* (Akron, 1854); William H. Perrin, *History of Summit County* (Chicago, 1881); and Harlan Hatcher, *The Western Reserve: The Story of New Connecticut in Ohio*, rev. ed. (Cleveland, 1966).

MARGARET GREENFIELD AND HER SON BENJAMIN

For sources that put Margaret Greenfield's life in perspective relative to selected topics, see the following: On the status of widows, Alexander Keyssar, "Widowhood in Eighteenth-Century Massachusetts: A Problem in the History of the Family," *Perspectives in American History*, 8 (1974), 83–119. On sex before and outside of marriage in eighteenth-century Rhode Island, John Demos, "Families in Colonial Bristol, Rhode Island: An Exercise in Historical Demography," *William and Mary Quarterly*, 3d ser. 25 (Jan. 1968), esp. 56–57. And on Baptists in Hancock, Mass., David Dudley Field, ed., *A History of the County of Berkshire, Massachusetts* (Pittsfield, Mass., 1829), 417–20.

Useful introductions to the Genesee Valley are as follows: *History of Monroe County, New York* (Philadelphia, 1877); Eleanor C. Kalsbeck, *Henrietta Heritage* (Private printing, 1977); E. W. Vanderhoof, *Historical Sketches of Western New York* (Buffalo, N.Y., 1907), 33–83; and Orsamus Turner, *Pioneer History of the Holland Purchase of Western New York* (Buffalo, N.Y., 1849).

Chapter Three:
UNFORESEEN DIRECTIONS, 1830–1850

The best one-volume biography of John Brown is Stephen B. Oates, *To Purge This Land with Blood* (New York, 1970), but for additional details about Brown's life prior to 1840 see Richard O. Boyer, *The Legend of John Brown: A Biography and a History* (New York, 1973). A solid introduction to the antislavery movement is Louis Filler, *The Crusade against Slavery, 1830–1850* (New York, 1960). Of particular interest, among the many more recent books on the subject, is Aileen S. Kraditor, *Means and Ends in American Abolitionism: Garrison and His Critics on Strategy and Tactics, 1834–1850* (New York, 1968). For Antimasonry see William Preston Vaughn, *The Antimasonic Party in the United States, 1826–1843* (Lexington, Ky., 1983). Still useful on the panic and depression of the 1830s is Reginald C. McGrane, *The Panic of 1837: Some Financial Problems of the Jacksonian Era* (Chicago, 1924).

BENJAMIN REMINGTON AND ADDISON WARD

In addition to the Remington-Bly references listed for Chapter 2, the following are helpful: Paul E. Johnson, *A Shopkeeper's Millennium: Society and Revivals in Rochester, New York, 1815–1837* (New York, 1978); and Neil Adams McNall, *An Agricultural History of the Genesee Valley, 1790–1860* (Philadelphia, 1952).

On Greene County, Indiana, in the pioneer period, see first Jack Baber, *The Early History of Greene County, Indiana* (Worthington, Ind., 1875); *History of Greene and Sullivan Counties, Indiana* (Chicago, 1884); and *Biographical Memoirs of Greene County, Indiana,* 3 vols. (Indianapolis, 1908).

BROWNS AND ADAIRS

For excellent sources on Western Reserve College and Oberlin College, see Frederick Clayton Waite, *Western Reserve University: The Hudson Era* (Cleveland, 1943); David French, "The Colonization-Abolition Controversy in Western Reserve College," *Western Reserve Magazine,* Nov.–Dec. 1979, pp. 48–53; Robert S. Fletcher, *A History of Oberlin College: From Its Foundation through the Civil War,* 2 vols. (Oberlin, Ohio, 1943); Geoffrey T. Blodgett, "Myth and Reality in Oberlin's History," *Oberlin Alumni Magazine,* 68 (May–June 1972), 4–10; Boyd B. Stutler, "John Brown and the Oberlin Lands," *West Virginia History,* 12 (Apr. 1951), 189–98; and Robert S. Fletcher, "Bread and Doctrine at Oberlin," *Ohio State Archaeological and Historical Quarterly,* 49 (Jan.–Mar. 1940), 58–67.

An invaluable source on the divisions within Hudson's First Congregational Church is Emily E. Metcalf, *Historical Papers Delivered at the Centennial Anniversary of the First Congregational Church of Hudson, Ohio, September 4, 1902* (Akron, 1902).

The Indiana Adairs and their environment may be studied through the following: Cass County, Ind., *Combination Atlas* (Kingman, Ind., 1876); Thomas B. Helm, *History of Cass County, Indiana* (Chicago, 1886); and John Z. Powell, *History of Cass County, Indiana . . . ,* 2 vols. (Chicago, 1913).

Chapter Four

IN THE SHADOW OF CONFLICT, 1 8 5 0 – 1 8 6 5

For an excellent introduction to the subject of women and the trans-Mississippi frontier, see Julie Roy Jeffrey, *Frontier Women: The Trans-Mississippi West, 1840–1880* (New York, 1979);

Lillian Schlissel, *Women's Diaries of the Westward Journey* (New York, 1982); Joanna L. Stratton, *Pioneer Women: Voices from the Kansas Frontier* (New York, 1981); and John M. Faragher, *Women and Men on the Overland Trail* (New Haven, Conn., 1979).

THE ADAIRS AND BLEEDING KANSAS

Of the standard sources on John Brown, Stephen B. Oates's *To Purge This Land with Blood,* cited earlier, has a good description of Brown's involvement in Kansas border warfare. On the early history of Osawatomie, see Charles A. Knouse, ed., *A Town between Two Rivers* (Osawatomie, Kans., 1954).

JERRY REMINGTON JOINS MR. LINCOLN'S ARMY

A starting point for the broad picture of the war is Bruce Catton, *This Hallowed Ground: The Story of the Union Side of the Civil War* (Garden City, N.Y., 1956). Sources for more specialized topics are as follows: on the life of rank-and-file Union soldiers, Bell I. Wiley, *The Life of Billy Yank: The Common Soldier of the Union* (Garden City, N.Y., 1971), on U. S. Grant, William S. McFeely, *Grant: A Biography* (New York, 1981); on Antietam, James V. Murfin, *The Gleam of Bayonets: The Battle of Antietam and the Maryland Campaign of 1862* (New York, 1965); and on the siege of Petersburg, Richard J. Sommers, *Richmond Redeemed: The Siege at Petersburg* (Garden City, N.Y., 1981).

JIM WARD: NO SOLDIER HE

For descriptions of antiwar and antidraft feeling and of the draft generally and conscription in Illinois, see Wood Gray, *The Hidden Civil War: The Story of the Copperheads* (Compass Books ed., New York, 1964); Eugene C. Murdock, *One Million Men: The Civil War Draft in the North* (Madison, Wis., 1971); Robert E. Sterling, "Civil War Draft Resistance in Illinois," *Journal of the Illinois State Historical Society,* 64 (Autumn 1971), 244–66; and Peter Levine, "Draft Evasion in the North during the Civil War, 1863–1865," *Journal of American History,* 67 (Mar. 1981), 816–34.

Chapter Five:
CHANGES OF MIND, 1865–1892

The introductory section on Emma Adair was based almost exclusively on primary sources. However, for background on Oberlin and Kansas pioneer life, see Robert S. Fletcher, *History of Oberlin College,* and Joanna L. Stratton, *Pioneer Women*—both cited earlier.

JERRY REMINGTON AND EMMA ADAIR

Two useful articles on the self-made men of the late nineteenth century are Marian V. Sears, "The American Businessman at the Turn of the Century, *Business History Review,* 30 (Dec.

1956), 382–443; and William Miller, "The Recruitment of the American Business Elite," *Quarterly Journal of Economics,* 64 (May 1950), 242–53. The article on Jeremiah Remington in *Portrait and Biographical Record of Southeastern Kansas* (Chicago, 1894), 490–91, places him in the self-made category. On Osawatomie, see the town newspapers, the *Osawatomie Gaslight* and the *Osawatomie Graphic.*

THE REVEREND SAMUEL ADAIR'S RELATIVES

On Samuel Adair's later life, see Lowell Gish, "Adair Center: Memorial to a Mental Health Pioneer," *Menninger Quarterly,* 16 (Fall 1962), 26–29; and *Osawatomie Graphic,* Nov. 3, 1966. Jerry Brown's career is summarized in Howard Clark to Boyd B. Stutler, Feb. 4, 1955, Brown-Clark Collection, Hudson Library and Historical Society. On Mary Brown's biography in the post–Harpers Ferry years, see M.H.F., "A Brave Life," *Overland Monthly,* 2nd ser. 6, no. 34 (October 1885), 364–65; Grace Gould Izant, "John Brown's Wives," in *Ohio Scenes and Citizens* (Cleveland, 1964), 221–25; Theron Fox, ed., *After Harper's Ferry: John Brown's Widow—Her Family and the Saratoga Years* (Saratoga, Calif., 1964); Daniel Rosenberg, *Mary Brown: From Harpers Ferry to California,* American Institute for Marxist Studies, Occasional Papers Series, no. 17 (New York, 1975); and Gerald W. McFarland, "A Legacy Left Behind: The Browns after the Execution," *American History Illustrated,* Mar. 1984, pp. 20–25. Glen S. Dumke provides an excellent introduction to *The Boom of the Eighties in Southern California* (San Marino, Calif., 1944). The Browns in southern California are discussed in C. Fred Shoop, "City's Early Days Recalled," *Pasadena Star-News,* Aug. 3, 1961, p. 28; Hiram A. Reid, *History of Pasadena* (Pasadena, Calif., 1895); and Dorothy K. Hassler, "Trail's End on Little Round Top," *Westways,* Sept. 1952, pp. 24–25. For background on the Illinois Central and on Marion County, Ill. (including Odin Township, where Addison and Mary Adair lived), see J. H. G. Brinkerhoff, *Brinkerhoff's History of Marion County, Illinois* (Indianapolis, 1909).

JIM WARD AND HIS SONS

For background on the sod-house frontier and the Homestead Act, see Everett Dick, *The Sod-House Frontier, 1854–1890* (New York, 1937); and Fred A. Shannon, *The Farmer's Last Frontier: Agriculture, 1860–1897* (Harper Torchbook ed., New York, 1968). More specifically, on the Wards and the places where they lived, see Estelle Baughn Marsh, "The Baughn and Ward Family Histories" (Mimeographed 92-page volume, 1962); and Anona S. Blackburn and Myrtle S. Cardwell, comps., *History of Republic County* (Belleville, Kans., 1964).

Chapter Six
JOE AND FLORA WARD: ON TO CALIFORNIA

On the history of Williams, Ariz., see James R. Fuchs, "A History of Williams, Arizona, 1876–1951," *University of Arizona Social Science Bulletin,* no. 23 (Nov. 1953), 20–35.

N o t e s

Chapter One
BEGINNINGS: THE COLONIAL ERA

1. Roger Clap, "Memoirs of Roger Clap, 1630," *Collections of the Dorchester Antiquarian and Historical Society,* no. 1 (Boston, 1814), 39, as quoted in Linda Auwers Bissell, "Family, Friends, and Neighbors: Social Interaction in Seventeenth-Century Windsor, Connecticut" (Ph.D. diss., Brandeis University, 1973), 15 n. 2.

2. Samuel Fuller to William Bradford, June 28, 1630, as quoted in Bissell, "Family, Friends, and Neighbors," 18 n. 1.

3. Henry R. Stiles, *The History of Ancient Windsor* (Hartford, Conn., 1892), I, 206.

4. Gilbert Arnold's essay in Jean Mason et al., *Southwick Congregational Church History, 1773–1973* (Southwick, 1973), 9.

5. Nelson Hull, *Reminiscences in the Settling of the Valley of the Little Hoosick* (Troy, N.Y., 1858), 11.

6. J. R. Cole, *History of Washington and Kent Counties, Rhode Island* (New York, 1889), 677.

7. Inventory of Estate (July 26, 1770) and List of Debts (Dec. 3, 1770), in File 11717, "Archibald Greenfield," Probate Court, Essex County, Mass. Greenfield owned his schooner on half shares with his stepson, Thomas Gautier, and its name is deduced from the Essex Institute, *Early Coastwise and Foreign Shipping of Salem* (Salem, Mass., 1934), 180, which carries the following entry: "SWAN, schooner, 36 tons, Thomas Gautier, to Virginia, November 20, 1762. . . ."

8. Deed RT B/53, Queen Anne's County Land Records, Hall of Records, Annapolis, Md. I am grateful to James E. Greenfield for sharing his research on this deed with me.   .

9. "Records, 1763–1768," Papers of the Baptist Church, Montville, Conn., Western Reserve Historical Society, Cleveland, Ohio.

10. Both quotations are from Randolph C. Downes, "Dunmore's War: An Interpretation," *Mississippi Valley Historical Review,* 21 (Dec. 1934), 319 and 327.

11. The "giant in size" quotation is from David E. Johnston, *A History of Middle New River Settlements and Contiguous Territory* (Bluefield, Va., 1906), 383. The "have ever since been known" item is from George W. L. Bickley, *History of the Settlement and Indian Wars of Tazewell County, Virginia,* as quoted by W. C. Pendleton, *History of Tazewell County and Southwest Virginia* (Richmond, Va., 1920), 407–8.

12. Pendleton, *History of Tazewell County,* 411.

13. Federal Assessment of 1798, Baltimore County, Maryland; Particular Lists, Gunpowder Upper and Mine Run Hundreds, Maryland Hall of Records, Annapolis, Md. entry 1562. Dr. Carson Gibb of Annapolis found this entry for me.

Chapter Two

TRANS-APPALACHIAN PIONEERS, 1805–1829

1. Daniel Scott, Esq., *A History of the Early Settlement of Highland County, Ohio* (Hillsboro, Ohio, 1890), 4–5, 113.

2. Both quotations are ibid., 109.

3. Ibid., 5.

4. Both quotations are ibid., 109–10.

5. For William Keys's use of the term *extermination,* see ibid., 148. The old-timer's boast is from Isaac J. Finley and Rufus Putnam, *Pioneer Record and Reminiscences of the Early Settlers and Settlement of Ross County, Ohio* (Cincinnati, 1871), 123. The "enemies to the advancement of man" quotation is from Scott, *Highland County,* 148.

6. Mrs. Ross's story is told in Scott, *Highland County,* 82; Mrs. Proud's appears in Finley and Putnam, *Pioneer Record,* 68; and the quotation on "little uncomfortable cabins" is from Scott, *Highland County,* 148.

7. For Mrs. Lamb's case, see "Rocky Spring Session Book" (Early Vital Records of Ohio, Rocky Spring Church Records, Highland County; 1952 typescript copy at the Ohio State Library and the Ohio State Historical Society, Columbus), 41–42.

8. Ibid., 31 and 34.

9. Ibid., 34–35, 35, and 36.

10. Ibid., 33–34.

11. Scott, *Highland County,* 109.

12. The letter is quoted in Cora C. Bowler Malone et al., "Jeremiah Root (Senior and Junior): Sketch and Genealogy," an undated typescript compiled by Root descendants. Various parts of the document were put together at different times, the latest date mentioned being 1927. Copy in Gerald W. McFarland's files.

13. Ibid.

14. Ibid.

15. Ibid.

16. Henry Trumbull, *Western Migration: Journal of Doctor Jeremiah Simpleton's Tour of Ohio. Containing an Account of the Numerous Difficulties, Hairbreadth Escapes, Mortifications and Privations Which the Doctor and His Family Experienced on Their Journey from Maine to the "Land of Promise," and during a Residence of Three Years in That Highly Extolled Country* (Boston, 1819).

17. There are two published versions, somewhat different in form and content, of "Owen Brown's Autobiography." See Franklin B. Sanborn, ed., *The Life and Letters of John Brown* (Boston, 1885), 4–10; and Oswald Garrison Villard, *John Brown: A Biography Fifty Years After* (Boston, 1910), 12–14. I have used Brown's original spelling, where a text is available.

18. The "solidarity" quotation is from Rebecca M. Rogers, *Hudson, Ohio: An Architectural and Historical Study* (Hudson, 1973), 18; on the "special compact" of "covenanted towns," see Page Smith, *As a City upon a Hill: The Town in American History* (New York, 1966), 6.

19. Sanborn, ed., *Life and Letters of John Brown,* 4.

20. Ibid., 6.

21. Lora Case, *Reminiscences: Hudson of Long Ago* (reprint, Hudson, Ohio, 1963), 49.

22. Christian Cackler, *Recollections of an Old Settler,* 3d ed. (Ravenna, Ohio, 1964), 7; and "Owen Brown's Autobiography," in Villard, *John Brown,* 13.

23. Cackler, *Recollections,* 31.

24. Case, *Reminiscences,* 40.

25. Owen Brown's statement is from Villard, *John Brown,* 13; John's words are in John Brown to Henry L. Stearns, July 15, 1857, as found in Sanborn, ed., *Life and Letters of John Brown,* 14.

26. Owen's words are from Villard, *John Brown,* 13. The inscription was recorded in this form in Case, *Reminiscences,* 49, but it may originally have read "delightful child." Thomas L. Vince (librarian and curator, Hudson Library and Historical Society) to Gerald W. McFarland, July 9, 1979.

27. Both quotations are from Sanborn, ed., *Life and Letters of John Brown,* 14 and 6.

28. Harlan N. Trumbull, "The Birth of Western Reserve University and the Ohio-Erie Canal (1825–1837)," in *A Short History of Hudson, Ohio* (Hudson, 1975), 11.

29. On the visitation program, see "Minutes of the First Congregational Church, Hudson, Ohio, 1802–1837" (Typescript, Hudson Library and Historical Society, 1966), 19; Case's statement is in his *Reminiscences*, 17–18.

30. The quotations and case histories are found in "Minutes of the First Congregational Church," 8–11, 12, 17, 22–23, and 28–34.

31. Both quotations are from Sanborn, ed., *Life and Letters of John Brown*, 9.

32. The Fitch statement is found in *Short History of Hudson, Ohio*, 4; and the church visiting committee quotation is in "Minutes of the First Congregational Church," 28.

33. "Van Rensselaer Survey Book," Box 4, Folder 6, Van Rensselaer Manuscripts, New York State Library, Albany, 26.

34. Timothy Alden, *Address from the Rev. Timothy Alden . . . to Such People in the New-England States As Wish to Avail Themselves of the Advantages to Be Derived from a Removal into the Western Parts of our Country . . .* (New York, 1813), 2.

Chapter Three
UNFORESEEN DIRECTIONS, 1830–1850

1. This letter, dated June 12, 1830, is reprinted in Ernest C. Miller, *John Brown, Pennsylvania Citizen* (Warren, Penn., 1952), 10–11.

2. John Brown to Frederick Brown, as reprinted in Louis Ruchames, ed., *John Brown: The Making of a Revolutionary* (New York, 1969), 50–51.

3. Robert L. Santon to Charles G. Finney, Jan. 12, 1872, as quoted in Paul E. Johnson, *A Shopkeeper's Millennium: Society and Revivals in Rochester, New York, 1815–1837* (New York, 1978), 95.

4. "David Ward, Will and Inventory," Tazewell County Will Book 1, pp. 221–22 and 228; reprinted in Netti Schreiner-Yantis, ed., *Archives of the Pioneers of Tazewell County, Virginia* (Springfield, Va., 1973), 191.

5. Jack Baber, *The Early History of Greene County, Indiana* (Worthington, Ind., 1875), 25.

6. Sanborn, ed., *Life and Letters of John Brown*, 10.

7. Ibid., 9 and 11.

8. *Ohio Star*, May 12, 1830.

9. Beriah Green, *Four Sermons Preached in the Chapel of the Western Reserve College on Lord's Days, November 18th and 25th, and December 2nd and 9th, 1832* (Cleveland, 1833), 1.

10. *Liberator*, Mar. 30, 1833.

11. From a letter published in the *Report of the Second Anniversary of the Ohio Anti-Slavery Society* (Cincinnati, 1837), 16–17.

12. My account is based on Lora Case, *Reminiscences*, 53–54. Another eyewitness, Edward Brown (John's cousin), gave a slightly different version of the incident. His piece is reprinted in Ruchames, ed., *John Brown*, 187–89.

13. Reginald C. McGrane, *The Panic of 1837: Some Financial Problems of the Jacksonian Era* (Chicago, 1924), 55.

14. Sanborn, ed., *Life and Letters of John Brown*, 10.

15. Owen Brown to Levi Burnell, Aug. 1, 1839, Microfilm Reel 6, Letters Received by Oberlin College, 1822–1866, Oberlin College Archives, Oberlin, Ohio.

16. As quoted in Robert S. Fletcher, *A History of Oberlin College: From Its Foundation through the Civil War* (Oberlin, Ohio, 1943), I, 227.

17. "Oberlin Free Church Record" (MS at the Hudson Library and Historical Society, Hudson, Ohio).

18. Both quotations are from Sanborn, ed., *Life and Letters of John Brown*, 10.

19. Benjamin R. Adair to Samuel L. Adair, Oct. 21, 1833, Samuel Lyle and Florella Brown Adair Family Collection, Kansas State Historical Society, Topeka (hereafter cited as Adair Family Collection, KSHS).

20. Benjamin R. Adair to Samuel L. Adair, Mar. 31, 1834, Adair Family Collection, KSHS.

21. George Adair and others to Samuel L. Adair, Mar. 15, 1833, Adair Family Collection, KSHS.

22. Ann Eliza Adair to Samuel L. Adair, Oct. 22, 1851, Adair Family Collection, KSHS.

23. The quotations, in the order they appear in the paragraph, are from the following sources: Benjamin R. Adair to Samuel L. Adair, Mar. 31, 1834; Ann Eliza and Benjamin R. Adair to S. L. Adair, Jan. 14–16, 1833; Ann Eliza Adair to S. L. Adair, Jan. 28, 1834; Ann Eliza Adair to S. L. Adair, July 13, 1833; and Ann Eliza Adair to S. L. Adair, May 16, 1834—all in Adair Family Collection, KSHS.

24. Ann Eliza Adair to Samuel L. Adair, Sept. 30–Oct. 1, 1833, Adair Family Collection, KSHS.

25. Ann Eliza Adair to Samuel L. Adair, July 7, 1837; and George and Ann Eliza Adair to S. L. Adair, May 23, 1838—both in Adair Family Collection, KSHS.

26. A. Eliza Adair to Samuel L. Adair, July 9 and 12, 1833; and A. E. Adair to S. L. Adair, Sept. 17–20, 1833—both in Adair Family Collection, KSHS. The definition of *tent*, is quoted from a letter by Dr. Richard Kerber (of the University of Iowa Hospitals and Clinics) to me, Aug. 7, 1984. I am very grateful to Dr. Kerber, Dr. Eric Weitzner of New York City, and my cousin Dr. Morris Adair of Nashville, Tenn. (a great-great-grandson of Peggy Adair), for their comments on this case history.

27. Ann Eliza Adair to S. L. Adair, Sept. 17–20, 1833; A. E. Adair to S. L. Adair, Jan. 25 and 30, Feb. 4–6, 1837; and A. E. Adair to S. L. Adair, Feb. 6, 1838—all in Adair Family Collection, KSHS.

28. Ann Eliza Adair and Benjamin R. Adair to Samuel L. Adair, Dec. 19, 1843, Adair Family Collection, KSHS.

29. George and Ann Eliza Adair to Samuel L. Adair, July 7–10, 1837, Adair Family Collection, KSHS.

30. Ann Eliza Adair to Samuel L. Adair, July 17, 1838, Adair Family Collection, KSHS.

31. Martha Adair to Samuel L. Adair, Dec. 6–7, 1849, Adair Family Collection, KSHS.

Chapter Four

IN THE SHADOW OF CONFLICT,
1 8 5 0 – 1 8 6 5

1. Robert S. Fletcher, *A History of Oberlin College: From Its Foundation through the Civil War* (reprint, New York, 1971), 373 and 640.

2. Ibid., 642.

3. Florella Brown's alumnae file, Oberlin College Alumni Office, Oberlin, Ohio; Florella Brown to Her Parents, Mar. 28, 1836, Adair Family Collection, KSHS; and Francis J. Hosford, "Oberlin Alumnae of the First Half-Century and Their Occupations," *Oberlin Alumni Magazine*, 25 (June 1929), p. 263, where the last two quotations in the paragraph are found.

4. Samuel Adair to Florella Brown, Mar. 3 and Apr. 7, 1841, Adair Family Collection, KSHS.

5. "Articles of Furniture delivered to Florella [by her father], Nov. 15, 1841," Adair Family Collection, KSHS.

6. Samuel L. Adair to S. S. Jocelyn, June 24, 1854, American Missionary Association Archives, Amistad Research Center, New Orleans (hereafter cited as AMA Archives).

7. Samuel L. Adair to S. S. Jocelyn, June 24, 1854, AMA Archives.

8. William S. Rodgers to Samuel Adear [*sic*], Dec. 14, 1831; and Ann Eliza Adair to S. L. Adair, Jan. 28, 1834—both in Adair Family Collection, KSHS.

9. Ann Eliza and Martha Adair to S. L. Adair, Jan. 11, 1842, Adair Family Collection, KSHS.

10. The "Buckeyed" quotation is in E. P. Bartlett to S. L. Adair, May 12, 1842; Samuel's "Journal" entry is for Sept. 3, 1854—both in Adair Family Collection, KSHS.

11. Florella B. Adair to Oliver O. Brown, Jan. 1, 1855, Oliver O. Brown Collection, Hudson Library and Historical Society, Hudson, Ohio; and Samuel L. Adair to S. S. Jocelyn, Jan. 20, 1855, AMA Archives.

12. Samuel L. Adair to S. S. Jocelyn, Mar. 13 and 31, 1855, AMA Archives.

13. Both quotations are from Samuel L. Adair to S. S. Jocelyn, May 3, 1855, AMA Archives.

14. John Brown to Owen Brown, Oct. 19, 1855, reprinted in Ruchames, ed., *John Brown*, 95; and John Brown to Wife and Children, Oct. 13, 1855, John Brown Collection, Kansas State Historical Society, Topeka (hereafter cited as Brown Collection, KSHS).

15. Florella B. Adair to Martha Brown Davis, May 16, 1856, Oswald Garrison Villard Collection, Columbia University, New York (hereafter cited as Villard Collection, CU).

16. Jason Brown to F. G. Adams, Apr. 2, 1884, Brown Collection, KSHS.

17. Samuel L. Adair to Bro. and Sis. Hand, begun on May 23, 1856, Villard Collection, CU; and Jason Brown to F. G. Adams, Apr. 2, 1884, Brown Collection, KSHS.

18. The sources for the quoted items are as follows: "d——d abolitionists," Samuel L. Adair to S. S. Jocelyn, July 10, 1856, AMA Archives; "hanging list," same to same, July 4, 1855, ibid.; and "That gun," Samuel L. Adair to Bro. and Sis. Hand, begun on May 23, 1856, Villard Collection, CU.

19. Unsigned letter from Florella B. Adair to Stephen and Martha Brown Davis, Sept. 2, 1856, in the Samuel L. Adair file, Villard Collection, CU.

20. Samuel L. Adair to S. S. Jocelyn, Sept. 26, 1856, AMA Archives.

21. The three quotations are in letters from Florella to Samuel Adair, Feb. 26 and Apr. 7, 1861, and Apr. 9, 1864, Adair Family Collection, KSHS.

22. Samuel L. Adair to John Brown, Sen., July 16, 1856, Brown Collection, KSHS; Marian Hand to Samuel and Florella Adair, Aug. 16, 1856, Adair Family Collection, KSHS; Martha Davis to Samuel and Florella Adair, June 8, 1856, ibid.; Jeremiah R. Brown to Brother Adair and Family, Aug. 18, 1856, ibid.; Florella B. Adair to Samuel L. Adair, Dec. 30–31, 1860, and Jan. 1–2, 1861, ibid.; and Marian Hand to Sister Florella, Apr. 25, 1860, ibid.

23. The quotations are found as follows: "weak nerves & broken health," Charles and Florella Adair to Samuel Adair, Aug. 18, 1860; "My own health," Florella Adair to Samuel and Emma Adair, Sept. 14, 1860; and "You speak as though," Florella Adair to Samuel and Emma Adair, Nov. 8, 1860—all in Adair Family Collection, KSHS.

24. The quotations are found as follows: "five years behind," Florella Adair to Samuel and Emma Adair, Sept. 6, 1860; "The Territory is cursed," Florella Adair to My Dear *Dear* Husband and Daughter, Nov. 21, 1860; "very strange," Florella Adair to Samuel and Emma Adair, Nov. 8, 1860; "drag out the rest of our days," same to same, Nov. 21, 1860; and "I have never loved my family," Florella Adair to Samuel Adair, Feb. 17, 1861—all in Adair Family Collection, KSHS.

25. Samuel Lyle Adair, "Journal," Jan. 5, 1861, Adair Family Collection, KSHS.

26. Ibid., Apr. 26, 1861, entry; and Florella Adair to Samuel and Emma Adair, Apr. 7, 1861—both in Adair Family Collection, KSHS.

27. Florella to Samuel Adair, Jan. 6, 1864, Adair Family Collection, KSHS.

28. J. Remington to his family, May 21 and Apr. 21, 1862, Adair Family Collection, KSHS.

29. J. Remington to his family, Sept. 9, 1862, Adair Family Collection, KSHS.

30. J. Remington to his family, Nov. 9, 1862, Adair Family Collection, KSHS.

31. James V. Murfin, *The Gleam of Bayonets: The Battle of Antietam and the Maryland Campaign of 1862* (New York, 1965), 276.

32. For the Confederate private's statement, see ibid., 279; "As we rose and started" is from *Battles and Leaders of the Civil War: North to Antietam* (reprint, New York, 1956), II, 661; and Remington's summary is in his letter to his family, Nov. 9, 1862, Adair Family Collection, KSHS.

33. J. Remington to his family, Jan. 24 and Aug. 17, 1862, Adair Family Collection, KSHS.

34. J. Remington to his family, Oct. 10, 1862, Feb. 9, 1863, and Aug. 17, 1862, Adair Family Collection, KSHS.

35. Robert Sims to Editor of Osawatomie *Globe*, June 8, 1912; J. Remington to his family, Apr. 23 and July 26, 1863, Adair Family Collection, KSHS.

36. J. Remington to his family, July 26, 1862, and Aug. 15, 1863, Adair Family Collection, KSHS.

37. J. Remington to his family, Aug. 17, 1862, and Feb. 9, Aug. 15, and Sept. 3, 1863, Adair Family Collection, KSHS.

38. J. Remington to his family, June 23, 1864; and Kansas G.A.R. proof (no date, but ca. 1900)—both in Adair Family Collection, KSHS.

39. J. Remington to his sister, Dec. 10, 1864, and Mar. 22, 1865, Adair Family Collection, KSHS.

40. J. Remington to family, Mar. 1, 1863; same to sister, Jan. 29, 1865; same to family, Dec. 1 and Oct. 15, 1862, and Jan. 24, 1863—all in Adair Family Collection, KSHS.

41. Sims to Editor of Osawatomie *Globe*, June 8, 1912.

42. Aretas A. Dayton, "Recruitment and Conscription in Illinois during the Civil War" (Ph.D. diss., University of Illinois, Urbana, 1940), 146.

Chapter Five

C H A N G E S   O F   M I N D ,   1 8 6 5 - 1 8 9 2

1. Florella Adair to Emma Adair, Dec. 14, 1860, included with Florella Adair to Samuel Adair, Dec. 13, 1860, in Adair Family Collection, KSHS.

2. Samuel Adair to Emma Adair, Feb. 12, 1863; same to Florella Adair, June 6, 1863; and same to Emma Adair, Feb. 12, 1863—all in Adair Family Collection, KSHS.

3. Emma Adair to Parents and Sister, Sept. 2, 1863; Florella Adair to Samuel Adair, June 3, 1863; and Samuel Adair to Florella Adair, Apr. 26, 1863—all in Adair Family Collection, KSHS.

4. Emma to family, Sept. 23, 1863; same to Parents and Sister, Oct. 8, 1863; and M. B. Hand to Florella Adair, July 6, 1863—all in Adair Family Collection, KSHS.

5. Emma to Parents, June 17, 1863; and M. B. Hand to Florella Adair, July 6, 1863—both in Adair Family Collection, KSHS.

6. Florella Adair to Samuel Adair, Apr. 30, 1863; Emma Adair to Samuel Adair, Nov. 3, 5–6, 1863; Emma to Parents, Dec. 14, 1863; Emma Adair to ? (address torn off), Dec. 17–18, 1863; and Florella Adair to Samuel Adair, Jan. 6, 1864—all in Adair Family Collection, KSHS.

7. Emma to Parents, Sept. 4 and 9, July 16, Jan. 30, and Aug. 2, 1864—all in Adair Family Collection, KSHS.

8. Florella Adair to Samuel Adair, Jan. 6, 1864, Adair Family Collection, KSHS.

9. J. Remington to Sister, Aug. 22, 1865, and Jan. 8, 1866, Adair Family Collection, KSHS.

10. H. L. Marvin to Mr. and Mrs. Benjamin Remington, Dec. 25, 1867, Adair Family Collection, KSHS.

11. J. Remington to Family, Jan. 3, 1869; and same to Sister, Apr. 18, 1869—both in Adair Family Collection, KSHS.

12. J. Remington to Sister, Nov. 28, 1869; same to Family, June 27, 1869; and same to Mother, Apr. 5, 1868—all in Adair Family Collection, KSHS.

13. Harvey Newcomb, *A Practical Directory for Young Christian Females* (Boston, 1851), 228 and 230.

14. Unsigned, undated poem postmarked Feb. 14, Charlotteville, New York, Adair Family Collection, KSHS.

15. Harvey Newcomb, *How to Be a Man: A Book for Boys, Containing Useful Hints on the Formation of Character* (Boston, 1847), chap. 27 and pp. 19 and 181; "Keep your feelings entirely under control" is from Newcomb's *Practical Directory,* 228; and "I am very well" is in J. Remington to Sister, Nov. 28, 1869, Adair Family Collection, KSHS.

16. Flora Remington Ward, "Autobiography" (Unpublished 13-page typescript; copy in G. McFarland's files), 1–2.

17. M. S. B. Hand to Lucy Brown Clark, Aug. 24, 1883, Brown-Clark Collection, Hudson Library and Historical Society, Hudson, Ohio.

18. A. T. Andreas, *History of the State of Kansas* (Chicago, 1883), 887.

19. Rachel van Meter to Reverend S. L. Adair, Dec. 12, 1870; and Addie Adair to "Folks at Osawatomie," June 20, 1872—both in Adair Family Collection, KSHS.

20. A. C. Brown to Samuel Adair, May 25, 1872; and J. R. Brown to Samuel Adair and Family, Jan. 21, 1874—both in Adair Family Collection, KSHS.

21. Mary A. Brown to Mrs. George L. Stearns, Aug. 4, 1863, Stutler Collection (microfilm version), Ohio State Historical Society, Columbus.

22. As quoted in Oates, *To Purge This Land with Blood,* 89; and Benjamin R. Adair to Samuel Adair, Oct. 21, 1833, Adair Family Collection, KSHS.

23. Marian Brown Hand to S. L. Adair and family, Jan. 13, 1889, Adair Family Collection, KSHS.

24. Marian Brown Hand to Lucy Brown Clark, Sept. 5, 1888, Brown-Clark Collection, Hudson Library and Historical Society.

25. Ann Eliza Adair to Samuel Adair, Sept. 1 and Oct. 6, 1863, Adair Family Collection, KSHS.

26. A. L. Adair to Samuel Adair, Dec. 5, 1865, Adair Family Collection, KSHS.

27. A. L. Adair to Samuel Adair, Oct. 2, 1882, Adair Family Collection, KSHS.

28. Estelle Baughn Marsh, "The Baughn and Ward Family Histories" (Mimeographed 92-page volume, 1962), 65.

29. Lelia R. Heil, *Genealogical Abstracts from "The Tecumseh Chieftain," 1873–1900* (Privately printed, 1970), Oct. 28, 1882, item.

30. Bertha Ward Van Nortwick, "Autobiographical Notes," (14-page typescript, in G. McFarland's files), 1.

31. Ibid., 7.

32. Ibid., 11.

33. Ibid., 8.

Chapter Six
JOE AND FLORA WARD:
ON TO CALIFORNIA

1. James R. Fuchs, "A History of Williams, Arizona, 1876–1951," *University of Arizona Social Science Bulletin,* no. 23 (Nov. 1953), 55.

2. Flora R. Ward, "Autobiography" (Unpublished 13-page typescript, copy in G. McFarland's files), 4a.

3. Gerald W. McFarland interview with Clara LaFetra Darling, Jan. 1979.
4. Flora R. Ward, "Autobiography," 5.
5. Ibid.
6. Ibid., 6.
7. Ibid.
8. Ibid., 7.
9. Ibid., 9.
10. Ibid., 7.
11. Ibid., 8.
12. Ibid., 9.

P i c t u r e   C r e d i t s

We are grateful to the following for providing or allowing us to use these illustrations:

The American Antiquarian Society, pp. 52, 63, 65, 66, 110, 163, 200

The Kansas State Historical Society, pp. 100, 101, 102, 120, 121, 122, 142, 143, 146, 148, 157, 181, 182, 188, 189, 192, 194, 197, 198, 204, 210, 211, 213, 214, 216, 217, 225, 226, 229, 230, 232, 234, 235, 238, 239

The Rare Books and Manuscript Division of the New York Public Library, Astor, Lenox, and Tilden Foundations, p. 9

Archives, History and Genealogy, of the Connecticut State Library, p. 12

The Library of Congress, p. 31,

The Maryland Historical Society, Baltimore, p. 45

The Hudson Library and Historical Society, p. 71

The New York Public Library, p 99

The New-York Historical Society, New York City, pp. 104, 159

Worcester Art Museum, Worcester, Massachusetts, p. 138

Missouri Historical Society, St. Louis, 1855 Boehl photo, number III-1, p. 144

Nebraska State Historical Society, p. 218

Ross County Ohio Official Records, p. 57

The Bettmann Archives, Inc., p. 219

The National Archives, p. 220

Other illustrations are from the author's collection.

Index

Italicized page numbers refer to illustrations.

ABOUT THE AUTHOR

Gerald W. McFarland is professor of history at the University of Massachusetts at Amherst, and lives in Leverett, Massachusetts. He is the son of Marguerite Ward, whose birth in California in 1900 closes this book. His other books are Mugwumps, Morals and Politics *and* Moralists or Pragmatists? The Mugwumps.